Enemy Within

Enemy Within

The Rise and Fall of the British
Communist Party

FRANCIS BECKETT

Merlin Press

First published 1995
by John Murray (Publishers) Ltd.
50 Albemarle Street, London W1X 4BD

This edition published in paperback 1998
in the UK by The Merlin Press Ltd.
2 Rendlesham Mews
Rendlesham Woodbridge
Suffolk IP12 2SZ

ISBN 085036 477 9

This book is for Paul Beckett (1976 - 88)
because ideas of fairness and
not exploiting others mattered to him.

Printed in Finland by WSOY

CONTENTS

Illustrations

Acknowledgements

M Y thanks are due to more people than I can count. Communist historians have been consistently kind, helpful, honest and supportive. Chief among them my thanks must go to the tireless Monty Johnstone who has been generous with his deep knowledge. Monty, a Communist who has spent many years of his life making sure that the darkest secrets of international Communism are not swept under the carpet, has also read large chunks of this book, corrected some factual errors and made a series of thoughtful and informed comments.

The CP's official historian, Noreen Branson, has also been kind and helpful, even to the extent of letting me read in manuscript her next volume, covering the years 1941 to 1951 and to be published in 1995. To another Communist historian, Mike Squires, I feel I owe an apology. It seems poor thanks for his generous help that I have firmly rejected the deeply felt view contained in his scholarly PhD thesis on the CP's early years – while shamelessly drawing on it for information. Another professional historian to whom I owe much is Kevin Morgan, Harry Pollitt's biographer, who has been generous with his considerable knowledge and understanding.

Two journalists have read some of the later chapters. I owe much to perceptive comments, as well as factual corrections, from Mick Costello and Andrew Murray. Four other people have read individual chapters and commented helpfully on them, as well as allowing me to interview them at great length and pick their brains:

Acknowledgements

Martin Green, Douglas Hyde, Wilf Page and Brian Pollitt. Douglas Hyde and Brian Pollitt have also been invaluable sources of guidance and information throughout; and Wilf Page has kindly allowed me to read and quote from his extraordinary and vivid autobiographical notes, which, if this were a society that valued an understanding of its roots, would be fought over by publishers.

The early chapters owe a great deal to my trawl through the Comintern archives in Moscow. I could only do this because Pieta Monks came with me, bringing her fluent Russian and her deep understanding of Moscow and its ways, gained from long study at Moscow University. She and her many Russian friends also translated some Comintern material for me.

I have been very grateful for the advice and encouragement of the custodians of the CP's archives, George Matthews and Francis King. The remarkable Comintern document quoted at length in Chapter 5, and more briefly again in Chapter 8, was not my find, but was obtained by the archives while I was researching this book. They kindly allowed me to use it, and to work from Francis King's excellent translation. Equally I have received nothing but help and encouragement from the staff at the Marx Memorial Library led by Tish Newland. The *Guardian* kindly allowed me to use its cuttings library, whose staff were unfailingly helpful.

I also want to thank Linda Cohen, for two reasons. First, as a highly efficient researcher, she did much of the preliminary work and drew up a marvellous chronology which has served to keep my mind as clear as there was any chance of it being; and second, as the mother of my children, she has kept them away from me through the long evenings when I was chained to the word processor.

Two people have helped me to get particular stories. Joyce Rathbone has been enormously helpful with information about her aunt, Rose Cohen. And former *Daily Worker* journalist Alison McLeod has generously given me access to her notes and memories of 1956 as well as her fascinating unpublished manuscript about it, *The Death of Uncle Joe*. Without her Chapter 8 would be much poorer.

This book owes a great deal to interviews – generally in person and taped, but sometimes on the telephone – with most of the above mentioned people, and also with Frank Chapple, Tony Chater, Dick Clements, Edith Constable, Marian Darke, Reuben Falber, Michael

Acknowledgements

Foot, Professor John Foster, Peter Fryer, Jack Gaster, Ken Gill, Anita Halpin, Kevin Halpin, Mike Hicks, Digby Jacks, Martin Jacques, Jack Jones, Roy Jones, Paula Lanning, Martin Linton, Denis MacShane, Mick McGahey, Gordon McLennan, Chris Myant, Steve Parry, Phil Piratin, the late Bert Ramelson, Mary Rosser, Sam Russell, John Saville, Phil Stein, Jim Tait and Nina Temple.

Arnold Wesker engaged in a most helpful correspondence with me. The late Bill Keys talked to me and gave me parts of his diary while I was working on another project and I have used the material here. Stanley Forman, custodian of the Communist Party's film archive, gave me free run of it and a characteristically urbane and exciting guided tour through it.

Talks over the years with many friends and colleagues have formed such understanding as I have of politics, Communism and the period of history in which the CP lived. I am not sure if I can still remember who they all are, but they certainly include Eddie Barrett, Clare Beckett, Jack Boddy, Mike Brereton, Marie Buchanan, Malcolm Clarke, Professor Colin Holmes, Jim Innes, Chris Jones, Chris Kaufman, Ellis Kopel, Jo Sinclair and Linden West.

I want also to thank Julian Alexander, a creative, exacting and supportive literary agent, and Grant McIntyre and Kate Chenevix Trench, who are careful, thoughtful and understanding editors.

Introduction

A middle-aged man in a shabby raincoat stood in drizzling rain outside the TUC's central London headquarters that cold November morning in 1991 selling the Communist newspaper, the *Morning Star*. The *Morning Star* has dedicated supporters prepared to turn out in all weathers to sell the paper. But this was a bad morning – he sold only eighteen copies.

Yet 213 people passed him on their way into the TUC for a meeting – the forty-third and last Congress of the Communist Party of Great Britain (henceforth CP). They were there to wind up their party after seventy-one years and create a new organization which rejected most traditional Communist beliefs and ways of working. And they were doing it just 50 yards down the road from the British Museum where, more than a century before, Karl Marx had worked out the Communist philosophy they were about to abandon.

These were people more likely to buy the *Daily Telegraph* than the *Morning Star*. The *Star* was run by those who were expelled from the Party in the mid-1980s. The CP, down to less than 5000 members from a wartime peak of 56,000, called the *Star* people 'Stalinists' or 'tankies' (because they were supposed to have applauded when the Soviet Union sent tanks into Czechoslovakia). The *Star* people for their part blamed the CP's leaders for betraying Communism. The bitterness between the two camps, comrades until a few years ago, was sharp and painful. Neither side could

1

summon up the same loathing for the Conservative government as they felt for each other.

The year 1991 was a lousy one for Communists. In the Soviet Union in August, Communist hardliners attempted a coup against President Gorbachev. Its failure hastened Gorbachev's decline and the rise of Communist turned anti-Communist Boris Yeltsin. As Yeltsin gained control over the dark vaults whose files contained Moscow's secrets, foreign newspapers mysteriously started to acquire tempting items of scandalous information about the misdeeds of the Soviet Union's former Communist masters. The timing often seemed designed to be as embarrassing as possible for Communist Parties throughout the world. Just a few days before the Congress, the *Sunday Times* man in Moscow obtained an old exercise book with records of payments to someone called R. Falber. This proved to be Reuben Falber, former assistant general secretary of the Communist Party, now retired, who after a little prompting confessed that he picked up cash from a Soviet embassy contact regularly in the years 1957 to 1979. Some years he collected over £100,000. The CP had denied it for years. The new secretary, Nina Temple, who knew nothing about it, was furious.

But it seemed to her proof that she was right: they had to throw out most of what their party stood for. They had to get rid of what remained of the Leninist system called democratic centralism – a system which ensured that effective decisions are taken at the centre and relayed outwards. Instead they had to create a party which, instead of being the tightest in Britain, would be the loosest: a federation of more or less autonomous branches. They had to remove all reference to Marxism and Leninism.

Temple is calm, thoughtful and engaging, if a little aloof. She was born into a Communist family in North London in 1956 – the year the dream finally turned into a nightmare for thousands of Communists. Now, Communist leader at 35, she was determined to ensure the Party's past never rose from its grave to haunt her.

The day the Congress opened Yeltsin signed a trade deal with Germany, his first ever with a foreign power, even though he was not yet the head of an independent state. At the same time, he took the chance to associate Communism with repression. His German hosts asked him to return East German Communist leader Erich Honecker to face German retribution for allegedly having his

2

troops shoot to kill at people who climbed the Berlin wall. But this, said Yeltsin, was not a matter for him. 'I have not handled the problem. I have taken enough of President Gorbachev's powers already, I don't want to take this from him as well.'

Britain was still Thatcher's, though Thatcher had gone. Trade unions were neutered, the frontiers of the state relentlessly pushed back, and beggars multiplied on London's streets. Politics had turned into a long and unexpected nightmare for socialists. The arguments in the 1970s about how a socialist society should be run seemed to mock those who had taken part in them. They now saw capitalism at its most triumphalist. Every time Norman Tebbitt sneered at trade unionists or Margaret Thatcher crowed about destroying the 'nanny state' it was a blow in the face from an already victorious enemy.

It was also the end of a decade that had seen a series of bitter splits inside the CP. Old comrades who for decades had stood shoulder to shoulder against the world now could hardly hear each other's names without spitting. If the government had planted *agents provocateurs* in all left-wing parties it could hardly have achieved better results. So on that winter morning it was not surprising that the *Morning Star* seller did not do as well as usual. Few people could bring themselves to speak to him.

Just inside the big glass door, some of the old timers were gathering. Noreen Branson, the Party's historian, who helped organize the squatters' movement in the 1940s, whose husband fought Fascists in Spain and died in the Second World War, and Phil Piratin, who joined in the 1930s to stop Mosley marching through the East End, and was Communist MP for Mile End from 1945 until 1950, were part of a small knot of men and women in their eighties. They wondered apprehensively what a new generation was going to do with the revolutionary party they gave their youth, their middle age and their declining years to build. These people had known Harry Pollitt, which gave them the aura of that earlier generation of Russian Bolsheviks who had known Lenin.

'All the old fogies were grumbling like hell,' said Noreen Branson. 'And the young people seemed to assume that the older ones were all encased and didn't know how to network and spread out.' Wanting to be loyal to the decisions of a new generation, she could not help adding: 'We knew how to organize and they do not.' But she enjoyed the day because she met a lot of old friends. 'It was a nice social occasion, every break you could go and sit with whomever you liked.'

In the TUC's spacious basement conference room, the chairperson Marian Darke tested her microphone by blowing into it and started the meeting: 'Order, please, comrades.' For the next three days, all the skills she had learned in twenty years as a secondary school teacher were to be fully tested, as she controlled angry debates and procedural wrangles.

Darke, at 42, was vice-president of the National Union of Teachers, due to become its president, and spoken of as a future general secretary of the Union. Just five feet tall, with high cheekbones and short brown hair, she is a powerful public speaker with a deep, attractive voice and an instinctive air of authority. She is the sort of woman – cool, sophisticated, fluent – who, had she chosen the Labour Party instead of the Communist Party, would in 1991 have probably been a member of Neil Kinnock's shadow cabinet, instead of presiding over the last Congress of a fast-diminishing Communist Party. She was also one of the Party's chief strategists, responsible for working out the new idea, and the new name, Democratic Left, which the conference would be asked to agree. Later she was to become a principal architect of the campaign which forced the Education Secretary to retreat over testing for seven year olds.

Communist congresses at the end of the 1980s were full of recriminations, and Marian Darke was prepared for a difficult three days. The Congress started, predictably, with a procedural wrangle. The very first speaker accused the executive of fiddling and gerrymandering a result. Another early speaker, Fergus Nicholson, tall, clever, cadaverous former Communist student organizer, inadvertently almost caused a nasty incident. The proposed organization to replace the CP would, he said, have 'a central executive with a central slush fund and no democratic structure. Everybody here is already a Communist, why else would he be here?' Political correctness had been the latest trouble to hit the Party, and the use of the unadorned 'he' caused instant protest. Nicholson, a man of long experience, had the sense to retreat fast: 'He or she – I misread my notes.'

Marian Darke and her colleagues on the executive were determined that things were going to change. 'We are dying on our feet as a Communist Party,' she told delegates. 'If you're stuck in a hole, the best advice is: stop digging.' She omitted to attribute the quote, which was probably just as well. Denis Healey, briefly a Communist in the 1930s, and the Chancellor of the Exchequer who imposed wages policies in the late 'seventies, was not a much-loved figure among Communists.

Marian Darke spoke for a new generation of Communists, men and women in their thirties and forties who were sure the future did not lie with the old verities. But she was addressing an audience heavily weighted towards the elderly. Wilf Page was almost 80 years old, a Communist farmworker in Norfolk for most of his adult life. He knew what it was to suffer for your beliefs: for years he had been blacked by farmers throughout the county, and had hardly had enough to eat. All his spare time went into his Communist Party work and into his union, the National Union of Agricultural and Allied Workers, where he was a much respected figure. Tall, erect, dignified, he was a widely read 'worker-intellectual' of the sort the Party prided itself on encouraging. Also a great orator of the old open-air school, with a voice that sounded as though he gargled with granite, his political history suggested he might be a powerful voice against change. At first he sounded like a man from another age.

'The heroic struggles of the Soviet people during the war, and the important role they played in destroying the Nazi war machine, convinced us that the USSR would be an important element in building post-war society,' he told delegates. Younger members remembered uneasily that they had to appeal to people to whom the Nazi war machine was about as real as Mr Gladstone's bag. But Wilf Page surprised his audience. 'When Russian tanks rolled into Prague [in 1968] the whole underlying [Soviet] system was seen to be full of contradictions,' he said. 'Our younger comrades are not conditioned by our experiences ... We older comrades must shed our nostalgia, including the name of the organization, and offer support and encouragement to these comrades ...'

Many at the Congress knew how much it cost Wilf Page to say that. Wilf confided afterwards that he had met too many 'old comrades clinging like hell to what they loved.' It was hard 'to give your life to something and find out you have been wrong.' It was

5

harder still when there was a nagging doubt about what the younger comrades intended to put in its place. Wilf wanted 'a disciplined Party based on Marxism.'

Reservations about the change came from two Marxist historians. Mike Squires wanted to ensure the new organization did not forget its socialist roots. A gentle, bearded London taxi driver with a PhD from Leeds University for a thesis on the early years of the CP, he said that without a clear commitment to public ownership, the new organization would not be socialist. But his attempt to get this commitment into the constitution was beaten by 112 votes to 77.

Monty Johnstone, a tall, thin, imposing figure who ran his fingers through his long dark hair as he spoke and sounded like an eccentric history professor, worried about proposals which could make the Party's aims compatible with capitalism. Johnstone, who played a major part in exposing the CP's past dependence on the Soviet Union, inflicted the only traditionalist defeat on the executive in the whole of the three days.

When Marian Darke asked delegates to vote to change the name to Democratic Left by holding up their orange credential cards, they accepted the change and disbanded the 71-year-old Communist Party by 135 votes to 72. The plan, in line with a new public relations image, was that delegates would come into the hall the next morning and see the name, Democratic Left, over the platform, in 18-inch-high letters, together with the smart new logo – three figures with outstretched hands, one red for socialism, one purple for women's rights, one green for the environment. Unfortunately the Party's past intervened: the comrade due to erect it overslept because his East German alarm clock failed, and it did not go up until lunchtime.

Mike Hicks read the news of the change in the *Morning Star*. He would have voted against it, but had been expelled six years earlier, in 1985. An official of the print trade union, he is also the general secretary of a new party formed in 1988 around the *Morning Star* called the Communist Party of Britain (CPB). 'I thought: at least now there's no doubt about who the Communist Party in Britain is,' he says. 'We've got them off our backs. Now we're the Communist Party and that's an end of it.' But for a few moments it brought back the anger and bitterness that keeps bursting out of this big, quiet man. 'These people who are now saying they haven't been Marxist-Leninists for five or ten years. Why did they stay in the Party?' Hicks believes they were more interested in the Party's substantial assets than in its politics.

Anita Halpin, the daughter of German-Jewish Communists who fled Hitler in the 1930s, was out selling the *Morning Star* in Watney Street Market, Tower Hamlets. Her cry of 'MOR-ning Star' could be heard from one end of a noisy market to another. She found a good many more buyers than her unlucky comrade outside the CP meeting. Like Marian Darke, she would soon become the president of her trade union, in her case the National Union of Journalists. She heard the news with bitterness. 'The money that went into doing all these things was money raised by us, the people they got rid of. We raised it over many years, doing the jumble sales, supporting the Party, selling the *Morning Star*. They used it to put forward political beliefs we didn't agree with.'

But inside the hall, the last secretary of the CP, and the first secretary of the Democratic Left, used her closing speech to mount an assault on everything Anita Halpin believed. 'Our Party cannot be revived by nostalgia, discredited ideology, rosy views of history, or unaccountable command structures,' said Nina Temple. She called for 'a rupture with past undemocratic practices . . . a break from the disastrous Soviet mould . . . an apology to all those who fought within the Party for radical democratic politics and who were marginalized and often left the Party in despair at its refusal to adapt or change.' Seldom has the leader of any political party been so unsparing of her colleagues and everything they stood for.

At the lunch break delegates walked past half a dozen demonstrators with a huge banner and a megaphone on their way to pubs and sandwich bars. The banner proclaimed the demonstrators to be the real Communist Party, and the tall, attractive woman with long dark hair who held the megaphone had picketed many CP meetings before. She believed the Communist Party had always been a traitor to the revolutionary working class, and led an angry, mocking chant: 'No matter how you change your name,' (and here her comrades joined in to scream out the second line) 'You still play the bosses' game'. George Matthews, who used to edit the *Morning Star* when it was the CP's paper, had to raise his voice to be heard as he told a *Guardian* reporter: 'I still believe Marxism has something to contribute, so I don't want to throw the baby out with the bathwater. The trouble is, there's a lot of dirty bathwater and a rather small baby.'

The problem of distinguishing baby from bathwater occupied delegates for two more days of anguished constitutional debate. But the deed was done. Britain's Communist Party, after seventy-one eventful and dramatic years, had ceased to exist.

1

The Hopeful Dawn

IT had all been very different seventy-one years earlier, in the summer of 1920. After days of pouring rain, a bright, cold sun shone on 160 revolutionary socialists with new hope in their hearts as they went into the Cannon Street Hotel, a railway hotel in the City of London near St Paul's Cathedral, immediately after lunch on 31 July.

Most were in their twenties or thirties, part of the generation most severely scarred by the 1914–18 war. Some of them had opposed it, and been abused and assaulted daily by men and handed white feathers by women. Some had fought in that most terrible of wars. What they saw in the trenches would haunt them all their lives. They had lost nearly all their friends, and would never quite get over the feeling of guilt that they had survived. They were determined that Britain should no longer be ruled – in a memorable phrase – by 'hard-faced men who did well out of the war.' They wanted an end to the system that enabled one man to amass huge wealth while another could not earn enough to feed his family. It seemed a betrayal of their dead friends to accept the injustices they found when they returned. Had men died so that their wives and children should be starved and exploited?

They came from a variety of socialist groups, and were there to sink their identities into one great Communist Party. The 28-year-old chairman of the conference, Arthur McManus, was already well known among the dockers and shipbuilders on the River Clyde –

the Red Clyde, as it became known – as a trade union shop steward. His father, an Irish Fenian, brought the family to Scotland.

McManus was now living in England. An eloquent man, with a reputation for exciting oratory and heavy drinking, he was to become one of the Russians' favourite foreign Communists when he started visiting the Soviet Union. After a hard day arguing with the leaders of the French, German, Bulgarian and other Communist Parties, he would lead them in drinking sessions described by a fellow British representative as 'gargantuan'. The sessions would start in a Moscow restaurant and end in the small flat of one of the Russian Communists, or in the Lux, the bare but modern and functional hotel where foreign Communists stayed. They toasted each other in vodka and good strong Georgian brandy, and threw the glasses over their shoulders. Even the hard-drinking Russians found it hard to keep up with McManus.

These were exciting times. It was two and a half years since the Bolshevik revolution, and Lenin himself had called on the socialist groups now assembling to sink their differences and form a Communist Party. The editorial in the Labour-supporting *Daily Herald* the morning the conference began expressed, not wild optimism, but something like conventional wisdom: 'The founders of the new Party believe – as most competent observers are coming to believe – that the capitalist system is collapsing.'

On the morning of the conference the *Herald* reported a commonplace story: 'An ex-serviceman was turned out of a job to make way for a girl, his pension temporarily withheld. One of his three children, owing to the effects of malnutrition, was sent to a poor law institution, and the father received a bill for 24 shillings for four weeks maintenance in hospital. Then another child was taken ill and in hospital seven weeks, and, with empty pocket and barely a crust in the house, the father received a demand for another 28 shillings.' Socialists were not the only people to predict that ex-servicemen, who had given so much for their country, would not long put up with this situation.

Above all, they would not go to war against the Russian Bolsheviks. And it looked very much as though the government was going to try to make them do just that. Any attempt to force them to war, Communists believed, could trigger revolution. Newspapers were campaigning for troops to be sent to support Poland against

Russia, a war which Russia was winning. Three days before the Unity Conference the Secretary of State for War, Winston Churchill, published an article in the *Evening News* suggesting that Britain should arm Germany so that Germany could fight Russia. The rhetoric was vintage Churchill – reading it, you can almost hear his voice: 'Eastward of Poland lies the huge mass of Russia – not a wounded Russia only, but a poisoned Russia, an infected Russia, a plague-bearing Russia; a Russia of armed hordes smiting not only with bayonet and cannon, but accompanied and preceded by swarms of typhus-bearing vermin which destroy the bodies of men, and political doctrines which destroy the health and even the soul of nations.'

The defence of the Soviet Union was clearly to be the Party's first task. It was largely for this that Lenin put so much time and money into bringing together the warring socialist groups in one united Communist Party. To do it, he had had to knock a great many British heads together – and to take quick decisions on the hoof about whom to include and whom to leave out.

He included the British Socialist Party (BSP) with perhaps 5000 members, which had been affiliated to the Labour Party since 1916. And he included McManus's party, the 1000-strong Socialist Labour Party (SLP), based where McManus's roots were on the Clyde. It was not affiliated to the Labour Party, believing that any contact with 'reformism' was corrupting. Most of its members also thought there were too many compromises to be made in merging with the BSP and tying themselves up with Lenin's Bolsheviks. They could not have imagined the compromises that the next seventy-one years would require. Despite the disapproval of other members, McManus and a few close colleagues carried on discussing amalgamation with the British Socialist Party, and his party disowned him.

A third party, the London-based Workers' Socialist Federation, was run by Sylvia Pankhurst. Other small groups such as the South Wales Socialist Society contributed handfuls of members.

During the First World War all these parties had led industrial battles over wages and conditions when more conventional trade unionists suspended normal hostilities in favour of the war effort. They welcomed Lenin and the Bolshevik revolution in Russia in November 1917 and organized the 'Hands Off Russia' campaign to stop Britain sending troops to fight the Red Army. Lenin had already secretly provided at least £55,000 – the equivalent of about £1 million today – to help get the Communist Party off the ground. He also channelled money through the CP to other organizations. McManus alone knew the full details.

The leaders of these tiny, warring socialist groups who had ploughed lonely and unpopular furrows for years suddenly found themselves after the 1917 revolution being courted by the rulers of Russia, and with money to spend. They were impressed that, amid all his other worries, Lenin found time to listen to them, to advise and to persuade. Lenin seems to have relied on his own knowledge of British politics, plus advice freely but secretly offered by several people in Britain's socialist groups jockeying for position in the new party. It seems incredible that Lenin found time to ponder the lengthy, ponderous and often self-serving papers that were sent to him. But he did.

In March 1920 Lenin was sent a long appreciation of British left-wing politics by Jack Murphy of the SLP. Murphy advised excluding what was by far the biggest group on the left, the Independent Labour Party, already becoming the established left wing of the Labour Party, with 35,000 members. There was, Murphy conceded, a group of left wingers in the ILP, but 'they are so entangled in reformism that they will not be of much value to the revolution until they cut loose from the ILP.' Murphy probably did not know that the left wing of the ILP was getting some of Lenin's money. But the ILP was left out of the negotiations, as Murphy advised.

That was a fateful decision. It set up years of trench warfare between the new Communist Party and its only rival on the left – warfare which was to ensure neither could pursue its goals effectively. When the ILP wrote to the Comintern – the Communist International in Moscow – it received in reply, the day before the Unity Conference, a thirty-five-page lecture on English and European history.

The British Socialist Party was a little better, said Murphy, but it was far too reluctant to break away from the Labour Party. This showed its 'lack of revolutionary temper.' It must have come as a nasty shock to Murphy when he found Lenin pressing the CP to seek Labour Party affiliation. He no doubt expected Lenin to be as dismissive of the British Labour Party as he was of social democratic parties in Europe. Lenin, however, thought the Labour Party was the authentic voice of the British working class, and that little could be achieved without it.

Murphy, like many British Communists, visited Moscow before the Unity Conference. Getting there in those days was dangerous, illegal, lengthy and uncomfortable. Though the Soviet Union paid the bills, the journey involved many days on the freezing seas between Norway and Russia. But it was the best and most exciting thing that had happened to this clever young Scotsman.

He later described how the Russian Communists tutored their foreign protégés. There were commissions (committees) for each country including a British Commission, which talked for as long as necessary. 'The Russians seemed incapable of exhaustion by discussion. We had got to learn that a Communist Party was the general staff of a class marching to civil war, that it had to be disciplined, a party organized on military lines, ready for every emergency, an election, a strike, an insurrection.' The Russians, having successfully organized their own revolution, believed they could teach everyone else how to organize theirs. British Communists grew to believe it too, and it was an illusion which was to cause them much misery in the next seven decades.

In Moscow Murphy was arrested under suspicion of being a police spy. The Comintern ran an enquiry and decided he was not guilty. He was much relieved because, as he wrote later, 'the Russians have a method of dealing with police spies which does not leave any room for continued activity.' The allegation surfaced again in 1928, and again as a dark rumour after he left the CP in the 1930s.

He returned to Britain, broke and out of work, and on Victoria Station he ran into a man he had known in Moscow: Mikhail Borodin, who was working in England as the Comintern's agent under the name of George Brown. Like most Comintern agents he had several identities. Borodin was no more his real name than Brown: he was born Mikhail Grusenberg in 1884 in Russia and joined the Jewish Socialist Party as a student. He was imprisoned in Tsarist Russia and then trained as a lawyer in America. Borodin gave Murphy a job as his secretary and together they guided the new party through the first months of its life.

McManus as chairman opened the first Congress. 'After today' he said, 'there will at least exist in Great Britain a reliable, rigid, straight and determined Communist Party.' It was almost three years since Lenin came to power in Russia and the conference was 'a more effective reply to the solicitations of Russia than anything else that has emanated from this country since the Russian revolution.' Lenin's ambassador was due in London. 'Kamenev and his comrades, the Russian commissars, are expected this evening. It is humiliating to think that, having triumphed in their own country, the Russian delegation will have to submit to the arrogance and vainglory of the capitalist politicians here.' But things were going to be different soon. 'If delegates rise to the standard of responsibility that I am setting before you, this will prove to be the most profitable weekend that the revolutionary movement has ever had in this country.' McManus and most of the others in the room believed that the revolution would happen in a matter of months. They swiftly agreed to establish the Communist Party of Great Britain and affiliate to the Third International – the Comintern, newly created by Lenin to organize world revolution.

The Party would aim at the 'establishment of complete Communism, wherein the means of production shall be communally owned and controlled.' But there would be a halfway house between capitalism and communism, 'the dictatorship of the proletariat.' This was 'the necessary means for combating the counter-revolution during the transition period between capitalism and communism.'

There was the first stirring of a debate which was to cause a lot of trouble over the next seventy-one years. Did the CP stand for armed revolution or not? One excited delegate proclaimed 'the historic and revolutionary value of a gun in the hands of a man of the working class', only to be magisterially rebuked by Bob Stewart of Dundee: 'A great many people talk about guns who would run away when they saw one. I am more interested in folks having brains in their heads.' Bob Stewart had spent several years in prison for opposing the First World War, and knew more about hardship and violence than most. He led the smallest and oddest of the groups which formed the CP, the Socialist Prohibition Fellowship. After the main resolution was carried, this stout, sincere man with a sober moustache walked solemnly to the platform to ask the new Party to come out in favour of suppressing the manufacture of alcoholic drinks. Few thought much of the idea, but they liked Bob Stewart, so they referred it to the executive for action. In seventy-one years no action was ever taken.

Yet banning the demon drink struck a chord with many Communists. Many hard, poverty-stricken lives were tolerable only through a haze of beer. Three Scottish founder-Communists, Stewart, Jack Murphy and Willie Gallacher, remembered their deprived childhoods being blighted further by drunken fathers. They not only abstained all their lives, but saw abstaining from alcohol as part of their socialism.

Stewart had a bigger, and unexpected, success the next day. He was one of the few who wanted the new CP to fight elections for Parliament and local councils, and to apply for affiliation to the Labour Party. The instinct of most delegates was to stay away from it. One delegate called Labour leaders 'the deadly enemy of the revolution which you and I are seeking.'

But a more powerful voice than any of those present was raised in favour of affiliation. That voice was Lenin's. While the issue was being debated in London, it was being decided in Moscow. Two key players were not at the London conference at all. They were at the second Congress of the Comintern in Moscow, both of them arguing strongly against affiliating to the Labour Party. They were Willie Gallacher and Sylvia Pankhurst.

Gallacher, though belonging to the British Socialist Party, was much more involved with the trade unions in Scotland. He had a reputation as a tough negotiator and an effective union leader. He was inclined to see parliamentary activity and the Labour Party as a diversion from the real business of the working class, which took place inside trade unions. It is a strand of thinking which persists in left-wing trade union circles to this day.

Lenin talked him round. Gallacher writes about his meetings with Lenin in the apocalyptic and almost mystical tones which Lenin seems to have inspired in many British Communists: 'It was on . . . the conception of the Party that the genius of Lenin had expressed itself . . . Before I left Moscow, I had an interview with Lenin during which he asked me three questions. "Do you admit you were wrong on the question of Parliament and affiliation to the Labour Party? Will you join the CP when you return? Will you do your best to persuade your Scottish comrades to join it?" To each of these questions I answered "yes."'

Sylvia Pankhurst, a member of the formidable suffragette family, felt that the new Communist Party was going to be too right wing for her taste, and was not prepared to have anything to do with the Labour Party. Lenin secured her uneasy adherence to the CP, but her conversion was less wholehearted than Gallacher's, and it did not last.

On the second day of the London conference Lenin's message arrived, a pamphlet called *Left Wing Communism – An Infantile Disorder*. It was translated into English by Mikhail Borodin, and was a direct appeal for the CP to seek affiliation to the Labour Party. An application for affiliation was agreed by 100 votes to 85.

McManus was elected chairman of the new Party. The secretary was to be Albert Inkpin, a thin, pale, intense, hard-working man with a reputation as an efficient administrator, who had been the full-time secretary of the British Socialists. He seems to have been thoughtful but ineffectual, and certainly deserved better of the Party than he eventually received. There was to be a weekly journal, *The Communist*, and the first issue appeared five days after the conference. The front page was entirely devoted to an article by McManus headlined 'The Task Awaiting the Communist Party'.

The Party claimed 5000 members and probably had rather fewer. Over the next few months it mopped up the remaining small socialist groups. Gallacher brought in most of the distrustful Scots socialists, and Sylvia Pankhurst came in, though with strong misgivings. She was soon expelled for refusing to hand over her publication, *Dreadnought*, to be controlled by the Party's executive. The long bureaucratic report of her expulsion sent to Moscow seems the work of a pernickety clerk rather than a revolutionary.

Without Lenin's continual encouragement, and the careful distribution of Soviet money among groups which had always been starved of funds, the Communist Party would not have existed. Lenin continued to take a close interest in its affairs. His first and strangest correspondent after the conference was the shadowy figure of Andrew Rothstein. Murphy had told Lenin that Rothstein was 'a theoretician of the old school, tending towards opportunism.' He was the highly intellectual son of Theodore Rothstein, a Lithuanian Jewish revolutionary who had fled Tsarist persecution and settled in Britain in 1891. When the Bolsheviks started their daily paper *Pravda* in 1912 Theodore Rothstein became its London correspondent and corresponded with Lenin regularly.

After the November 1917 Bolshevik revolution, Theodore arranged secret contacts in Britain for Lenin's ambassador and later became Lenin's chief agent in London. He published Lenin's works in Britain; he sent information to Moscow; he secretly received money from Moscow and distributed it to British socialist groups. He was the Comintern's representative at the unity talks, and after the Unity Conference he went straight to Russia and began a new life as a senior Soviet diplomat.

Andrew, just 22, went with him. While in Moscow he wrote an account of the Unity Conference for the Comintern. It is a remarkable document. It reads like that of a small boy anxious to impress upon his teacher that he is better behaved than his classmates. It also illustrates the preoccupation with ideological rectitude which bedevilled the left throughout the twentieth century. The editing of *The Communist*, he wrote, 'betrays serious defects, in the shape of waste of space on non-revolutionary material, occasional lapses from revolutionary thought in the middle of a theoretical article ...' Perhaps the Comintern might care to instruct the CP to improve it. It was not his father who suggested he should write the paper, wrote Rothstein: 'My sole object is to do my duty to the Communist movement in England and to the International ...' Andrew Rothstein returned to Britain and played a key part in Communist politics throughout his life, travelling regularly to Moscow and once finding himself in a Soviet prison and hours away from execution. He chose, however, never to discuss any aspect of his long and curious life.

In addition to giving money directly to the CP, Lenin was funding all sorts of related activities via a number of routes. Bob Stewart, for one, was travelling to Moscow and returning with wads of banknotes hidden in a belt round his ample waist. Jack Murphy wrote a lengthy account to the Comintern of how he disposed of £12,600 entrusted to him, which illustrates the way money was handled.

Murphy received a mandate for money which he took to the Comintern's banker in Berlin. He entered England, like Bob Stewart, with cash stashed about his person. £2,600 went to the National Council of Shop Stewards and Workers' Committees, and £5,600 to the British bureau of the Red International of Labour Unions, the Soviet-inspired trade union international.

Then someone from the Irish Communist Party came to see him and told him that its money from the Comintern had not arrived. Murphy was troubled: 'While I was not satisfied with his explanation of the disposal of the £300 entrusted to him and Connolly ... I felt that [the Comintern] would not want the work delayed,' so he handed over £150. Murphy demanded a receipt and told the Comintern: 'Others with a greater sense of responsibility and with better prestige in the working-class movement of Ireland will have to be found to conduct and direct the work ... The work in Ireland, as far as I can find out, is yet to commence.'

Smuggling cash in this way was a dangerous and uncomfortable business. It was even more dangerous to be a Comintern agent – the people who travelled secretly from country to country, helping and advising Communist Parties, making sure they worked efficiently, spent Moscow's money wisely, and followed the Moscow line. Police surveillance was close and Comintern agents kept their identities secret even from CP members. Mikhail Borodin was at a meeting in Glasgow with Bob Stewart, Willie Gallacher and others when the room was raided by a dozen or so policemen. 'Who's he?' asked the policeman in charge, pointing at Borodin. Stewart replied – truthfully, as far as it went: 'A Yugoslav journalist.' 'He's the man we want,' said the policeman.

Borodin found his six months in Glasgow's Barlinnie Prison hard. It was colder than Siberia, he said, and he knew what he spoke about. The food – almost exclusively porridge – was excruciating. He scalded his legs badly with boiling water in the prison laundry and could hardly wait for the six months to be over so that he could be deported.

A Comintern agent who called himself 'Comrade Robinson' (which just might have been his real name) sent to Moscow a hair-raising account, in Russian, of one of his many attempts to enter Britain illegally. He was carrying money for the CP in December 1921 and stowed away on a cargo boat with the help of a friendly sailor. Landing in a small, quiet Scottish port, he was picked up by police after four days and pretended to be a Russian engineer fleeing to America who spoke no English. He spent five days in prison before police put him back on board, telling the captain to hand him over to the authorities in Bremen, where he had boarded. 'It was with relief that I finally felt the Scottish shores receding in the distance. My false identity saved me from the greater danger.'

On the boat he was held in a locked storeroom with reinforced metal doors and only let out during the day when the ship was at sea. In Denmark he hoped to escape by breaking the door, but 'the minute we arrived there the authorities arrived and shut me up in a holding cell. I was kept there for four days on "Kremlin" rations.' He failed again at the Kiel canal.

'I managed to escape in Hamburg. Police chased me with dogs. Now I am free in Berlin. I am tired – completely exhausted. As before I am without papers.' He was also, no doubt, terrified, holed up somewhere in Berlin and expecting the door to be kicked down any moment. 'Any new illegal attempt [to enter Britain] is out of the question. Legally? God knows. I can't wait for papers. Comrade Klishko arrived from England. He represents the view of our London friends when he says he is categorically against any new attempt. The police are looking for me under my real name. With our talkative English comrades . . . this is not surprising. He says that I won't be able to hide long and failure will make things very complicated. Again, knowing our English comrades and the way they operate, I agree with him.'

He desperately wanted permission to return to Moscow. 'My staying in Berlin is dangerous, but most important, it is useless. I don't have the right to return without higher authority . . . I must return to Moscow as quickly as possible and immerse myself in vital work in the interests of the movement.'

Robinson probably did not know that he had already been replaced in England. The same month his successor Peter Vassiliev's report begins: 'It is now almost exactly six months since I took over the work begun by Comrade Robinson.' In this report he accounted to the Comintern for the money he brought with him. Most of it – nearly £20,000 – went into books, pamphlets and journals. But more than £2000 went into cloak-and-dagger operations. An underground printer was acquired and a garage and car to distribute illegal material such as 'seditious' pamphlets. Some of the money went to 'a comrade who is a first-class forger' so that he could produce passports. After some hesitation Vassiliev turned down the forger's offer to produce banknotes. While 'this might conceivably be of value at a critical moment in the political process', it needed more consultation.

The police also paid close attention to the Communist Party leaders themselves. In May 1921 they raided the new offices at 16 King Street, Covent Garden, a fine property bought with Soviet money which, more than half a century later, was to save the Party from bankruptcy. They rounded up the entire staff and sent raiding parties to everyone's homes, including the secretaries. Inkpin asked to see a warrant, to which the inspector replied: 'I don't need a warrant. I am acting under the emergency regulations.' The police were mainly interested in the Comintern statutes. Inkpin explained that these were a record of Comintern decisions, and demanded to know why his staff were being intimidated and his office turned upside down. He was arrested and received six months hard labour for publishing the statutes in English, because they were said to be seditious. The police left Bob Stewart behind in the office. But they came back for him the next day and took him to Cardiff on a flimsy sedition charge arising out of a speech he had made in Aberdare. He went to Cardiff Gaol for three months.

The effect the Comintern's money had on the leadership at this time seems to have been wholly undermining. They were not corrupt, but they were human. Not used to having money, they believed, with Lenin, that revolution was around the corner and they had a duty to prepare for power. They also wanted to stay on the right side of their benefactors. It is easy to see how their organization could have quickly become flabby, complacent and bureaucratic.

One visitor to Communist Party headquarters, who came to seek money for the National League of Ex-Servicemen, wrote afterwards: 'We were led through the bookshop in front, and a number of underground passages, into a dim room thick with the aroma of good cigars. After the kind of greeting which the millionaires federation might offer to a deputation of office boys, the chairman read a lengthy manifesto of which the chief points were that the National Union of Ex-Servicemen would affiliate to the Moscow

International and take its orders from the British branch of that body; that we were both to become paid officials ... and we were to join the Communist Party. There was also a provision that our Executive Committee must be confined to members approved by the CP. We asked for a copy of this document in order that we might consider it at our leisure. This was refused but the main points were recapitulated to us and we were instructed to return in the afternoon for further examination.'

It could not go on like this, and it did not. 'Comrade Robinson's' report in December 1921 included a plea to get money quickly to the CP. Its funds, he said, are exhausted. 'The publishers [the front company set up to publish CP material] will go bankrupt unless money is immediately forthcoming.' Peter Vassiliev wrote to Moscow that the subsidy to the CP had 'after tremendous efforts been reduced to £2,500 a month.' In addition, another £2500 a month was needed for other tasks, not subsidized through the CP but directly by the Comintern, such as running the British section of the Red International of Labour Unions. So for 1922, the Comintern must put into Britain £5000 a month, or £60,000 a year, plus £5000 for 'emergency situations'. In today's terms, that is well over £1 million a year.

The same month, the Comintern dispatched another representative, Norwegian Communist Jacob Friis, to tell the CP to prepare for an end to all subsidies. Friis had long, anguished meetings with McManus, who told him that the Party had only enough money left for two weeks on the current operating basis. Immediate collapse was imminent, said McManus. Friis told Moscow: 'My general impression is that the Party in the last year has been fighting more with its financial difficulties than with political problems ... The strain and worry over matters of finance naturally prevents the Party officials from devoting as much time to political thinking as might otherwise be the case.' Nonetheless he considered the administration to be very weak.

McManus, it was agreed, should go to Moscow to talk about the situation. The executive met early in January 1922 to look at ways of reorganizing on the basis of no subsidies. It was handed a remarkably frank paper: 'There is £5000 in hand – and no prospect of more, apart from what the membership can raise by their own exertions ... The executive has before it the task of bringing the

Party down to a self-supporting basis, not gradually, but in a fortnight or three weeks at the outside.' The subsidies had 'created the impression that there was an unlimited supply of finance' and hence branches 'shirked their responsibility to the Central Office.' Subsidies were 'responsible for a staff of full-time officials being taken on that was out of all proportion to the membership.' Members left everything to paid officials. The principle now proposed was that salaries should never exceed contributions.

Subsidies did not dry up completely. Money continued to come from Moscow until the mid-1930s. But the sums received after 1922 were smaller. In addition to a regular subsidy there were sums allocated for specific purposes: £2000 to fight the 1922 general election, for example. In 1923 there was £2000 for 'safe-keeping of documents, lines of communication, passport facilities, propaganda and undermining work in government institutions, special intelligence.' At the end of 1922 Albert Inkpin was again writing to Moscow for more money. Without it, 'our Party will be faced with disaster within a fortnight.'

Inkpin tried to get Labour Party affiliation, as Lenin wanted. But the CP had an implacable enemy at court who was to become more powerful as time went on. This was Herbert Morrison, a cunning Cockney with one almost blind eye and the narrowest possible political vision. Morrison was a machine politician. He did not like anything that interfered with a complicated structure which he knew how to work. For his rooting out of heresy – not just Communist heresy – he became known as Labour's 'chief witchfinder'. His power base was the London Labour Party, which over thirty years he did more than anyone else to shape.

At Labour's June 1921 conference in Brighton Morrison was the backroom organizer who delivered the crucial trade union block votes against the CP. The conference did not reject the Communists outright. It left some room for negotiation. But by the time of the following year's conference in Edinburgh, Labour leaders were hardening in their conviction that Moscow pulled McManus's strings – which, generally, it did. A left winger, Frank Hodges, said the Communists were 'the intellectual slaves of Moscow ... taking orders from the Asiatic mind.' Labour leader Ramsay MacDonald said that not only was the Communist Party controlled by Moscow, it also held out the right hand of friendship while in the left it concealed a dagger 'to stick into your back.' Communists poured scorn on this melodramatic image, though earlier in the year a leading Communist, Tommy Jackson, had said the CP would take Labour Party leaders by the hand 'as a preliminary to taking them by the throat.'

The proposal for affiliation was lost decisively, and was lost again in 1923 and 1924. There were no further attempts for eleven years.

That did not prevent the CP from having three MPs in the 1920s. The most unexpected was the aristocratic, handsome Cecil L'Estrange Malone. Malone's father came from an Anglo-Irish landowning family, his mother from the English aristocracy, and he counted Liberal cabinet ministers among his relatives. Educated at the Royal Naval College, Dartmouth, he later commanded several ships. His war record helped carry him into Parliament as a Liberal in 1918, aged 28. This stately, conventional progress came to an abrupt halt the next year after a visit to Russia.

On his return he called Parliament 'a machine for fooling democracy.' He appealed to workers for 'direct action' to stop the government's 'criminal policy' against Russia. He said a solution to the Irish question would come 'when the workers in Ulster realise that they have been the tools of the Ulster capitalists . . . Salvation will come when they awake to class consciousness.' This must have come as a nasty shock to his Irish landowner relatives. In July 1920 he joined the British Socialists, less than a month before the Unity Conference merged them with the CP.

And that is how the newly formed Communist Party found itself with a sitting MP on the first day of its life. Some of his new comrades thought he was a police spy. But police spies are usually less conspicuous than Malone. He took his new faith to heart, and was wilder and more immoderate than other CP leaders. He went to prison for six months for a speech in which he said: 'What, my friends, are a few Churchills or a few Curzons on lampposts compared to the massacre of thousands of human beings?' He was caught by the police with known Comintern agents outside his Hampstead flat.

But by the end of 1922 he had left both Parliament and the CP. He was a Labour MP from 1928 until 1931, moving rapidly towards the right of the Party, then spent the rest of his life as a businessman and nautical expert. He died in Kensington in 1965, a retired naval officer with rather right-wing political views.

Shapurji Saklatvala was a wealthy and aristocratic Indian who came to the CP by way of the Independent Labour Party. He won Battersea North at the general election of November 1922 as an official Labour candidate, despite being openly a Communist. (It was not until 1924 that the Labour Party decided Communist Party members could not be endorsed as Labour candidates.) At the 1925 election, disowned by the Labour Party nationally but supported locally by the Battersea Labour Party, Saklatvala managed to hold his seat, but he lost it to Labour in 1929.

The third MP was J. Walton Newbold, who, like Saklatvala, joined the CP with the left-wing group of the ILP. He won Motherwell in 1922 but lost it in 1923, leaving the CP soon afterwards.

In 1924 Ramsay Macdonald became Labour's first Prime Minister, but without a majority and reliant on Liberal support. Left wingers in the Labour Party were ecstatic. David Kirkwood, a newly elected left-wing MP and a Clydeside friend of McManus's, told his cheering Glasgow constituents as his London-bound train pulled out of the station: 'When we come back, all this will belong to the people.' But the Labour government behaved no differently from its Conservative predecessors, and the CP was able to say, with some justification, we told you so. MacDonald – with much less justification – blamed the CP for the fall of his government, and its failure in the ensuing election. What happened was this.

In July 1924 the *Workers' Weekly* – which had replaced *The Communist* – published an 'Open Letter to the Fighting Forces'. It asked them to 'let it be known that, neither in the class war nor in a military war, will you turn your guns on your fellow workers.' The editor, Johnny Campbell, was charged with incitement to mutiny. Campbell was a talented writer and propagandist, another Scottish 'worker-intellectual' and one of the few CP leaders who was liked and respected outside the Party. He fought in the First World War and lost all the toes from one foot, which left him with a pronounced limp. He was thin and quick-witted and had a sense of humour which was not always appreciated in the rather humourless Party hierarchy.

24

Labour's Attorney General, Sir Patrick Hastings, decided to withdraw the charge. Campbell, he said, was a man of otherwise excellent character with a fine war record. The Conservatives seized the chance to level the charge that Labour showed bias towards Communists. The Liberal Party offered a face-saving formula: a Select Committee to look into the affair. MacDonald turned down this chance to save his government and a general election was called for October.

Four days before polling day, the *Daily Mail* came up with a sensational story designed to harm Labour's chances, a trick it still generally manages to this day. Moscow, it claimed, had told CP leaders to paralyse the British army and navy by forming cells inside them. The proof was a letter from Zinoviev, general secretary of the Comintern, which the *Mail* published – and which the Foreign Office declared genuine. It was almost certainly a forgery, probably by Russian exiles. But it helped secure a massive victory for the Conservatives under Stanley Baldwin.

The new government at once started to prepare for a general strike. The Samuel Commission, set up to examine the coal industry, recommended a reduction in miners' wages, already near starvation levels, and an increase in already back-breaking hours. The new miners' leader, Arthur Cook, had been in the South Wales Socialist Society, one of the organizations which merged into the CP, and had been elected to lead the miners with Communist support. Cook was an extraordinary man. Slight and unimpressive to look at, with a high, squeaky voice, his speeches broke all the rules of oratory and had little logical structure. Yet in that Indian summer of British oratory he was the most effective public speaker in the country, perhaps because he accurately reflected the anger his members carried in their hearts. His slogan was 'Not a penny off the pay, not a minute on the day.'

The government subsidy to delay lowering miners' wages ran out in May 1926, and by that time the government was ready for a general strike. It had set up the Organization for the Maintenance of Supplies. It had volunteers ready to take on essential work. And it had put Britain's twelve most prominent Communists in prison.

In October 1925, thirty detectives had again raided the King Street offices. The unfortunate Albert Inkpin found himself in prison for the second time since he became Party Secretary. This time he was joined, among others, by Johnny Campbell, Willie Gallacher, Arthur McManus and Jack Murphy. Police guarded every room in King Street. Busts of Lenin, Zinoviev and other Russian Bolsheviks were carried away, as also was a mysterious metal object which turned out to be the lavatory ballcock. The twelve were charged with seditious libel and incitement to mutiny. Five went to prison for a year, the other seven for six months.

The general strike started on 4 May 1926. The TUC had made no proper preparations for it and was desperate to settle. Three million people went on strike; 2500 were arrested, of whom several hundred were Communists. At the end of nine days, with no concessions won, the TUC General Council called off the strike. Thousands of miners, convinced they had been betrayed by the Labour Party and the TUC, joined the CP. But did it have the ideas and the organization to keep them?

2

The Instrument of Steel

L ENIN wanted the Communist Party of Great Britain run his way. To achieve this the Comintern brought together the two men who came to dominate the Party for most of its life: Harry Pollitt and Rajani Palme Dutt. Comintern instructions for Communist Parties, drawn up in 1921, demanded 'democratic centralism'. Parties must be run from the centre. Party leaders must be able to take decisions which bind all members. So Communist Parties must have iron discipline, and all Comintern decisions must be binding on all Communist Parties. A three-man Commission was set up to translate this into practice for Britain. In addition to Pollitt and Dutt there was Harry Inkpin, brother of Party secretary Albert Inkpin, but he seems to have had little influence.

Harry Pollitt was born in 1890 in a tiny terraced house in the grim industrial town of Droylsden, between Manchester and Ashton-under-Lyne. His mother, like many working-class women of the time, lost as many children in infancy as she brought up, for want of sufficient care, the right food, and enough time off from her exhausting job to look after herself or her babies. Mary Louisa Pollitt, known as Polly, left for work each day at 4.30 am. She rushed home during the breakfast half hour to give the children their breakfast. She then left again, even when one of them was ill, otherwise she would lose her job. Without a second income the family would starve. Harry always remembered 'watching for her to come home from the mill, the once rosy cheeks in which my

27

father so delighted, faded by ten-hour day after ten-hour day in the hot, noisy weaving shed, by frequent confinements and by never-ending poverty.' But she was never too tired to greet her children with a smile, he said.

A founder member of the ILP, she joined the Communist Party when it was founded in 1920. Harry loved and admired his mother, with the desperate, powerless, angry love which wants to protect and to revenge. It remained always at the root of everything he did. In 1960, the year he died, on a plane to Singapore, he met a former Communist and started talking about his mother: how he saw her standing in her clogs all day in several inches of water and thought: 'They mustn't be allowed to do this to my mother.' He could still not speak of it without tears in his eyes.

Harry saw two of his mother's dead babies. Too young to understand the first time, he did not like the solemn face and black clothes of the undertaker and begged his mother: 'Hide the coffin behind the curtain, then Mr Rayment won't find it.' The second time he was 13. It was his little sister Winifred, his angel. He thought as he watched her die: 'I would pay God out. I would pay everybody out for making my sister suffer. He wrote in 1940, 'I was unconsciously voicing the wrongs of my class.'

At 12 he started working with his mother: 'Every time she put her shawl round me before going to the mill on wet or very cold mornings, I swore that when I grew up, I would pay the bosses out for the hardships she suffered. I hope I shall live to do it, and there will be no nonsense about it.'

When he was 27, in November 1917, he read about the event which shaped the rest of his life. The Russian revolution brought the Bolsheviks to power and Pollitt saw that 'workers like me and all those around me had won power, had defeated the boss class.' By then he was a skilled craftsman, a boilermaker, an experienced strike leader, a member of Sylvia Pankhurst's Workers' Socialist Federation, an effective public speaker, and the proud owner of a copy of Marx's *Capital*, given him by his mother on his 21st birthday.

Sylvia Pankhurst brought money from Moscow for a 'Hands Off Russia' campaign, instigated and funded by Lenin and involving most of the future leaders of Britain's Communist Party. Pollitt became its full-time organizer, but became restless in a desk job and went back to work in the Port of London. There he helped persuade dockers to refuse to fill the SS *Jolly George* with coal, because the ship was loaded with munitions intended to help Poland fight Russia. Another supply of Moscow money, this time brought in by Jack Murphy, now the CP's man in Moscow, enabled the British bureau of the Red International of Labour Unions to employ Pollitt as its London district organizer in 1921, and in the same year he travelled to Moscow for the first time and met Lenin. 'That handshake meant everything in the world to me.'

At the Labour Party conference that year, Pollitt was a delegate from the Boilermakers Union and spoke powerfully in favour of allowing the newly formed CP to affiliate to the Labour Party. He already had an instinct for the right buttons to press. He described the CP as 'an integral part of the English working-class movement.' Labour in government, he said, 'will not depend on the Fabian Society for their power; they will depend on the men in the mine, the mill and the shipyard, and that is where the bulk of the Communist Party happens to be.'

Pollitt was short and heavily built, with a Lancashire accent, a ready laugh and that precious political gift, a warmth towards people that communicated itself instantly. He was never able to acquire the ruthlessness which many Communists considered essential. His greatest weakness in the straitlaced world of Labour movement politics was his inability to control his irreverent sense of humour – a weakness which, in later years, may have been the only thing which sustained him.

Palme Dutt could not have been a greater contrast. Personal ruthlessness was an article of faith for him. Tall, shy, intellectual, seemingly cold, he was once accused of lacking a sense of humour, and replied irritably: 'When a comrade tells me a joke, I laugh.' He had a deep, precise, academic's voice. Words like 'stand' came out of his mouth as a tightly controlled 'stind'.

He was born in 1896. His father was an Indian doctor, his mother a Swedish writer with highly placed connections, including a future Swedish Prime Minister, Olaf Palme. But the families had quarrelled and Dutt never met his distinguished relation. Emotional influences leading him towards socialism included the unthinking racism of the English upper classes, and the comparison between his father's poor patients in the working-class part of Cambridge where he lived and the rich at the other end of the town. But emotional influences were not Dutt's style. Exceptionally academically gifted, by the time he went to Balliol College, Oxford, he had thought his way to socialism.

In 1916, aged 20, he insisted on his right to go to prison for refusing the draft. He was told that conscription did not apply to him, on racial grounds. He appealed, his appeal was successful, he was conscripted, he refused, and he spent six months in prison. This self-imposed penance almost broke his health, which was never good. Expelled from Oxford for organizing a meeting in support of the impending Bolshevik revolution in Russia, he was allowed back to take his finals and won a first-class degree, the best of his year.

Palme Dutt was to become the most rigid Communist of all. He explained why fifty years later by recalling an international student meeting he attended in Geneva with Ellen Wilkinson, then a Communist, who soon left to join the Labour Party and who became a cabinet minister in the 1945 Labour government.

'As so often in international conferences there arose an "English problem": in this case whether to accept us in the proposed international organisation of socialist students or not. Accordingly that night a fraction meeting was called of the Communist representatives ... to decide what to do with the English; we were allowed to be present as silent spectators. The discussion was held in an attic and continued into the small hours; at one point the police arrived in the house ... we adjourned through the attic window into a neighbouring attic and the discussion continued ... Our organisation and line was analysed relentlessly like a body being dissected on a mortuary slab; at the end the decision went against us ... As we came away into the cold air of the December night Ellen Wilkinson said to me: "This is the most ghastly, callous, inhuman machine I have ever witnessed." I said to her: "At last I have found what I have been looking for: socialists who mean business."'

To Dutt these solemn student deliberations were the real stuff of life. 'Meaning business' meant rigorously and faithfully interpreting the line laid down centrally, without deviation, until it was changed; and then following the new line, without deviation and without question. That is what he did for the rest of his long life, and he had neither time nor sympathy for anyone who failed to do likewise.

It meant the same to Salme Murrik, an Estonian woman eight years older than Dutt. She had already fought for Bolshevism in Russia and Finland, and paid for her involvement in the attempted 1905 revolution in Russia with Siberian exile. In 1920 she asked Lenin to send her 'where the struggle is toughest' and he sent her to England to help create the British Communist Party. Her first friend and ally, and future husband, was Dutt.

In 1921 her Finnish friend Otto Kuusinen became secretary of the Comintern. So when, the next year, Lenin ordered the creation of a theoretical journal – dedicated to analyzing Marxist ideas – in Britain, and *Labour Monthly* was born, the Comintern choice to run it was Dutt. Money for it probably came from Moscow via Salme. The next year a reliable theorist was needed to translate the Comintern theses into proposals for action in the Britain. Dutt was again the Comintern choice.

Pollitt and Dutt wrestled with the task in the evenings and through the nights, for Pollitt had by now returned to his daytime job on the docks. They grew to like and admire each other. People would never love and follow Dutt as they did Pollitt, but Pollitt admired Dutt's intellect. Here, he thought, was the pure Marxist-Leninist theorist the Communist Party needed. Usually he distrusted middle-class intellectuals, but Dutt was different, as Pollitt's son Brian explained: 'Dutt was half Indian and half Swedish, he had a brown face, he did not come out of the British class system – and so he did not trigger [Harry's] class instincts, he could neutralize them.'

Their report called for the Bolshevik system known as 'democratic centralism': a Central Committee divided into a Political Bureau (Politburo) and an Organizing Bureau (Orgburo). The Central Committee would communicate decisions to District Committees, which would then communicate them to local groups. On any representative body, like a trade union executive, Communists would form a 'fraction' to work together, preparing their policy in advance of meetings. In factories Party members would meet as a 'nucleus'.

CP leaders were used to a much freer sort of organization. So Moscow demonstrated the importance it attached to Britain's tiny CP and to conformity by applying some Comintern discipline. It invited the whole Central Committee to Moscow for 'consultations'.

Apart from being expensive, this left the CP leaderless for more than a month, but the committee returned to England after listening to Lenin himself for hours on end, convinced, as Willie Gallacher had been before them, that the experienced and successful revolutionaries in Moscow really did know best.

Yet Arthur McManus and Albert Inkpin still dragged their feet, leading Pollitt and Dutt to form a secret group of 'young Turks'. Apart from Pollitt they were mostly young intellectuals. One of them was Rose Cohen, with whom Harry Pollitt fell passionately in love. He asked her to marry him several times. She always refused but they remained friends even after she married and went to live in Moscow. He could not have guessed in 1922 that fifteen years later he would plead with Comintern officials for her life, in secret and without success.

If Pollitt's love was thwarted, so was Dutt's. Salme was living in England illegally. She had to stay in her room overlooking Regents Park, going out, if at all, only after dark. Dutt hardly ever saw her: it was too dangerous. Salme was a key figure in the conspiracy – for that is what it had become: a conspiracy to remodel the Party on Russian Bolshevik lines, and put Pollitt in charge. They both deferred to her views. But Dutt overplayed his hand. As editor of *Workers' Weekly* he published a fictional piece about a Manchester metalworker who moved to London ready to give his all for socialism, and who bore a startling resemblance to Pollitt. This wholesome young hero saw the worthlessness of the old guard, including one who bore the same initials as McManus and was 'definitely demoralising, with all his old habits, including drinking.' It sunk the conspiracy. From then on, however much he admired Dutt's brain, Pollitt had no doubt which of them was the political leader.

Now, though they had their new structure, and Pollitt went to King Street as national organizer responsible for the Party's industrial work, the Party was split. Inkpin felt under attack. Jack Murphy and Andrew Rothstein were irritated by the way the Comintern were pushing Pollitt and Dutt. Murphy spoke of Dutt's 'incapacity, bankruptcy and confusion' and referred to Pollitt as Dutt's 'sheepish acolyte'.

Shortly before the general strike both Dutt and Pollitt changed residence. Pollitt's move was involuntary. He was one of twelve

Communists to be arrested, the week after he married a Communist schoolteacher, Marjorie Brewer. He spent a year in Wandsworth Prison. Dutt, together with Salme who was now his wife, went to live in Brussels, where he stayed until 1935.

To judge from their own accounts Pollitt had more fun in his new abode than Dutt in his. He laughed at the prison chaplain, who looked at the pictures on his cell wall of his sister's two children and said: 'Tch! Born out of wedlock, I suppose.' He was put to work with Albert Inkpin, who, he found, had 'a great sense of humour.' A professional burglar berated him for having no respect for private property. The worst part was doing without cigarettes. The day of his release 'I smoked 14 Gold Flake straight off . . . and promptly paid for my folly by vomiting violently. But it was worth it, all the same.'

As for Dutt, quite why he spent the next eleven years in Brussels no one has ever known for sure. He said he went there for his health. His health was certainly bad – he had spinal tuberculosis – but Brussels was as unlikely a health resort then as it is now. It made Salme's position a little easier: she could at least go out in Brussels. It also made it easier for Dutt to make frequent trips to Berlin and Paris to meet Comintern agents. There was speculation that the Dutts were working as international spies. This seems to be an exaggeration. Their home certainly became a link in the chain for Comintern messages. Salme kept in close touch with her sister Hella, whose home in Helsinki was nicknamed locally the 'spy centre' because of the constant flow of foreigners who passed through it, including top-ranking Soviet soldiers and diplomats. If they were spies, the Dutts were grossly underpaid, for they lived very frugally.

Yet when all this has been said, an extraordinary mystery remains. Dutt was one of the leaders of the CP. He was consulted on everything and expected to be informed of everything. He was consulted by the Comintern on matters relating to Britain. He edited *Labour Monthly* and wrote the column Notes of the Month, which was accepted as the authoritative statement of the Party line. Yet he lived in a foreign capital and never visited England.

The extra factor may lie in his personality. Beneath the cold, logical Dutt everyone knew, there was a seething mass of nervous jealousy. He saw personal slights everywhere. It probably seemed sensible to the more experienced Salme and her contacts further east to remove Dutt from the centre of CP politics. He could be most use if he was not always on his colleagues' backs, fretting about what they were doing.

Meanwhile, to end the general strike of May 1926 the TUC, led by J. H. Thomas of the railwaymen, struck an unwritten deal with Lord Samuel, who claimed to be an unofficial emissary for the government. The miners would go back to work, on lower wages and with worse conditions, and the mineowners would take them all back. There would be no victimizations.

Miners' leader Arthur Cook, ill with anxiety and overwork – he was the miners' only full-time official – appealed desperately to the TUC general council not to call off the strike on these miserable terms. He was right: the no victimization agreement turned out to be a deception. Miners stayed loyal to Cook, who was close to the CP although not a member of it. 'Part of his brain' writes his biographer Paul Davies, 'told Cook that the miners would be beaten; the rest of his body, particularly his heart and guts, told him they must fight.'

Soviet money was put to a new use. At least £270,000 went into the mining communities. Without it hundreds of mining families would have watched their children starve. Labour MPs in mining constituencies knew who was keeping food in the mouths of their constituents, and some of them, too, warmed towards the Communists for a while. After seven months the miners were starved back to work – those whom the mineowners felt were no threat. The bitterness in mining areas was passed down the generations. It is still there today.

CP membership more than doubled between 1925 and 1926, reaching over 10,000. But a year later it was down to just over 7000 and by the end of 1929 it had plummeted to 3200. How did the Party lose its advantage? It had backed the miners to the hilt. Soviet money stopped them from starving. It had fought for an embargo on coal (on one occasion headlining an article in *Workers' Weekly* ALL COAL IS BLACK). But it systematically destroyed the goodwill it had amassed by its determination to show that the miners had no other friends than the CP. The obvious rival for the miners' affections was the Independent Labour Party, which was by now so much more radical than the Labour Party itself that it was almost a separate party, and believed that the miners had been shamefully betrayed by the TUC and the Labour Party. But the CP, instead of welcoming the ILP as allies, set out to prove to the miners that the ILP was really an enemy in disguise. In June acting-secretary Bob Stewart (Inkpin was still in prison) wrote to the ILP calling for a joint campaign around four Communist Party slogans. ILP leaders resented being asked to play second fiddle and carried on with their own campaigns. This enabled the CP to level the absurd accusation that the ILP was really against the miners.

A headline in *Workers Weekly* in July read: WILL THE ILP JOIN IN THE FIGHT FOR THAT EMBARGO? The paper claimed that the Communist Party was fighting for the miners 'even though it is absolutely alone.' 'Isn't the ILP just simply too wonderful?' began a long heavy-handed piece of satire on 30 July. The real enemies, it appeared, were not those who opposed the miners, but those who supported them without supporting the CP.

In September *Workers' Weekly* turned on Arthur Cook himself – and forfeited all the CP's support in the mining communities. Miners knew that Cook was rapidly destroying his health by working seven days a week without a break and refusing to take more in salary than a miner was getting in strike pay. The CP accusation that he was 'not only losing faith in the workers, but allying himself with their enemies' seemed to miners not only absurd, but a wicked calumny against a man they revered.

How could the CP have been so stupid? The answer lay in Moscow. Lenin died in 1924. Power was now in the hands of Kamenev, Zinoviev and Stalin, and the struggle for absolute power lasted until Stalin's total victory in 1929. Trotsky led the 'left opposition' and was expelled from the Politburo in 1926. The honour of proposing his expulsion from the Comintern executive fell to a British Communist, Jack Murphy. Now the CP's man in Moscow, he tried to keep his colleagues in touch, but did not always understand what was going on.

The Moscow power struggle affected everything the CP did and every attitude it struck. You might have thought that the power brokers in Moscow had better things to do than watch what their tiny British outpost was up to, but you would be wrong. The CP found itself being lectured like a naughty child for failing to follow the 'correct' line – as most recently laid down. A typical closed letter during the general strike explained that 'the British events have DEFINITELY SETTLED the controversy over the problem of capitalist stabilisation. The viewpoint of Comintern has been fully and splendidly confirmed. The Praesidium was correct and the British were wrong ...' The 'controversy' was about the arcane question of how far capitalism had stabilized after the upheaval of the First World War.

After the general strike some British Communists like Johnny Campbell continued their supportive relationship with their old friend Arthur Cook. But this was in contradiction to the emerging Comintern line. As Stalin consolidated his victory, the Comintern was adopting what was called the 'new line' – a policy called Class Against Class, which outlawed such relationships. Nonetheless, as late as 1928, when Cook and ILP leader James Maxton launched a joint manifesto, Cook's speech was actually prepared by Campbell.

Maxton was a brilliant and captivating public speaker, painfully thin, a chain-smoker with long wavy black hair, and one of the most popular and romantic figures in British politics. He commanded great affection and loyalty. Many of his followers were fellow Scots from the 'Red Clyde', with backgrounds similar to McManus, Gallacher and Campbell. Many worked closely with Communists.

Maxton could see the division in the CP. A revealing secret memorandum from Willie Gallacher to the Comintern says: 'Maxton and his friends are barely on speaking terms with me, but they are very friendly with Johnny Campbell and [South Wales miners' leader and Communist] Arthur Horner. Maxton needs the CP for material but wants it from Johnny and Horner.... Cook is as cunning as they make them and as unscrupulous ... We can I think just about finish off the ILP ... Poor me, I'm in bad, with [trade union leader] Hicks also. Both meetings he has attended I keep insisting that he has got to admit his part in betraying the general strike and in the break with the Soviet Union.' He talks of the appeal for funds for the Cook-Maxton campaign, adding: 'What about some Moscow Gold? ... Ask Bukharin to send a couple of bob to the Cook-Maxton fund.'

Class Against Class, the new line, meant in practice that the CP must stop trying to affiliate to the Labour Party and instead attack it relentlessly. It called for an end, worldwide, to collaboration with social democrats. In particular, Labour left wingers must be denounced vehemently. The most bitter abuse must be reserved for the ILP, whose views and aims were closest to those of the Communist Party, and its leaders must be denounced – Moscow even laid down the exact phrase – as 'social fascists'.

Those like Dutt whose ears were most sensitively attuned to the Moscow tune had been operating Class Against Class since soon after the general strike, which was why *Workers Weekly* had so abruptly turned on the ILP and Arthur Cook. Dutt was impatient for Communist leaders to adopt the new line, detecting, as he often did, foot-dragging on the part of his colleagues when it came to obeying the Comintern. They could not pretend they did not know about Class Against Class. They often travelled to Moscow. They had their own representative there and a Comintern representative in Britain.

So in February 1928, while Campbell and Gallacher were in Moscow at the Comintern executive meeting, Dutt devoted his Notes of the Month to a criticism of the leadership for their tardiness in formally adopting the new line. Although *Workers' Weekly* was doing its duty by pillorying Maxton and Cook, Campbell was still being permitted to behave as though Maxton and Cook were friends. This would not do. The CP Politburo passed a 'severe censure' on Dutt for his 'thinly disguised attack on the Party.' At once his friends and enemies alike, in Moscow and in London, were besieged with long, detailed, hurt missives from Brussels, each one bearing testimony to the fury of a thin-skinned man unable to confess to human weakness.

Dutt was under enormous strain. He was ill and in constant pain. Salme was even iller and due to have a serious operation. He felt that the sole burden of keeping the British Party in line rested on his shoulders. He wrote first to the Politburo, three closely typewritten pages demanding that they must rescind the resolution and formulate 'a specific charge to which I may reply.' They must do it at once 'in view of the damage that may already have been caused in the Party.'

Another letter followed. Andrew Rothstein had criticized Notes of the Month in a private conversation with Dutt's brother. Dutt did not know if anyone else was present. Rothstein must 'take steps to correct this so as to remove any injury he may have done to the *Labour Monthly* by the spreading of such statements ...'

37

Dutt noted that Pollitt had voted for the censure. Here was betrayal. Six pages went to Pollitt, covered in Dutt's small, precise hand. 'I refused to believe it, and guessed there must be some trick ... I stand under severe censure, before the whole Party, completely unjustified... have not even yet received any specific charge or opportunity to answer it, stand under censure for what I believe to be some of the best political work I have done for the Party ... Since you have taken the position with the others of political censure and condemner of what I have written, will you please tell me, what I have in vain asked for from the others and failed to get any answer, what passages, by line and by word, you condemn, and why? Will you please tell me if there is anything in the existing Party line on the Labour Party as it then was, i.e. ....' And so on.

It was not personal, of course. 'Good God, Harry, I wouldn't write like this if it was only a question of me personally involved.' But 'I feel this, that you feel as a burden your association with me and Salme and that you want to be free of it ...' Salme wrote, too. 'Harry, Harry, this time I wish from all my heart that you may never see that I have once more been right on a big thing. Your conscience will prick you ever so much harder. And I shall cry.'

Harry replied in April. The Dutts were hurt that his dictated reply began 'Dear Reggie' instead of 'Dear Raji'. Salme replied at once: 'Some time it had to come, as fighting in our work is inevitable, and we don't know how to fight with kid gloves on ... Raji represented a definite policy for which it was necessary to fight and hit everybody hard who didn't understand.' Dutt wrote the same day: 'I am very sorry that you have not troubled to treat my letter seriously ... I do not think you can have seen the resolution for which you voted' and he painstakingly typed it out, no doubt from memory.

What on earth was going on in the Dutt household? The answer lies in a long series of letters Dutt wrote to his friend Robin Page Arnot in Moscow. Page Arnot was an academic, an expert on the British mining industry. He was a Scot with a deep, melodious voice and bottomless cunning. He had been part of the Pollitt-Dutt conspiracy and was now Britain's representative at the Comintern.

In these letters, Dutt's handwriting gets worse and there are more and more afterthoughts added in boxes at the top, the bottom and the sides of the paper. 'Please answer IMMEDIATELY on this letter as it contains my serious urgent points for your view on' and 'Why no letter, NOT ONE WORD, after all promises?' 'Still no word from you since you left. This is very serious. I have no knowledge whatever what is happening, I do not even know if my article has reached, or, if reached, whether it is being used . . . I know nothing. The "avis de reception" with which my article was sent has not been received here.' Then after a day or two, back to the matter in hand: 'The question of the discussion in the Party seems to me to be very serious. Consider the facts . . .' and he recites in fine detail over several pages the history of the Comintern's policy and the CP's failure, in his view, to implement it.

He writes again the very next day. The Politburo resolution 'has a terrible effect on *Labour Monthly* circulation. (It is really damnable that for their own personal spite they must smash whatever is living in the Party.)' In mid-April there is a hint of what is to come: 'Have just had a bad time with work due to trying too hard.' And then it came, in the form of a telegram from Brussels: REGRET BREAKDOWN THROUGH OVERWORK COMPELS ABANDON ATTEMPT WRITE BOOK . . . RAJI. The book was to have been called *Reformism in England*, and the Comintern had asked for it. A letter followed. 'During the past fortnight I have been desperately struggling to face pressure of other work, but have failed all round. The three days when I couldn't work or do anything was a warning. I am now in danger of going to pieces completely. A period of too much pressure and activity all round since the question of the new line.'

Yet by this time Dutt's victory was complete. Arnot wrote from Moscow to Inkpin: 'In my opinion Comrade Dutt has shown great self-control in his notes. It is quite obvious to me that your "severe censure" will be treated . . . as a "political act". This . . . may give the impression of a campaign against the Comintern resolution and against all who defend it.' There was no greater crime than a campaign against a Comintern decision. By April Inkpin's letters to Dutt consisted of headlong retreat. He sent a telegram to Moscow: CENTRAL COMMITTEE UNANIMOUSLY ACCEPTS PLENUM RESOLUTION AS MEANING COMPLETE CHANGE POLICY STOP WITHDRAWS OWN THESIS GROUNDS INADEQUACY MISTAKES . . . It was the humiliating climbdown Dutt and the Comintern demanded, but it was still not good enough for the senior theoretician. He demanded more apologies, more grovelling, more statements about how he was right, more 'self-criticism' from everyone else for being wrong. In June, the censure was at last withdrawn in sufficiently grovelling terms to satisfy Dutt. He wrote at once to Arnot with the news: 'Do please write more than a few lines. Many old points on letters remain unanswered.'

The Comintern successfully used the Young Communist League, led by Bill Rust and Dave Springhall, to impose its will on the CP. These were now the young Turks, as Pollitt, Dutt and Page Arnot had been just four years earlier. Rust and Springhall were young working-class Londoners who had grown up in the Party. It was their life and their career. To them obedience to Moscow was as natural as eating.

Rust was described by a colleague in 1928 as 'round and pink and cold as ice.' He was tall, plump and just 25. Few people saw him smile and no one seems to know what made him tick. Springhall was big and muscular and noisy, the sort of man who always knows best, and he walked with the rolling gait of a former sailor, which he was. Together they turned the Young Communist League into a Comintern watchdog, looking over Inkpin's shoulder and ensuring there was no shilly-shallying. It was to be the new line, all the new line, and nothing but the new line or Bill Rust would know the reason why.

In Moscow in July 1928 at the Comintern Congress, Rust took on the role of prosecutor, denouncing the British leadership. Manuilsky, the Ukrainian Communist leader and the main Soviet representative, added that Dutt and Page Arnot were the only correct theoreticians it possessed. The existing leadership, he said, had made serious mistakes and been too sympathetic to non-Communist left wingers like Maxton and Cook. Throughout that summer the unfortunate, inoffensive Inkpin had been under constant attack from Moscow. Everything he did, even a sentence in a speech by Saklatvala, all were sticks to beat him with. In May Dutt had still not accepted the climbdown, and Inkpin had to grovel further. In June a Comintern committee decided in strict secrecy that 'the financial affairs of the CP must no longer be handled through Comrade Inkpin . . . Up to now he has not realised the reasons for his mistakes and the consequences of the false measures in the handling of the financial affairs.' Whether or not there was the slightest justification for the report's implication that he was not discreet about the CP's financial affairs, it is now impossible to establish with certainty.

The Comintern instructed the CP to hold a special Congress in November. It sent a letter to this Congress: 'The opportunist elements in the Party leadership ... must be brought out into the open and ruthlessly exposed.' A new method of electing the Central Committee was adopted, called the 'Bolshevik method' though it had never been used by Lenin. This meant electing a nominations commission which put forward a recommended list. The Congress would then be invited to vote for the whole of the recommended list.

Moscow was looking, not just for obedience, but for all key positions to be filled by devoted adherents of the new line. There were disturbing reports of doubts being expressed by Campbell and Inkpin. Rothstein, surprisingly, had got it wrong. Even Gallacher, who had tried throughout to make sure Moscow thought he was reliable, had equivocated too much and was suspect.

Arthur McManus had died in 1927, at only 38. His ashes were embedded in the walls of the Kremlin, where old drinking companions could pay their respects every day. The Comintern favoured a new leadership of Dutt as theoretician and Pollitt as practical politician. Inkpin tried to reassert himself. He told the Comintern that Page Arnot no longer represented the British view in Moscow and should be withdrawn. Page Arnot did, however, represent what the Comintern wished to become the British view, and he stayed. Inkpin registered 'a most emphatic protest against a decision of this character being made without the slightest reference to the British Party' but he was ignored.

Andrew Rothstein grovelled in an unsuccessful attempt to save his job as editor of the *Sunday Worker*. 'I wish to remind the Politburo that, when I was unfortunate enough to totally misunderstand the 9th Plenum decision [about the new line] ... I was the first to propose the strongest possible correction in the following week's paper.'

Inkpin, Rothstein, miners' leader Arthur Horner and other 'opportunists' were thrown off the Central Committee. Campbell and Gallacher were thrown off the Politburo. Pollitt became general secretary, combining Inkpin's duties with McManus's leadership role.

The Instrument of Steel

Inkpin had been full-time secretary since well before the First World War – first for the British Socialist Party, then for the Communists. He had served two long prison terms. It was unlikely that he could find other work. Pollitt thought Inkpin should be offered a Party job. Rust, ruthless and unsentimental about people who got the line wrong, wanted to leave him to rot. Someone started a false rumour that Inkpin was keeping a pub on the side. But the Comintern surprised everyone by agreeing with Pollitt, and Inkpin became secretary of the Friends of the Soviet Union.

The Comintern was still not satisfied that the CP had sufficiently repented of its headstrong ways. At a Comintern Congress in 1929 Manuilsky attacked the CP for failing to follow Moscow politics closely enough: 'How does it happen that all the fundamental problems of the Communist International fail to stir our fraternal British party? ... All these problems have the appearance of being forcibly injected into the activities of the British Communist Party ... The German comrades carefully weigh every word spoken by anybody. They allow no deviation from the line, they attack the least deviation, respecting no persons.' But the British party, he said contemptuously, 'is a society of great friends.' It was a sad state of affairs, not completely rectified until the 1980s when the British CP adopted Manuilsky's prescription to the letter and tore itself to pieces.

At the general election of May 1929, Labour emerged as the biggest single party, but without an overall majority, and MacDonald formed his second Labour government. A hard core of seventeen ILP MPs under James Maxton formed the left-wing socialist opposition in Parliament to MacDonald's right-wing Labour government. Far from making common cause with Maxton's group, the new line required the CP to denounce them as 'social fascists'. Indeed, it reserved special venom for them, reasoning that they were leading the working class away from the true path of revolutionary socialism.

In August 1931 the cabinet was told that the only way to save the pound was a 10 per cent cut in the already inadequate levels of unemployment benefit. But why, asked the left, was the only solution to take money away from the poorest and most vulnerable people in Britain? No one had a satisfactory answer,

42

except that it was said to be a condition of a loan from a New York banker.

As August ended, the cabinet resigned, but MacDonald remained Prime Minister in a national government. Sixty-eight year old Arthur Henderson became Labour leader. When the election came in October the Maxton group were sent forms to sign promising always to obey the Labour whip. Most refused to sign, and Labour put up official candidates against them in their constituencies. Only Maxton and two other Glasgow MPs were re-elected. Labour went down to a massive defeat. The National Government (mostly Conservatives, together with MacDonald and the few Labour people who had followed him) won 556 seats, a majority of 500 over all opposition parties. Soon the ILP and the Labour Party formally parted company.

The left fragmented. Some people on Labour's left, like John Strachey, started down the road which led to the CP. Some, like Stafford Cripps, wanted ILP policies and Labour Party membership; they formed the Socialist League. Oswald Mosley and Robert Forgan led a group of socialists into the British Union of Fascists. Some stayed in the ILP, but this was quickly ground to death between the Labour Party anvil and the CP hammer. Communists targeted its candidates for abuse in the 1931 election and ran organized campaigns to disrupt its meetings.

Jack Jones, later a powerful trade union leader, was then a left-wing Labour councillor in Liverpool. He remembers the CP in this period: 'Their methods were the same as the Socialist Workers' Party in the 1970s. They make a long statement with demands which are completely removed from reality, and then condemn you for not implementing it.'

The ILP still had 20,000 members but was fatally split. Its Revolutionary Policy Committee was close to the CP and was led by a law student called Jack Gaster, the 22-year-old son of a rabbi. His political friends were Bill Rust and Dave Springhall. The older generation saw Gaster's group as infiltrators, there only to damage the ILP from within. Gaster denies this, but when in 1935 the Committee dissolved itself and its members joined the CP, he took care to ensure that they acted together for greatest effect.

Infiltrators there certainly were, whether Gaster's group was among them or not. Several keen young Communists joined the

ILP 'as a means' wrote one of them, Douglas Hyde, 'of taking my communism into the enemy camp.' Hyde became an ILP secretary in North Wales, where most members were elderly folk who could remember working with Keir Hardie or Ramsay MacDonald. When the ILP left the Labour Party, he demanded that they all tear up their Labour Party cards. When they refused, he expelled them from the ILP.

The CP's daily newspaper, the *Daily Worker*, was born into Class Against Class. It was founded on Comintern instructions and edited by Bill Rust. In the first issue, on 1 January 1930, Dutt wrote an article headed SHAM LEFT'S NEW ALLIES. Maxton and Cook were speaking in Maxton's constituency when Communists disrupted the meeting. The police arrested three Communists. Therefore, 'Cook and Maxton are now the recognised leaders of the "police socialists."'

Later issues explained how Cook was tricking the miners into not fighting for a seven-hour day, and spelled out the tactics of 'the Lloyd George-MacDonald-Maxton alliance.' The headline BOW WORKERS BOO LANSBURY - POLLITT GREETED WITH GREAT ENTHUSIASM probably did not convey the full flavour of the event it reported.

The *Daily Worker* was the first newspaper to identify Oswald Mosley as a Fascist, while he was still in the Labour Party. This achievement is not as remarkable as it sounds. If you call everyone a Fascist you must hit a winner eventually.

Running a daily paper, Pollitt had to do what Inkpin had spent so much time doing: begging for money from Moscow. In his last two years as secretary Inkpin had spent a lot of his time pleading with an increasingly hostile Comintern. The CP had an allowance of £54,000 in 1927. Inkpin wrote to Page Arnot in Moscow at the end of the year. The Comintern was saying he must take a reduction of £9000 for 1928, with agreement to consider special sums for particular work. He haggled. Moscow seems to have been capricious about money. Dutt suffered from this – the odd small cheque he received never appeared to relate to anything, and never seemed to be adequate payment for his long, painstaking articles.

In 1930 Pollitt was writing to his representatives Campbell and Alec Herman in Moscow about 'a financial problem that I do not know how to face'. In a handwritten note at the bottom he wrote: 'Last Saturday I threatened to commit suicide to Ward, he staved off my death by giving me £500 but the *Daily* is eating money . . . Dorritt [the printer] is at a standstill . . . Get the Old Man [the Comintern] to do something. If things don't perk up I am coming to see him myself.' 'Ward' was probably the code name of a Comintern courier.

Pollitt knew that the money he got to run the *Daily Worker* depended on Moscow's approval of its contents. He wrote to Herman just two weeks into the paper's life to say that finances were a problem, and asked Herman to seek the views of 'the responsible comrades you are in touch with' about its contents. Should there be more non-political news? Could Herman initiate a debate in Moscow 'on the content and makeup of the paper?' What do they think of 'the character of the sports pages?' Unfortunately the Comintern's comments on the sports pages have not survived. But there is little doubt that it would have had something to say, perhaps on the tone of the cricket reports. The Comintern had comments on most things, and ignorance of the subject was never an inhibiting factor.

Gradually the futility of Class Against Class was born in even on the faraway Comintern. Soon after the 1931 election Pollitt began lobbying in Moscow to be allowed to change the line again. Dutt opposed this. His letters to Pollitt are calmer than those of 1928 – he seems to have recovered from his breakdown – but they convey distress and irritation that the pupil thinks he knows better than the master.

There were meetings with Maxton and the ILP secretary Fenner Brockway. Dutt was almost pathological about the kindly, hard-working Brockway. He wrote a long briefing note to Pollitt before Pollitt and Brockway were due to debate in April 1932. The three closely typed pages end: 'NO POLITENESS! No mere 'difference of opinion.' No parliamentary debate. No handshakes. Treatment is CLASS ENEMIES throughout. You speak for holy anger of whole international working class against the foulness that is Brockway. Make that whole audience HATE him.' Brockway wrote afterwards: 'He declared war to the knife on the ILP.'

But the damage done to the British left by Class Against Class was nothing to the damage it did in Germany. The German Communist Party's adherence to Class Against Class was crucial in helping Hitler to power.

3

Fascism and Spain

M oscow theorists were sure that Germany would be the next country to turn to Communism. The German Communist Party, the biggest in the world outside Russia, won nearly 6 million votes in the November 1932 election. The social democrats won 7.2 million and the Nazis 11.7 million. So there were over 13 million votes for the left – enough to beat the Nazis. But the new line, Class Against Class, prevented the Communists from allying with the social democrats against Hitler's National Socialist Party. This stunning Comintern miscalculation was one of the reasons why Adolf Hitler became Chancellor on 30 January 1933.

September saw the trial of four Communists accused of burning down the German parliament, the Reichstag. One of them was a Comintern agent, the founder of the Bulgarian Communist Party, 51-year old Georgi Dimitrov, who decided to defend himself in court, although German was a foreign language to him. He was so effective that most of the world ended up convinced the Nazis had burned down their own Parliament (which they had). The four were acquitted and freed, and Dimitrov went to Moscow in triumph.

There he determined to convince Stalin and the Comintern that Class Against Class was a mistake. The Comintern's seventh world Congress was delayed while the battle raged, for no one in Moscow wanted a debate until they had decided on the outcome. The Congress met eventually in August 1935. As usual, no one admitted

46

that the Comintern had made a mistake. Dimitrov's report *The Working Class Against Fascism* was presented as a response to a new situation. But it stood the policy on its head and called for a united front of all left-wing parties against Fascism. Dimitrov's credentials in the battle against Fascism were now assured. He led the Comintern after this, and his prestige was crucial in keeping the CP in line in later years. In 1945 he returned to his native Bulgaria as head of the government.

The world had not waited for the Comintern to sort out its internal politics. In France, an alliance between the Communist Party and the Socialist Party, the Popular Front, was already more than a year old. And in Britain, Harry Pollitt had quietly discarded much of the ideological baggage of Class Against Class. A few days after Hitler's triumph the ILP and the CP held a joint demonstration against Fascism. Pollitt and Campbell started to meet frequently with Maxton and Brockway. Maxton was understandably suspicious and resentful, though Brockway recalls: 'Pollitt was as skilful a negotiator as he was a speaker.'

Sir Oswald Mosley made unity urgent by founding the British Union of Fascists in 1932. Mosley was not to be taken lightly. Behind him lay a meteoric Labour Party career. A favourite of Labour leader Ramsay MacDonald, he was tipped to become foreign secretary in 1929, but instead was given the task of assisting the cynical, decaying Jimmy Thomas to find a remedy for unemployment. His proposals were rejected. He resigned and left the Labour Party to form the New Party, which he soon turned into a Fascist organization.

Mosley in 1932 was not yet 40. He was an impressive public speaker and an establishment figure, with powerful establishment support – including that of Lord Rothermere, whose *Daily Mail* hailed the British Union of Fascists with the headline HURRAH FOR THE BLACKSHIRTS. Most important of all, Mosley had money – a vast inherited fortune which he now used to further his political ambitions.

The fact that Mosley left the Labour Party because it was too conservative made him more dangerous. Mussolini had come from the left. France's future Fascist leader, Doriot, was in 1932 one of the leaders of the Parti Communiste Français. With the left fractured and despairing after the traumas of 1931, and with unemployment, poverty and injustice still rampant after a post-war decade of unfulfilled promises by Labour, Mosley could attract support that, in better times, would go to the left. His supporters included former ILP members. His chief ideologue was a former Communist, Raven Thomson. Working-class recruits included two unemployed Communists who had just finished prison terms for distributing Communist leaflets to soldiers.

The CP pioneered the policy of disrupting his meetings. At a vast meeting at Olympia in June 1934, Mosley was prepared for disruption. He stood under a spotlight, surrounded by twenty-four amplifiers. Whenever he was interrupted, Mosley would pause, the spotlight would swing on to the hecklers, and uniformed blackshirts would throw them out. The violence alienated establishment figures and helped to ensure Mosley's decline.

Fascist support was now concentrated in the East End of London and increasingly reliant on anti-semitism. Mosley planned a big march through the East End which the CP aimed to stop. Its slogan was 'They shall not pass.' The Labour Party advised people to stay away, but this time the Communists were more in tune with the feeling of East Enders, especially the Jewish community, than Labour leaders. The CP strategy succeeded: the police told Mosley he could not go ahead with his march.

Among Jews who joined the Communist Party because they saw it as a bulwark against Fascism were Phil Piratin, who became a Communist MP in 1945; Sara Wesker, a future Central Committee member, whose experiences partly inspired the first and best plays by her nephew, Arnold Wesker, thirty years later; and Reuben Falber, who was to become assistant general secretary and, in 1957, took on the task of secretly bringing Soviet money to the aid of the Party.

Communists were also seen as the only effective opposition to Spanish Fascism. In July 1936, a group of Spanish army officers led by General Franco staged a rebellion against their newly elected government, an alliance of republicans, socialists and Communists. Franco asked Mussolini and Hitler for help. The two dictators responded with ammunition, aircraft and troops. The Spanish government asked for help from western democracies, Britain and France, but was refused. The British Conservative government pioneered the policy of non-intervention, preventing anyone from selling arms to Spain. The only place from which the Spanish government could get weapons was the Soviet Union.

The CP denounced non-intervention. Sales of the *Daily Worker* soared as its star reporter Claud Cockburn filed moving reports of the struggles of the Spanish people against overwhelming odds. Several Communists went to work behind the front line as doctors, ambulance drivers and nurses. A few joined the Republican army. Then the Comintern backed the formation of International Brigades: units of anti-Fascist volunteers from all countries, willing to fight and die alongside the Spanish government forces.

On 5 December 1936 Harry Pollitt appealed through the *Daily Worker* for volunteers to go to Spain and fight. By the end of the month, nearly 500 men had gone, and the next month the British Battalion was formed. The British government at once tried to stop it. The foreign office declared that enlisting in the Spanish forces was illegal under the 1870 Foreign Enlistment Act. So recruitment went underground. Groups of recruits assembled at constantly changing venues in London. More than once frantic search parties were sent out from the CP's Covent Garden headquarters to find, say, a lost group of Scots.

In London the volunteers were given a weekend ticket to Paris. From Paris, they were sent to different towns near the Spanish border, in the hope of confusing the French authorities. Some were told to get a train to the walled city of Carcassonne. Others went to Perpignan, others to Sète. There they hid for a night or two in the home of a local Communist before being given a pair of rope-soled shoes in which to cross the Pyrenees.

Every night groups of men were led across the mountains, using smugglers' routes and led by smugglers. They walked for about sixteen hours, in total darkness and often freezing cold, through narrow mountain passes sometimes deep in snow. 'You could only see the man in front,' recalled Dave Goodman half a century later. 'You relied totally on following him. Once someone crashed down into the ravine. I never found out who it was.' The wind was often so strong that it almost tore the clothes from their bodies. The men had to hug the ground, thousands of feet up a mountain, until it died down.

Between 1936 and 1939, about 2200 volunteers went from Britain. Between a third and a half of them were Communists;

526 volunteers were killed. The CP, like other Communist Parties, also sent political commissars. 'The political commissar is the collaborator of the commander, the political adviser and friend of the men, and his work extends to the smallest details that contribute to their material well-being,' wrote Bill Rust. 'He does not issue circulars from an office, but fights alongside the men.' They were said to be necessary because this was a fundamentally different sort of army from a capitalist army. In the latter, the attitude was summed up by Lord Tennyson: 'Theirs not to reason why; theirs but to do and die.' In the International Brigade, volunteers needed constant, day-to-day information on the political situation, so that they fully understood the significance of what they were doing. In the First World War it was deemed sufficient to tell the men they were fighting for king and country. These volunteers needed to know rather more than that.

Rust was officially in Spain for the *Daily Worker*. In reality he was Britain's senior commissar and a Comintern representative, with an office in Barcelona. Working with his old Young Communist comrade Dave Springhall, he directed the work of the commissars who were with the men at the front. As the front was forced back towards Barcelona, Rust took to visiting it each day.

Commissars were a mixed blessing. Certainly they helped keep up morale, both by reminding the men what they were there for, and by helping with the sort of problems which are bound to arise when men are under constant strain, exhausted, short of weapons and supplies. Sometimes their role was more sinister: they were also witch-hunters. About forty British volunteers fought, not with the International Brigade, but with the POUM – Workers' Party of Marxist Unity – militia. POUM had broken away from the Spanish Communist Party in 1931 and was close to Trotsky, who had been expelled from the Soviet Union. Behind the lines in Republican Spain, this internal Soviet conflict flared up into open warfare, with deadly results.

In May 1937 there was fighting behind the Spanish Republican lines. Historians have struggled ever since with the exact rights and wrongs. Government forces, supported by the Communists, fought anarchists and POUM supporters for the Barcelona telephone exchange. Communists branded POUM as Trotskyist wreckers and Fascist agents. POUM supporters denounced Communists as

Stalinist killers. At this time conflict inside the Soviet Union was at its sharpest, and in Moscow the slightest suggestion of Trotskyism was enough to send anyone to their death. In Madrid, the government outlawed POUM. In London the evils of POUM and Trotskyism became almost an obsession with CP leaders – and remained so for the next half century.

The chief foreign commissar, the French Communist André Marty, was memorably – and accurately – pictured in Ernest Hemingway's *For Whom the Bell Tolls*. A Spanish Republican soldier is speaking to the hero, an American brigader:

'He is as crazy as a bedbug. He has a mania for shooting people.'

'Truly shooting them?'

'That old one kills more than the bubonic plague. But he doesn't kill fascists like we do. He kills rare things. Trotzkyites. Divagationers. Any type of rare beast.'

Hemingway describes Marty (disguised in some editions as Massart) as a 'tall, heavy, old man ... His face looked as though it were modelled from the waste material you find under the claws of a very old lion.' Before men were shot, he 'did not mind the men cursing him. So many men had cursed him at the end. He was always genuinely sorry for them as human beings. He always told himself that and it was one of the last true ideas that was left to him that had ever been his own.' He describes Marty sticking his finger on to a hill on a map he did not understand: 'Later, men who never saw the map ... would climb its side to find their death along its slope ... the general would think: "I should shoot you, André Marty, before I let you put that grey rotten finger on a contour map of mine ... Go and suspect and exhort and intervene and denounce and butcher in some other place and leave my staff alone."'

Fred Copeman, who commanded the British Battalion, wrote many years later: 'There were too many bastards running round giving orders and not enough of them fighting. And those that were giving orders, they were useless silly orders and irresponsible to human life.' But his successor as British Battalion commander, Bill Alexander, paints a slightly different picture of Marty. Though 'irascible, suspicious, unpredictable' he remembered also his 'drive, determination and single-mindedness.' Perhaps it is another way of saying the same thing.

POUM was eventually suppressed, its leaders arrested and many of them killed in prison. The ILP supported POUM, and it was therefore in Spain that the new CP-ILP alliance broke apart. Having called the ILP 'social fascists', horrified CP leaders now jumped to an even more appalling and equally wrong conclusion. They were not social fascists after all. They were much worse. They were Trotskyists.

The forty or so Britons sent to fight with POUM by the ILP included George Orwell and 19-year-old Bob Smillie, grandson of a legendary miners' leader with the same name. Smillie ended up dying, not from a Fascist bullet, but in a Republican prison, where he was sent after being arrested on the border, suspected of Trotskyism. He was on his way home on leave after three months with the POUM militia. The government claimed he developed appendicitis in prison and died of it, and perhaps he did. The British ILP representative in Barcelona was refused permission to see his body. Orwell wrote:

'Here was this brave and gifted boy, who had thrown up his career at Glasgow University in order to come and fight against fascism, and who, as I saw for myself, had done his job at the front with faultless courage and willingness; and all they could find to do with him was to fling him into jail and let him die like a neglected animal.'

For the remaining fifty years of its life the Communist Party insisted that POUM was either being paid by the Fascists, or might as well be. Communist volunteers had no reason not to believe what they were told: that POUM people were Fascist spies. To them Spain was as morally simple as it was for Smillie. They had volunteered to live in constant fear, to expect death or serious injury, in a dirty, brutal, vicious war, because they loved liberty and equality and hated Fascism. None of them knew how close to them was that other conflict in far-away Moscow, the power struggle which Stalin was eventually to win, and which was poisoning the sacrifices of the young men who thought they had found a pure and truthful cause to fight for.

In March 1938 Franco finally succeeded in splitting the Republic in two. In April Harry Pollitt paid his fifth and last visit to the men of the British Battalion. This time there was no disguising the way the war was going. All the places he had visited before were now controlled by Franco's troops. He drove to Barcelona and visited the men on a hillside outside the city, near the banks of the River Ebro. There, dispirited survivors trained, waited for orders, and occasionally caught a glimpse of Franco's heavy guns going into position on the other side of the river.

Harry Pollitt cut an odd figure. Now tubby and middle-aged, wearing a trilby hat and a three-piece suit that had not stood up well to the rigours of his illegal journey into Spain, he stood on a bare, scorched hillside, feet slightly apart, thumbs in his waistcoat, and orated, much as he might have done at a Party Congress. He seemed to belong to a different world from the grubby, emaciated, weary young men lying listlessly on the ground, smoking the cigarettes he had brought with him and reading the letters he had carried over from parents and girlfriends they might never see again.

But the men liked him. He was one of theirs – an ex-boilermaker who liked a drink and a joke. You couldn't imagine Harry shooting a man dead in cold blood because he was suspected of sympathizing with Trotskyists, as Comintern people like Marty did, or carrying a handgun and analysing your politics with cold brutality as Bill Rust did. And it was Harry, mostly, who dealt with the human consequences of their decision to go to Spain, which often meant talking to widows and bereaved parents. When he finished speaking, he got out his notebook and took down the messages they had for home. He never failed to deliver them.

But Pollitt's last visit had another purpose. Franco now controlled most of Spain. British politicians and newspapers had given the Republican cause up for lost. Modern weapons in the hands of trained regular soldiers seemed inexorably to be defeating clumsy Soviet weapons in the hands of hastily trained volunteers. That month Hitler marched his troops over the border to Austria, and in a few hours made it part of Germany. And British Prime Minister Neville Chamberlain signed an Anglo-Italian Treaty which gave Italy a free hand in Spain and Abyssinia. This treaty, wrote Winston Churchill in a private letter to foreign secretary Anthony Eden, was 'a triumph' for Mussolini.

Comintern and Stalin wanted the International Brigades to stay in Spain for a little longer. To Stalin, Spain had ceased to be the issue. What mattered now was the Soviet Union itself, and

Stalin needed time. Time to re-arm; time, secretly, to find out whether he could do a deal with Hitler. If he was to deal, he needed something to bargain with. He knew Hitler wanted the International Brigades out of Spain. He could have it – at a price.

It was up to Harry Pollitt to inspire the men of the British Battalion, to get them to make some sense of what they were doing. He could not leave them with the feeling that they were likely to die in pain, far from home, for nothing. He could not tell them they were winning. Many of these men were not soldiers when they came to Spain, but they were all soldiers now. They could see what was happening around them.

Pollitt, as he usually did, found the right note. Those who survived remembered his argument all their lives. It made sense of everything they suffered. Pollitt was the only Communist leader who could have done it. He had personally persuaded many of them to go to Spain. He was exempt from the charges of brutality, cynicism, and simply living it up in Barcelona, which were levelled, often with justice, against the top-level Communists on the spot.

One of the young men sitting on that hillside was Dave Goodman, a salesman from Marlborough and a member of the Young Communist League. Half a century later he explained how Harry Pollitt foretold the future that day. Harry told them they were holding up the march of Fascism to give other countries time to prepare. 'The Spanish Civil War was the first battle of the Second World War. In Spain we held out against Fascism for three years. This gave other countries time to re-arm and develop opposition to Fascism. That is how the people of Spain and the international brigades made their contribution to victory in the Second World War.'

Goodman, alive today, is tall, thin and ascetic, and speaks about the horrors of war in a detached way, as though it all happened to someone else. He became a full time CP organizer, then a college lecturer. Thirty years later a BBC interviewer asked him: 'When did you realize the futility of it?' Dave laughed at the stupidity of the question for months afterwards.

Bill Alexander, the stiff, unbending and brave commander of the British Battalion, sternly warned the men against defeatism. He sent round a directive deploring 'in a certain number of our

54

comrades a map-conscious ideology. This has to be broken down.' The time of retreat was over.

Many men were sent home – especially those who were not members of the Communist Party who, it was felt, might find it harder to keep faith in the face of the facts. One of these was Liverpool Labour councillor Jack Jones, who wrote from a filthy Barcelona hospital to the new Labour leader, Clement Attlee, begging him to campaign for Britain to reverse its non-intervention policy. But Attlee could do nothing. He had succeeded the pacifist George Lansbury, and was at that time almost obscured by the vast shadow of the violently anti-Communist Ernest Bevin.

Just over 300 British brigaders, almost all of them CP members, saw out the next three months on the hill outside Barcelona where they heard Pollitt speak. At last came the order which he had prepared them for. In July the British Battalion was told to force Franco's troops off a hill on the other side of the Ebro. They crossed the river at night in small open boats, guided by local peasants who knew the currents and the best landing places, and launched their attack at dawn.

But the enemy was well dug in, with powerful machine guns, and could pick the men off like flies. It was burning hot on the bare rocks in the height of summer. The men who had boots found that these were soon cut to pieces. The majority wore traditional rope-soled shoes which gave no protection at all. Day after day for a month Bill Alexander led his men in charges at the hilltop. There was a nauseating smell of blood and bodies everywhere. And there was not enough food or drink. The men became thin and exhausted. Hospital beds were in caves in the rocks.

Once or twice, one of the men got close enough to throw a grenade before being forced back by machine-gun fire. In London Jack Jones led a delegation to Downing Street asking for an end to non-intervention. They had to leave their letter with a policeman at the door. Prime Minister Neville Chamberlain was irritated with the British brigaders. Hitler and Mussolini had told him, through their ambassadors, that if Britain was serious about peace it ought to prevent its citizens from fighting in Spain.

On 18 September 1938, while Hitler was waiting for Chamberlain to arrive, Franco was opening a new offensive against Barcelona, and the Spanish Prime Minister, Negrin, was pondering a message from Chamberlain telling him to send away the International Brigades. Franco's troops were closing in. There was near civil war on the streets of Barcelona. There was just one slim hope.

Negrin did what Chamberlain asked. The day after Chamberlain returned to London after meeting the German Chancellor and told reporters that he had 'a piece of paper signed by Herr Hitler – it means peace in our time', he heard of another triumph for his diplomacy. Negrin was sending away the International Brigades, in an attempt to persuade Chamberlain to put pressure on Hitler to get his troops out of Spain. It did not, so far as anyone knows, occur to Chamberlain to raise the matter with Hitler.

A week later the British who were left alive marched for one last time down the Ramblas, the wide, elegant, tree-lined central street in Barcelona. Then they took the train to the French border. It did not save Republican Spain. On 7 March 1939 Madrid surrendered. It was all over.

Tom Jones did not leave. He was in prison. He told me about it in a Barcelona bar in 1989, after celebrating the fiftieth anniversary of the end of the International Brigades. He was then a short, thick-set, quietly spoken man in his seventies, a retired official of the Transport and General Workers Union. He told his story in the same quiet, slightly monotonous voice he used for everything else. You would not know that the memories had any terror for him, except that he chain smoked as he talked.

He was on the hillside, the only man left alive of a dozen men in a machine-gun company. The hillside was littered with the bodies of his friends. His own right arm was almost torn off, and he was covered in blood – his own and that of his friends. A patrol of Franco's troops picked him up. They put paper bandages on his arm and locked him in a room with half a dozen others. The bandages at once started to poison his arm, and it started to stink. So they took him to the hospital and cut the flesh off, without anaesthetic.

'I held the bed with my left arm and the nurse told me afterwards that she was waiting for me to scream, but I didn't. That afternoon she came in with a paper bag full of oranges and bananas. She said: "I thought you were very brave, though I still hate you for coming to Spain to kill Spaniards." I said: "I wouldn't have come if the Germans and Italians hadn't come to fight for the other side." '

In Swansea, Tom's parents were told he had died in hospital. There was even an obituary in the local paper. In fact he was sent to Burgos prison. Built for just a few hundred, it was housing 5000 Spaniards and 600 International Brigaders of all nationalities. Tom was in a tiny cell with five others, and they spent their days killing lice in the hope of sleeping at night. Six hundred Spaniards were shot or garrotted in Burgos over the next few months.

Not all the stories surrounding this mass incarceration are wretched. A Polish brigader in the prison was a doctor, and although he had virtually no medicines and spoke little English, he treated several of the British brigaders, including one young Liverpudlian, who told him on the fifth day of treatment: 'No shit for five days.' The doctor stared at him in amazement, then said: 'Today, you shit.' He had been treating him for diarrhoea.

On 2 January 1939 Tom Jones was sentenced to death by a military tribunal. Later that day he was called to the court again and told that the sentence had been commuted to thirty years imprisonment. 'I explained that I'd rather die than spend thirty years in prison,' said Tom in the tone of voice he might use for saying he prefers the programme on the other television channel.

Every day men were being taken out and shot. Tom said: 'I had learned at the front not to get too close to anyone. If you make a friend he might be killed tomorrow. If you are too sentimental, you can't do your job. An angry man is not a good fighter.' But Tom's friends knew – though he did not tell me – that he made the closest friend of his life in that prison. When they moved him to a death cell, he shared it with three Spaniards and Frank Ryan, former IRA officer, former editor of an Irish Republican newspaper, former student of Celtic philology and archaeology, and the only other English-speaking brigader left in Spain. They slept side by side on the floor, Frank sharing with Tom and the Spaniards the food parcels he received through the Irish ambassador. Through the same channel, he helped Tom get news out.

That was how Harry Pollitt found out that Tom was still alive. It was 1939, the Second World War was starting, and Pollitt had troubles of his own and was temporarily out of office. But he had a word with some friendly Labour MPs, who started asking questions.

Tom and Frank listened to the screams of Spaniards being

garrotted. 'They used to tighten the garrotte until a man passed out. Then they threw cold water over him and started again. The lieutenant in charge decided how often you would be garrotted before you were allowed to die. He was a bastard,' Tom added calmly, lighting another cigarette from the butt of the one he had just smoked.

Ryan scratched his name on a comb. The day he was to be executed, he planned to throw it into a cell where the men were only sentenced to imprisonment, as some sort of clue to his friends in Ireland about what had happened to him. One officer offered Frank a cigarette. 'Have you got one for my friends?' asked the Irishman. 'No, this is officer to officer.' So Frank turned it down.

Tom was released in April 1940, after the British government, prompted by parliamentary questions, demanded his release. Back in Britain, he tried to get into the army, but failed the medical. He found a job in a brewery. 'It was the best job I could have, because my arm still wasn't right, and lifting sacks of malt helped it to get better. I came home three years to the day after I left with a weekend return ticket to Paris.'

There was an emotional parting with Frank Ryan. Both men were in poor physical shape. Ryan by now had rheumatism and chest pains, and was almost completely deaf. Tom never saw him again. Later in 1940, Ryan was transferred to Germany. The Nazi government calculated that it would make a good impression in Ireland if he were released by their efforts. He was by then totally deaf, emaciated, and looked nearly twice his 38 years. You would not have recognized the brigade officer of three years ago.

The Germans had a use for Frank Ryan. Together with another IRA man already in Berlin, Sean Russell, they put him on a U-boat bound for Ireland. They hoped that the two IRA men would act as German agents inside Ireland, and co-ordinate IRA activities with German military activities. Ryan was a popular and romantic figure in Ireland. Russell fell ill with a burst gastric ulcer on the U-boat and died in Ryan's arms 100 miles from Galway. Ryan, still ill from his Spanish imprisonment and not thinking clearly, allowed the U-boat to turn round and take him back to Germany – a decision he later regretted bitterly.

He spent the short time left to him trying by every possible means to get back to his native Ireland. In January 1943, with Berlin under heavy bombardment, he started to suffer from a series of illnesses. He could hardly move from his bed and could not hear the air raid warnings. He died of pleurisy and pneumonia in Dresden in June 1944. His body was brought back to Ireland and buried in Dublin in June 1979.

Dave Goodman also spent some months in a Spanish prison, together with Maurice Levitas, a square-jawed Dublin Jew with a clipped voice. Guards wanted to make them read English translations of Fascist literature, and two men who refused were savagely beaten. So they gave Maurice a pamphlet to read, and Maurice, relying on the guards being unable to speak English, so distorted the meaning that his friends were hard put to it not to laugh. They remember being told to dig. 'I thought we were digging our own graves,' says Maurice. 'I looked at the sun and I thought, this was the chance I took when I volunteered.'

Nan Green, one of the first Britons in Spain, who nursed behind the lines until the British were sent home, heard a rumour that her husband had been wounded. She searched every hospital in Barcelona. He was not in any of them. Years later their son went to Spain to try to find out what happened to the father he hardly knew. He is pretty sure that George Green, musician and Communist, one of the keenest of the brigaders, the man who founded an activist movement to keep their morale high, died on that hillside. He thinks his father did not want to come back without victory. He tries to think it was not a waste, but he cannot get out of his mind the fact that when George died, Stalin and Negrin had already taken the decision to get the International Brigades out of Spain.

The CP's record against Franco and against Mosley changed the Party's fortunes. In the darkest days of Class Against Class, in 1930, membership was down to under 3000. It had reached almost 18,000 by the start of the Second World War.

4

Who Was Not in the Thirties Red?

B Y the mid-thirties, Harry Pollitt had every reason to be rather pleased with himself. He had rid himself of Class Against Class. The Comintern was signalling that national Communist parties would have more autonomy than before – a move which Pollitt heartily welcomed. Class Against Class took its ideological baggage away with it, with the result that the CP's influence in the unions grew. It achieved a symbolically important success when Communist Arthur Horner was elected president of the South Wales miners. The CP was seen to be in the vanguard of the great issues of the time: Fascism, the war in Spain, and unemployment.

Every government since the First World War, including the two Labour ones, had promised to reduce unemployment, and had failed. All they reduced was the pittance on which the unemployed had to live. In the 1930s unemployment approached the 3 million mark, a figure which had been thought inconceivable. It would not reach this level again until the 1980s. In unemployment blackspots, near starvation was commonplace.

A tough and effective Party organizer, Wal Hannington, ran the National Unemployed Workers Movement. Although Ellen Wilkinson, a former CP member, is remembered for her part in the hunger marches of the 1930s, they were largely organized by Communists.

Membership was steadily increasing. The *Daily Worker* was becoming a much better paper, belatedly able to distinguish between Adolph Hitler and James Maxton, and its circulation was rising steadily. It started to escape from the dead grasp of Class Against Class and run stories which people actually wanted to read.

Some time in the early to mid-1930s Moscow stopped directly subsidizing the Party, reckoning that it could now stand on its own feet. The Soviet Union was in dire financial straits. What money it could afford went to countries where the Communist Party had been forced underground. And the British Party was not in great need. Thanks to its image as the main bulwark against Fascism, it was receiving considerable sums from the Jewish community.

Some indirect subsidies remained. Copies of Party literature were bought in bulk to boost circulation and income; books were sent from the Soviet Union at knockdown prices; direct deals on travel were made with the Friends of the Soviet Union; young and promising CP members were sent to Moscow's Lenin School; Party officials subsidized their low wages with cheap holidays in the Soviet Union, and when they were ill they were treated in Soviet nursing homes. But the direct subsidy to headquarters ceased, and for more than twenty years the Party almost stood on its own feet.

The Party's new image was crowned by an electoral success. In the 1935 general election it put up only two candidates – and one of them was elected, the second person ever to be elected to Parliament under Communist colours. There was some irony in this, because the new Communist MP for West Fife was Willie Gallacher who, in Moscow in 1920, had stood out against having anything to do with Parliament.

Gallacher had been talked round by Lenin, who is therefore directly responsible for Britain's only real Communist parliamentarian. Gallacher held West Fife for fifteen years, becoming by far the longest-serving Communist MP, and the only one with a real Westminster reputation. He was an unlikely Communist. Proud, sensitive, fiercely independent, emotional and unpredictable, Lenin was only the first of many people in Moscow to find him exasperating. There is in the Moscow archives a furious handwritten note from Gallacher, probably written about 1926: 'In view of the treatment I have received from the Praesidium and the lack of support I received in carrying out Praesidium instructions, I ask leave to withdraw from the Praesidium.' It is not clear what the issue was, but the note is typical Gallacher. As he showed during the Class Against Class period, he was not above sounding like a hardliner in Moscow and a liberal in London when it suited him.

Nearly a decade older than Harry Pollitt, born on 25 December 1881, his first job and his political education were on the Clyde, the region that threw up many leading Communists including Arthur McManus, as well as James Maxton and most of the ILP leaders. An engineering worker, he was short, stocky, square-chinned and strong, and smoked thick black tobacco in his pipe. He was a class warrior who still kept a sense of humour about class. When George VI's daughter – the future Queen Elizabeth II – was born, he told the House of Commons: 'When I was born, the bells rang out all over Britain, too. It was Christmas Day.' When invited to visit the Queen, he wrote back that in Scotland it was the custom for the older lady to invite the younger one, and his wife Jean would gladly welcome Her Majesty in their two-room Paisley flat. But some things he did not joke about. To his dying day he never knew what every other leading CP member knew: that when he and Pollitt were together, Pollitt drank his whisky from a teacup so as to avoid sparking off a Gallacher lecture on the evils of drink.

He was, rather improbably, a great authority on the Bible, a spare-time poet, and addicted to detective stories. His poems were private, written mostly on trains, and expressing what he felt. They may have been his way of escaping stifling Communist discipline. A poem on Dartmoor Prison, whose sentiment would not have been approved by the Politburo, ended:

> Tear down these fearsome walls, down to the ground.
> Give to these men the chance to build anew.
> Till in their hearts some joy of life is found
> And welcome dawn becomes their portion too.

The election of 1935 was Gallacher's third attempt to win West Fife, and his victory owed more to his personal popularity and record of support for the miners than to his party label.

Pollitt was now able to work with the other groups on the left – the ILP and the Socialist League – to try to create a Popular Front. France showed what could be achieved. A Popular Front between the Parti Communiste Français and the Section Française de l'Internationale Ouvrière (SFIO, the French social democrats) brought a victory for the left in 1936 and a Popular Front government under Léon Blum.

Pollitt had as good a relationship with ILP leaders as could be expected given the abuse his Party had heaped on them. Brockway found him thoroughly reasonable. By 1937 there were regular meetings between the ILP, the Socialist League and the CP in the offices of the Socialist League's newly founded *Tribune* magazine. Maxton led the ILP side but Brockway did the work. Stafford Cripps, later a Labour Chancellor of the Exchequer, and former Communist William Mellor, editor of the *Daily Herald*, were the main representatives for the Socialist League. As for the CP, whoever attended the meetings, only Pollitt mattered.

ILP secretary John Paton wrote of him: 'He was conciliatory, he was deft, he was diplomatic, he knew to a hairbreadth just how far to press and when to give way.' When another member of his team tried to push things too far Pollitt would intervene decisively: 'We'll let that go.' But the meetings were made difficult by the CP's suspiciousness. Apparently they thought both the ILP and the Socialist League had been infiltrated by police spies whose task was to snoop on Communists. The ILP spy, they thought, was Brockway. And the Socialist League spy was worse, for he was an apostate. The League had appointed as its secretary the same Jack Murphy who was a CP leader throughout the 1920s and represented it in Moscow. Murphy lost patience with the CP in its Class Against Class period, after he put forward a modest, but unauthorized, policy suggestion, and was ordered to sign a public recantation. He refused and resigned from the Party in 1932. The Party knew that the police had an informer at its heart throughout the 1920s, and privately its main suspect was Murphy. Perhaps they recalled the breath of suspicion in Moscow in the early days, when he had briefly found himself in a Moscow prison cell before the Comintern cleared him.

They were almost certainly wrong, says Michael Foot, who discovered the CP's suspicions of Brockway and Murphy. 'Jack Murphy was a perfectly sincere and dedicated socialist and a clever one too, even though there was something uneasy about him.' But people who left the Party were not lightly forgiven. 'Pollitt and his companions lost all sense of dignity,' wrote Murphy, who probably never knew they had revived the whisper that he was a spy. 'No slander was too big.' Twenty-four years later, in 1956, a *Daily Worker* journalist met him and passed on to Dutt the good news that he was alive and well. Dutt shook his head gravely and whispered: 'It was his wife, you know.'

All three parties had powerful members who would have liked to see the talks founder. Maxton had been desperately hurt by the things old friends in the CP had written about him during Class Against Class. Cripps knew that the resentment of some of his supporters went even deeper. Jennie Lee, who became an ILP MP in 1929 when still in her early twenties and later married Aneurin Bevan, never forgave the Communist Party for trying to brand her father a blackleg during the general strike. 'It was a shocking thing to say and her hatred of the Communist Party could never be eradicated,' says Michael Foot. 'That was the ruthless way some Communists behaved. Some of them – not Pollitt – thought it was required of them to prove their Marxism.' Pollitt had to deal with people who really wanted Class Against Class back, with all its sour, sectarian self-righteousness: people like Dutt and Rust, who in their hearts still believed that any association with those who were not of the pure faith tainted and corrupted, but were silenced for the moment because the Comintern favoured a popular front.

The ILP, the Communists and the Socialist League called their attempt to work together the Unity Campaign, and it was a final desperate attempt to change the course of British politics in a leftward direction. It was effectively killed when the Labour Party, with its usual eagle eye for heresy, disaffiliated the Socialist League and declared its members ineligible for Labour Party membership. Cripps decided that Labour Party membership mattered more and dissolved the League.

The Unity Campaign would probably have failed anyway, even if the Second World War had not come along and swept out of the way every dream that Pollitt, Cripps and Maxton had ever dreamed. But it formed the basis for a wartime coalition and some post-war work. For that the credit goes to Pollitt. His biographer Kevin Morgan puts it this way: 'If Pollitt owed what authority he had to the Communist Party, it is equally true that the CP owed much of its credibility to its charismatic leader and to the trust and esteem in which he was held by many on the left.' There were few others in the CP with whom Cripps and Maxton could or would have done business.

Dutt, too, played his part in the revival of the Party's fortunes. Many intellectuals were desperate in the early 1930s for an idea they could believe in: a faith which would come ready-wrapped, with all the intellectual angles covered and no questions left untidily unanswered. They wanted to believe Communism offered this, and, for them, a grand tour of the prodigious, if mummified, contents of Dutt's remarkable mind could feel like the intellectual equivalent of seeing the seven wonders of the world.

One of these was John Strachey, Oxford-educated son of the editor of *The Spectator*, one of those young Labour MPs who became utterly disillusioned with their Party in the 1929–31 Parliament. Strachey was to become one of Labour's most coherent socialist philosophers, but in 1931 he had a lot of thinking to do before he could get there. He attached himself to Mosley's New Party for a while, then sought the help of the sage of Brussels.

Dutt had by now been elevated from senior theoretician to legend. The initials RPD at the end of the Notes of the Month were those, readers were told, of an 'outstanding Party theoretician' who 'plays a decisive part in Central Committee discussions through his articles and letters.' Few people knew where he lived. Strachey, one of Dutt's most avid readers, had somehow picked up the romantic notion that the great man was dying in Paris. Finding out the truth, he wrote to Brussels in the gloom which followed the 1931 election, asking for a meeting. He was rewarded with 'one of the most intellectually exciting conversations I have ever had,' and his book *The Coming Struggle for Power* was heavily influenced by Dutt.

Dutt signalled the new mood of optimism by reappearing in London in 1936. The police were now more relaxed about Communists, so Salme could enter Britain without being arrested. Also, Dutt was facing understandable criticism for pontificating from Brussels, divorced both from the reality of life in Britain and from the life of the Party itself.

Strachey became a regular *Daily Worker* columnist and was central to the foundation of the Left Book Club, launched by publisher Victor Gollancz in 1936. The club offered a book a month for half a crown, which was between a third and a half of the normal cost. The list was selected by Gollancz, Strachey and

Harold Laski. All three were members of the Labour Party, so no one could claim it was run by Communists. But all three were close to the CP, and the first book they chose was Dutt's *World Politics 1918-1935.*

The club was a clever idea, and massively successful. By 1939 its books were reaching 57,000 people. It could only have happened in the 1930s, when the CP and left-wing intellectuals felt close to each other. It would have been inconceivable in the Class Against Class period, when Communists mistrusted intellectuals, who were mostly right wing; but the flowering of socialism in the universities at this time was unexpectedly embraced by the Party. It was then that the Oxford Union elected its first Communist president, Philip Toynbee, and many of its students turned to Communism, though with the self-conscious irony that led them to write satirical songs about it:

> Dan, Dan, Dan
> The Communist Party Man
> Working underground all day
> In and out of meetings
> Bringing fraternal greetings
> Never seeing the light of day.

Poets, novelists, playwrights, actors and musicians, as well as economists and political philosophers, tried to make themselves comfortable inside the CP. Not all succeeded. Decades later, in languid, patrician tones, the poets Cecil Day-Lewis, Stephen Spender and W. H. Auden offered half-embarrassed apologies for their brief flirtations with Communism. Day-Lewis said: 'We had a kind of officer class mentality that we are privileged people and we should feel some responsibility for the under-privileged.' He thought this 'woolly-minded but respectable.' Auden disowned his early socialist poetry, and Sir Stephen Spender talked curiously of being 'in love with the idea of the working class and wanting to have a working-class friend, you know, and so on.'

Other promising young poets from patrician backgrounds fought in Spain, wrote poetry there, and sometimes, like John Cornford, died there. Cornford died trying to reach the body of a friend and novelist, Ralph Fox. A few days before, he wrote a remarkable love poem to another Cambridge University Communist, Margot Heinemann, who later became a distinguished literary historian and novelist, and who never left the Communist Party. For her, the Party was an answer to the question 'How can I devote myself to creating a society without poverty and exploitation?'

Virginia Woolf wrote for the *Daily Worker*. Ted Willis, then a *Daily Worker* journalist and, much later, the creator of *Dixon of Dock Green*, was national secretary of the Labour Party Young Socialists and secretly a Communist. He later became a leading figure in the Young Communist League.

The Communist Party introduced many working-class activists to the idea that they could write, and made the first serious assault on the idea that creative writing was essentially a middle-class activity. Many of these wrote plays and poems graphically describing the struggle to keep bread in children's mouths. Walter Greenwood's novel, *Love on the Dole*, was in 1935 turned into a highly successful play. He was one of many who turned to writing when he became unemployed. In his novel, as in many others, the hated means test is an ever-present character. Harry Hardcastle discovers that his benefit has been stopped: 'Ha! Means test, eh? They can't knock me off. Blimey, it's tekkin' us all our time t'manage as it is ... Now him as lives next door; Ah could understand 'un knockin *him* off. He's got more coming in than me. Yaach, they won't touch the likes of us. They daren't. There'd be a bloody revolution.'

The Unity Theatre remained a heavily Communist-inspired theatre until the 1950s, and many people who worked there were sympathetic to Communism. It launched the careers of several well-known names: writers like Ted Willis, Lionel Blair and Eric Paice (who later created *The Avengers*), and actors like Alfie Bass, Warren Mitchell, David Kossoff and Bill Owen (now best known for *The Last of the Summer Wine*).

Communists were prominent in creating *Left Review*, which was encouraged by the party leadership and quickly became one of the best-selling cultural magazines of the day, publishing Auden, Spender and Day-Lewis but also less well-known names, including new working-class writers. The Party launched the journal *New Writing*, which later became *Penguin New Writing*, and it launched the Workers Music Association.

Two small publishing firms run by sympathizers amalgamated to form Lawrence and Wishart, the CP's publishers right up to the end, which still publishes for the CP's successor, the Democratic Left. Progressive bookshops were founded, among them Collet's of Charing Cross Road. Thus the Communist Party in the 1930s found itself in the vanguard of culture, and its achievements were real and lasting. By 1937 the Party had a steadily increasing membership, a leader who was respected and admired by many people across the political spectrum, a reputation as the leader of the fight against the main scourges of the day – Fascism and unemployment – and it was the cultural vanguard of the left. Its record as the organizer of the British Battalion in Spain earned it respect among people whom it could not otherwise have attracted at all. It looked as though it had an excellent chance of leading a united left in a series of popular crusades. But it was not to be. For just at this time it started to become difficult not to notice the terrible things happening in Stalin's Soviet Union.

The excuse for the purges was the assassination, on 1 December 1934, of a senior Soviet official, Sergei Kirov. The killing was probably ordered by Stalin. In 1936, when everything in Britain seemed to be going the CP's way, two very senior Bolsheviks whom the CP had taught its members to admire were shot as traitors. One was Zinoviev, the man who, as Comintern chairman, had guided the CP in the 1920s, and to whom was attributed the forged letter printed in the *Daily Mail* during the general election in 1925. The other was Kamenev. The CP was told that these venerated Bolsheviks were in fact traitors. They had been in league with the hated Trotsky (whom CP members had also once been called upon to admire).

In the year of Kirov's assassination, 139 people were elected to the Central Committee of the Communist Party of the Soviet Union. Three years later, ninety-eight of them – 70 per cent – had been executed. Of the 1966 delegates to that Congress, 1108 – 56 per cent – were executed. And that was just the tip of the iceberg. The purges reached down into every part of Soviet society. No one knows how many died, but it ran into many millions. Stalin's was not even a rational despotism, where you at least knew what the rules were. Staying alive was a matter, not just of being careful and of smart footwork, but simply of luck. Many of those executed had fought in the 1917 revolution beside Lenin.

Foreign Communists in the Soviet Union died too. Those from countries where the Communist Party was outlawed were massacred wholesale: their governments could be relied on not to protest. They came to Moscow as refugees to escape persecution in their own countries, only to perish miserably in Soviet labour camps. Poles suffered worst because many were Jews; they had openly defended Trotsky before Lenin's death; their party was illegal; many of them were old comrades of Lenin; and Stalin loathed Poles anyway. Manuilsky explained it away: 'Agents of Polish fascism managed to obtain positions of leadership.'

By and large – there were exceptions – Communists from Britain, France, Czechoslovakia and the Scandinavian countries were spared, probably largely because the Communist Party was legal in those countries and their governments might have objected.

Stalin's successor Khrushchev admitted much of the truth twenty years later. 'Confessions of guilt ... were gained with the help of cruel and inhuman tortures.' One typical testimony cited by Khrushchev read: 'Not being able to suffer the tortures to which I was submitted by Ushakov and Nikolayev – who utilised the knowledge that my broken ribs have not properly mended and have caused me great pain – I have been forced to accuse myself and others ...'

British Communist leaders came very close to these events. Because of the time they had spent in Moscow, they all had friends and many had relatives in the city, and everyone was at risk. Perhaps Harry Pollitt came closest at first. How this self-possessed man lived with himself and what he knew after 1937, we can never know, but it was surely the personal crisis of his life.

In the early 1920s he fell in love with Rose Cohen, and proposed marriage – on her account, several times, and on his exuberant and perhaps exaggerated account fourteen times. They never lost their affection for each other. Rose Cohen's oldest brother and sister were born in Poland, near Lodz, where her father worked as a tailor. When they fled Polish anti-semitism her father set up as a tailor in the East End of London. Rose was born in Mile End, in 1894. She was a remarkable woman. She had to work for her living from an early age, yet managed to become fluent in three languages and to learn enough about politics and economics to be a welcome recruit at the Labour Research Department, the research organization on which trade unions have always relied extensively, where she met Dutt and Robin Page Arnot. She was clever, fluent, entertaining, and attractive. Everyone who knew her talks of her smile, but says she was quite unaware of its power.

She was a socialist and a suffragette. A founder CP member, she was part of the Pollitt-Dutt-Page Arnot circle which intrigued in the 1920s to change the Party leadership and Party policy. It was at this time that she got to know Harry Pollitt.

She turned him down for Max Petrovsky, Comintern representative in Britain from 1924 to 1929. No other Comintern representative managed to evade the British police for anything like so long. He lived in England under the name of Bennett. Petrovsky was not his real name, any more than Bennett was. A Ukrainian Jew who often went by the name of Goldfarb, his real name was David Lipetz. Everyone knew him as Max. Leading revolutionaries before the First World War generally had several names: that was how they stayed alive. The son of a wealthy Jewish merchant, he was one of the leaders of the Jewish Socialist Bund. Forced into exile, he took a doctorate in Brussels and became a leading Jewish political writer in the USA. He returned to Russia after the 1917 revolution, and in 1918–19 as president of the Ukrainian city of Burdichev he was twice sentenced to be executed, first by the Ukrainian army and then by the Soviet military command.

Max was about fifteen years older than Rose, a big, thick-set man with a long, drooping nose: ugly but charming according to Ivy Litvinov, an Englishwoman married to the Soviet foreign commissar, Maxim Litvinov. He was a close friend and confidante of everyone in the CP leadership. 'He was the comrade in the Comintern with whom I (and the rest cf the British comrades) had the closest links and personal friendship,' according to Robin Page Arnot. Bob Stewart recalled that he influenced, not only CP members, but miners' leader Arthur Cook as well. 'All our leading comrades visited him whenever they were in Moscow.'

Max and Rose moved to Moscow in 1929, the year their son Alyosha was born. They were, as far as anyone knows, very happy. Max had a high-powered job at the Commissariat of Heavy Industry. Rose became foreign editor of the English language paper

Moscow Daily News. They had a splendid flat. Alyosha, says Ivy Litvinov, looked just like Max.

Rose visited England briefly in 1936, and stayed with her older sister, Nellie Rathbone, in London. She came by herself and, although she said nothing, Nellie felt that things were not right in Moscow. She was sure that if it were not for the child, Rose would have stayed in London. Nellie's daughter Joyce, then 7, remembers Rose teaching her some Russian words and a Russian pioneers' song. They never saw her again.

Early in 1937 Petrovsky was arrested. The atmosphere of terror in Moscow at once ensured that his wife became an outcast. Maxim Litvinov forbade Ivy from going to see her, but Ivy's teenage daughter brought Rose and Alyosha to Ivy. Rose was lonely and terrified. 'Not a single one of my friends has been to see me,' she said. In April, knowing of Max's arrest, Harry Pollitt wrote her a chatty letter obviously intended to cheer her up: 'My visit to Spain gave me great satisfaction. There is quite a story about how I got there, which will make you laugh. Seeing the war on the ground made a great impression on me, and I think that my visit had a good effect on the lads ... We all send our love. Don't lose heart.'

She never saw the letter, or laughed at Harry's story. The letter was opened, and the information in it considered too sensitive for her to see. It went into a dusty Moscow archive. Nellie also wrote. Her letter was returned.

Just before Petrovsky's arrest, the Soviet authorities asked Rose to give up her British citizenship and apply for Soviet citizenship. Innocently, she agreed. As soon as her husband was arrested she realized her mistake, and frantically tried to retrieve British citizenship, because British passport holders were relatively safe. But it was too late. Max was shot, and they came for Rose in August 1937, seven months after his arrest. Alyosha was taken from her and sent to a children's home. Rose broke down completely in prison, mainly for fear of what would happen to him. For eight months, no one knew where she was. Nellie asked Harry Pollitt and Willie Gallacher to do what they could.

Pollitt pressed his protest further than his colleagues thought was wise. He had long and troubled interviews with Dimitrov and Manuilsky. He made so many waves that Comintern officials floated the idea with other CP leaders of replacing him with someone more malleable. Another English Communist, Pearl Rimmer, went to see him to beg him to intercede on behalf of her husband, Dutch Communist George Fles, then languishing in a Soviet prison. 'What can I do?' he said to her. 'They won't listen to me. They've arrested Rose Cohen. I know she's innocent; I've known her from a child.' Fles died in prison.

Gallacher went to see Georgi Dimitrov in Moscow about Rose and other foreigners who had disappeared. Because Gallacher was an MP, he probably got a politer hearing in Moscow than that accorded to Pollitt. That at any rate is what he told Nellie Rathbone. Years later he told his friend and literary executor Phil Stein that Dimitrov looked at him gravely for a few moments, then said: 'Comrade Gallacher, it is best that you do not pursue these matters.' And Gallacher did not pursue them.

In April 1938 the British newspapers learned of Rose Cohen's arrest. The foreign office protested – ironically, the protest had to go to Maxim Litvinov. But Litvinov said she was now a Soviet citizen and no concern of Britain's, and had been sentenced to ten years' imprisonment for espionage.

The day after the news came out, the *Daily Worker* published an editorial: 'The National Government is starting up a new attack on Anglo-Soviet relations. As a pretext for this they are using the case of the arrest of a former British subject on a charge of espionage. The individual concerned, it is understood, is married to a Soviet citizen and thereby assumed Soviet citizenship alike in the eyes of Soviet law as of international law ... The British Government has no right whatever to interfere in the internal affairs of another country and of its citizens.' It noted that the *Daily Herald* supported the 'attack upon the country of socialism ... This is not the first time that the *Daily Herald* has lent itself to the most poisonous attacks on the Soviet Union.'

The article must rank as one of the most weasely and discreditable pieces ever written, with its fastidious refusal even to mention the name of a woman whom every leading Communist in Britain counted as a friend. The only possible excuse is that CP leaders thought this was the only chance of saving her. If so, the hope was forlorn. She was tried in secret and sentenced to ten years imprisonment without the right of visits. This was Moscow code for: she will be shot at once. And she was.

There were some sad postscripts to the Rose Cohen episode. In 1956, after Khrushchev denounced the crimes of Stalin, Harry Pollitt wrote to the Soviet judicial authorities asking for Rose to be rehabilitated. As far as we know, nothing happened. About the same time, Ivy Litvinov wrote to Nellie Rathbone. Alyosha had traced Ivy. He had had a hard childhood in two orphanages where the names of his disgraced parents could not be mentioned. Eventually elderly relatives of his father's took pity on the boy and adopted him. Now the regime was a little more liberal, he had permission to visit Moscow and see Ivy. Could she possibly obtain a picture of his parents from Nellie?

Nellie sent the pictures but they never arrived. She wanted to make contact with her nephew, but was discouraged by people who knew Moscow well, and who told her that it would embarrass him. Alyosha was a geologist, and scientists were discouraged from having contact with people from the west. He would not want it, they said.

In the early 1980s, after Nellie's death, her daughter Joyce Rathbone decided to make a determined effort to find Alyosha. It took her two years. When she finally arrived in Moscow, Alyosha's son Misha met her and said his father had changed his mind: he did not want to see her, believing that she was an imposter. Misha eventually persuaded him that he was wrong, and Alyosha saw Joyce and was thrilled with the few small mementoes of his mother she brought with her.

The strangest and saddest thing about the meeting was Alyosha's attitude to his parents' fate. He was most anxious for Joyce to understand that his parents were not Trotskyists at all. It was all a terrible mistake, he said. Even then, like most Russians, he considered Trotskyism a terrible crime.

When Stalin's purges began, the CP declared its support for 'the measures taken against the Trotsky-Zinoviev terrorists, whose treacherous activities against the Workers' State have met with well-merited sentences of death.' Later it congratulated 'the workers and peasants of the Soviet Union, their party and their government, on the drastic measures which they are taking to root out wreckers and spies from their midst.'

Did intelligent men like Pollitt, Dutt, Rust, Campbell and Gallacher really believe any of the garbage they wrote to justify events in the Soviet Union? They were in and out of Moscow for meetings several times a year. They had many Soviet friends. Johnny Campbell was the CP representative in Moscow. It is not credible to deny that he had a pretty shrewd idea what was going on. His close friends believe, from hints he dropped towards the end of his life, that he told Pollitt, but no one else, what he knew.

Many British Communist leaders had personal ties with Moscow. Some of them, like Bill Rust, married Russians. Campbell had close relatives in Moscow. After Bob Stewart represented the CP in Moscow in the early 1920s, his daughter stayed there and married a Russian who disappeared during the purges. Stewart managed to bring his daughter home before she, too, was arrested.

Many lower-ranking Communist Party members, and many non-Communists, believed the Soviet version – that the people going into prison were wreckers and spies and had fair trials. Two senior British lawyers went to see the trials of leading Bolsheviks and professed themselves satisfied that justice was being done. The British press which reported the purges was discredited in left-wing circles. They had worked people into a fever of hatred against Germany during the First World War with concocted stories of atrocities. They had seized on anything which would discredit the Soviet Union. They had told lies about International Brigaders in Spain being paid mercenaries. Why should they be telling the truth now?

Noreen Branson, the CP's official historian, says: 'The fact that thousands were being detained and *not* being brought to trial but simply disappearing into prison camps was not known to the leaders of the British Party any more than to the rank and file members.' Willie Gallacher told his family years later that even in Moscow, not speaking the language and being shepherded about everywhere, it was hard to know what was really going on. Certainly British visitors saw little from the hotels, dachas and nursing homes they stayed in.

But they saw enough. They had to get used to not asking the whereabouts of old friends whenever they visited Moscow, for deep in their hearts, they knew what had happened. They may have feared that asking questions would put friends and relatives at risk.

Whatever the reason, they seem, incredibly, to have convinced themselves that Stalin was doing the minimum necessary to protect the workers' revolution against Trotskyists. And if a few mistakes – such as Rose Cohen – were made, were mistakes not inevitable when the revolution was fighting for survival? And were not a few innocent lives the inevitable price to pay for the end of exploitation, injustice and inequality?

Noreen Branson writes of 'the belief – held by all Communists – that all persecution, tyranny and injustice had their roots in the capitalist system, and in capitalist property relations ... insofar as they still manifested themselves in Russia, this was simply a hangover from tsarist days, soon to disappear.'

The silence of CP leaders also derived from a sense of inferiority. Dutt felt this keenly. What right had the British Party, with its puny membership and its utter failure to bring about revolution in Britain, to lecture successful revolutionaries about human rights? Soviet Bolsheviks had created the first successful socialist revolution and they must do whatever they thought necessary to defend it. And that was an end to the matter. Harold Laski once asked the CP to take up the case of the Russian husband of an Englishwoman he knew. Dutt wrote to him: 'Least of all have we in other countries who have made a complete mess of our own Labour movement ... any right to pose as superior critics and censors of those who have shown in practice that they are able to judge correctly the necessary measures to defeat the capitalist enemy.'

Pollitt's faith went back to the time when, as a 12-year old, he had sworn revenge on the capitalists who made his mother and his sister suffer. Two years after Rose Cohen's death he wrote about the Russian revolution: 'The thing that mattered to me was that lads like me had whacked the bosses and the landlords, had taken their factories, their lands and their banks ... These were the lads and lasses I must support through thick and thin ... for me these people could never do, nor ever can do, any wrong against the working class.' So step by step, Pollitt became an apologist for one of the most savage tyrannies in the savage history of the twentieth century.

Pollitt had been one of the most independent minds in international Communism – a thorn in the Comintern's side, as he once privately boasted. He refused to join in the absurd deification of Stalin, and he had an awkward tendency to insist that he knew more about British conditions than all-wise Russians studying documents in Moscow. He never lost the habit of thinking for himself. But after the purges, and more particularly after the Second World War, this critical independence seemed slowly to ebb out of him.

Meanwhile the *Daily Worker*'s brief renaissance was snuffed out by the need to defend the Moscow trials and it became once more an apparatchiks' plaything, relentlessly analysed for the correctness of its political line by terrified Comintern officials, and therefore rather boring. Comintern once complained that pictures it printed of the CP Congress betrayed the fact that there were empty seats in the hall.

CP leaders took from Stalin the hysterical hatred of Trotsky and Trotskyists which became a Communist obsession. Trotskyists became equally hysterical about 'Stalinists', and the conflict was to poison the whole British left for sixty years.

The first British Trotskyists were former CP members in South London – the Balham Group. Beginning in 1932 with a tactical difference on the role of trade unions, the split developed into one which affected the very core of the CP's philosophy: the idea of the Soviet Union as the first workers' state whose interests must be protected above all things.

It was in Spain that dislike of Trotskyists hardened into hatred. POUM was not strictly a Trotskyist organization, but to Communists its line had a Trotskyist feel. POUM wanted the Republican government replaced by a socialist government. The Communists held to the common-sense view that the immediate job was to defeat Franco, and only then would it be appropriate to worry about the ideological purity of the government. Trotskyists favoured the tactic of 'impossibilism': setting an impossible objective, then attacking everyone else on the left for not achieving it. The Communists' difficulty was that it was only a couple of years since the CP had itself been taking the sort of line it now denounced as 'impossibilist'.

At first the CP claimed that, by their mistaken views, Trotskyists were unwittingly aiding the cause of Fascism in Spain. But eventually it came to believe that Trotskyists were conscious agents of Fascism. The dispute was bitter and unrestrained. And the declining, vulnerable ILP found itself drawn in. To the Communists' fury, the ILP journal *New Leader* started to give space to Trotskyists.

So the CP redoubled its efforts to destroy the ILP. Hundreds of Communists were ordered to infiltrate its ranks. Douglas Hyde was one of them. After his triumph in destroying the ILP in North Wales, in 1938 he moved to Surrey, joined his local Labour Party, and was quickly elected to its executive. 'It was not long before I had got every likely man or woman at executive level into the Communist Party. Then, one night, I got them together . . . When all had arrived I revealed that everyone present was already a Communist Party member and suddenly they realised what had happened and just what strength the Party already had in the local Labour movement. Then we got down to business.'

One of the Balham Group's leaders, Reg Groves, a gentle, thoughtful man and a self-taught intellectual, was a historian and writer. He could compete with Dutt for analysis but, free from the shackles under which Dutt laboured, wrote far more interestingly. Groves is responsible for one of the few trade union histories which is worth reading, a history of rural trade unionism called *Sharpen the Sickle*. Also in the Balham Group was Harry Wicks, a founder Communist Party member who had spent three years at the Lenin School in Moscow and worked in one of the Soviet trading agencies in the City of London until his political activities brought dismissal and he was out of work for five years. The group scraped together enough money to send Wicks to Copenhagen to confer with the exiled Trotsky himself. At first the hated Trotskyists were no more than thoughtful idealists like Groves and Wicks. It was only later that British Trotskyism started to ape the worst features of the Stalinism it sought to replace.

5

Spies

T HE Communist Party was born on the fringes of legality. For dedicated revolutionaries, the inside of prison cells, spying and being spied on, were part of life. Mostly, they went to prison simply for being Communists or Comintern agents, or for putting out Communist propaganda. But amid all the hysteria about spying there had to be some real spies, and there were.

The CP was convinced it was being spied on, and it was, but it was generally wrong when it tried to identify the spies. MI5 was convinced that Communist spies were active in Britain, and they were, but it unerringly focused its attentions on innocent people or small and unimportant spies, and missed those who mattered.

Police surveillance was not always sophisticated. At one CP meeting in 1924, the speaker opened a trapdoor under the stage to discover two men taking shorthand notes. The police were called and they arrested the men, only discovering later that they had arrested fellow policemen. In the 1930s Harry Pollitt boarded a bus one day and told the conductor in a loud voice that he was paying for himself and 'that man in the front of the bus, because I'm the only person who knows where he's getting off.'

Wilfred Macartney, a former army intelligence officer, was one of the first Communists to go to prison for spying, in 1927. His arrest was achieved by the use of an *agent provocateur*, and came after a police raid and an armed search of the Soviet Trade Delegation which caused Moscow temporarily to sever diplomatic relations with London. Macartney was a remarkable man: a dedicated Communist, an accomplished soldier and spy, and a writer and journalist with admirers throughout the left, not just in the CP. He was sentenced to ten years in prison. After his release he fought in the Spanish Civil War, becoming commander of the British Battalion, wrote two well-received books, and helped run a spy network against Germany during the Second World War.

In 1930 the neurotic, manipulative Maxwell Knight was put in charge of MI5's plan to penetrate the Communist Party. He started routinely by tapping telephones and arranging for the dismissal of Communists working in what he considered to be sensitive areas of industry. One of these was Percy Glading, a former member of the CP Central Committee who worked at Woolwich Arsenal. By this means Knight may well have created a spy. Glading was now out of work and finding alternative work hard to come by. But he was also a man of considerable ability, and rather likeable, with an open face and a keen sense of humour, who knew a good deal about maps and photography. Unwilling to waste his talents, the CP and the Comintern agreed that he should spend his enforced idleness at the Lenin School in Moscow. There, in addition to the school's normal syllabus of Marxist and trade union studies, he learned the rudiments of espionage. Arriving back in 1930 he worked in the CP's colonial department, which meant in practise that he carried Comintern cash and messages to India.

Meanwhile Maxwell Knight found an agent to infiltrate the CP. Olga Gray worked for the CP for six years, from 1931 to 1937, first as a volunteer and then full time at King Street. She was surprised to find herself growing to like these Bolsheviks of whom she had heard such hair-raising things. When she began to help Percy Glading with a scheme to convey plans of a British gun to the Soviet Union, she found herself liking the man. Although Olga wanted to give up her job with MI5 Knight managed to persuade her to stay on until Glading was in the net. Glading went down for six years and Olga suffered agonies of guilt about his wife and daughter.

Pollitt would have taken care not to know much about Glading's operation. Such things were always kept separate from the Party's political work. Neither he nor Glading suspected Olga Gray. Their suspicions were focused on Jack Murphy, former Communist leader and one of the CP's founders, who left the Party in 1932 and was by now active in Stafford Cripps's Socialist League. As the Second World War grew closer and the purges in Moscow created paranoia and spy-fever, other suspects were also discussed in low voices in King Street. But the first thing to make King Street suspicious in those frantic days was divergence from 'the line', and a real spy would be unlikely to draw attention to himself in this way.

Hence one of the CP's more laughable suspects was Fenner Brockway, who had encouraged people going to Spain to volunteer for the POUM militia rather than the Communist-controlled British Battalion. He had written bitterly of atrocities committed behind the lines by the Communists. In fact, Brockway had little access to information about the CP, even if he had been a spy, but several former CP members were among his friends.

The atmosphere of intrigue in which the CP operated is illustrated by an unsigned memorandum in the Moscow archives, written late in 1928. The writer was visited by 'D, a left-wing social democratic journalist of Berlin' who 'let it be seen that in Russian matters his sympathies were left-oppositionist' (code for Trotskyist). He said he wanted the writer of the memorandum to help Trotskyists in Britain to obtain confidential information, especially from the foreign office.

'I asked: to whom will the information go? He said: to certain people in Russia. I said: Have they an organisation now? He said: no, that was the mistake Trotsky made. Now it is a question of individuals. Money would be available to buy informers, he said. I then pretended surprise. How could individual oppositionists in Russia have funds? He said at last: if it were from the government, would that make any difference to you? ... Yes, it really is from the government.'

The writer asks for instructions on a picture postcard. 'The day of writing shown on it will be the code, as follows: Sunday: he is really our man, co-operate with him. Monday: continue contact and investigate further. Tuesday: break off all contact and tell them it is impossible to do anything. Wednesday: Come to Berlin [where the Comintern had its west European headquarters] for consultation.'

As the war approached, MI5 seems to have devoted a lot of time to compiling information about the International Brigades in Spain, and lists of those who fought in them. Some were blocked when they tried to get into the British army, others found their promotion blocked. In this way the British intelligence service deprived the army of the most battle-hardened anti-Nazis the country possessed.

But it was in Moscow that the most wildly wrong and absurd guesses about spies were made, especially during the paranoid atmosphere of the purges. By then, the atmosphere in Moscow was fetid with fear and suspicion. British Communists, still travelling regularly and frequently in and out of Moscow, were in greater danger than they realized of being caught up in the hysteria and shot. Their British passports may have saved them.

In January 1939 an anonymous Comintern official drew up a report on the CP which was obviously intended to form the basis for executing its leading members, in case that should be thought desirable. The official who drew it up almost certainly knew that writing this sort of murderous nonsense was the only chance he had of staying alive himself.

'The leadership of the CP,' he began 'contains a number of people who were formerly connected with enemies of the people, and in some cases are currently connected with politically dubious people.' Many of them 'have made serious political mistakes in the past.' These mistakes were relentlessly itemized. Eleven years ago Johnny Campbell 'adhered to a so-called majority of the Central Committee which underestimated the revolutionary strength of the working class and overestimated capitalist stabilisation.' Twenty years ago Willie Gallacher 'displayed left-sectarian tendencies' by opposing Labour Party affiliation. And so on. No one was spared. Even the faithful Dutt and Rust had been known to display 'sectarian tendencies', though Rust 'overcame them in his work in Lancashire, according to Comrade Pollitt.' Nonetheless there was a question mark over Rust: he was married to a Russian whose father, an architect and a former Soviet citizen, 'left in 1927 on a business trip to Germany and refused to return to the USSR.'

Even more serious, there were 'materials on the connections between the leading Communists in the British Communist Party with Petrovsky and his wife Rose Cohen, who turned out to be enemies of the people. It is clear from the materials that some of the leading comrades in the British Communist Party, particularly Comrade Pollitt, did not just have a business connection with Petrovsky and Cohen, but also a personal friendship with them.' The document quotes written statements given (under what circumstances we will probably never know) by Robin Page Arnot and Bob Stewart, confirming this. Page Arnot's statement says Petrovsky 'was the only comrade on the Comintern with whom I and the rest of the British comrades had the closest links and a personal friendship.' Rose Cohen 'was a close personal friend of most of the leading comrades.' Stewart says Petrovsky 'had great influence not only on us . . . but also on such people as Arthur Cook and other left leaders of the MFGB [the miners' union].'

It also quotes Pollitt's friendly letter to Rose Cohen, which she never saw. Pollitt had clearly not been forgiven for making waves about her case. He told her too much, says the document: 'One may conclude, among other things, that the position of conspiratorial work in the CP is far from satisfactory, if the general secretary shows such an irresponsible attitude to conspiracy.' And then, insinuatingly: 'The letter ends with these words addressed to Rose Cohen: "We all send our love. Don't lose heart."'

The Young Communist League must also be purged. 'Some doubtful elements were found in the Kensington and Paddington YCL organisations, suspected of links with Trotskyists.' Communists on the Glasgow Trades Council had committed the crime of electing a delegate to an Aid Spain conference who was in the ILP – which meant, of course, that he must be a Trotskyist. 'Corrupting and demoralising Trotskyist ideas enjoy fairly wide credit . . . the following books have been published in England written by enemies of the USSR Trotsky and his fellow travellers of the German Gestapo . . .' It also mentions 'a Trotskyist organisation – the ILP, led by Brockway, McGovern and Maxton.'

The German wife of a Macclesfield CP member was pinpointed as having been a Trotskyist in Germany. She had 'a lot of literature in the German language, presumably produced by a Trotskyist publishing house,' and her husband agreed with her about all important political questions. Yet the Macclesfield CP branch had taken no steps 'to protect its ranks from penetration by Trotskyist influences, or to investigate under what circumstances this German Trotskyist came to England and based herself in a textile area with a large working-class population . . .' The circumstances, with Hitler in power in Germany, hardly needed investigation. Fortunately Bill Rust was on hand to 'warn the comrades that such quietism and political indifference borders on rendering assistance to the most malicious enemies of the Party – the Trotskyists . . .'

But all was not lost. 'All CP district committee members attend Sunday classes to teach them the importance of Comintern decisions and gain a deeper understanding of the lessons of the Moscow trials.' Nonetheless, shamefully, 'there are still over 1000 copies of the pamphlet on the history of the Soviet Union by the enemy of the people N. N. Popov in the Party organisations.'

Recommendations included: 'Particular attention must be paid to exposing the Trotskyists, *provocateurs* and spies who have penetrated the Party's ranks, and discovering their method of penetration . . .' The *Daily Worker* 'is making the most serious political mistakes.' It staff must be urgently 'checked and purged.' Another report to Dimitrov, again anonymous but written in German, talked of a mistake by the *Daily Worker*, which welcomed Chamberlain's visit to Hitler under the mistaken impression that this was Comintern policy. Calling again for 'a purge' in the *Worker* office, the report said that the newspaper 'makes itself enemy propaganda and instils poison drop by drop.'

It is hilarious stuff, viewed from the safe distance of more than half a century. But it is also infinitely sad. Was this what it had all come to, the Russian revolution which signalled to Harry Pollitt that the workers were on top at last and that the wrongs of his class would be avenged? Was this litany of paranoid fairy-tales what it had all come to?

MI5 was quite capable of similar delusions. It tapped the Communists' phones, it raided their offices and published the documents it found, it planted spies, it put leading Communists in prison, it rushed to declare the Zinoviev letter genuine on virtually no evidence. But because it did not monitor the changes in Communist policy and work out their significance, it missed the important spies.

In the early 1930s the CP changed its policy towards intellectuals. One of the many absurdities of Class Against Class was that, in addition to condemning ILP people as 'social fascists', Communists were required to make the CP unwelcoming for intellectuals and students. This was not entirely without reason. CP leaders had watched students helping to break the general strike by doing the jobs of striking workers, and had concluded that universities were producing élitists and reactionaries. The people who needed to be recruited to the Party were industrial workers. Communist academics, writers and the rest were forbidden to try to organize among other intellectuals. This was also the Comintern line.

Abandoning Class Against Class allowed the Party to discover all the useful things Communist intellectuals could do for the Party. There was also the fact that intellectuals were organizing anyway, and what was the Party to do – break them up? In 1931 Communist groups were formed at Cambridge University, the London School of Economics and University College, London. In 1932 groups were formed at Oxford, Reading, Durham, Leeds and Manchester universities.

Communist students felt obliged to sound more like workers than the working class. Denis Healey writes that in the Class Against Class period 'Communists were very sectarian, got drunk, wore beards and did not worry about their examinations.' They 'affected the glottal stop, which they regarded as essential to the proletarian image. "Ours is a par'y of a new type," they would say.'

But when CP policy changed, this affectation became unnecessary. Willie Gallacher visited the Cambridge CP group in 1934 and told them the opposite of what the Party had been telling students just two years before: 'We want people who are capable, who are good scientists, historians and teachers ... We need you as you are ... it's pointless to run away to factories ... We want you to study and become good students.' Denis Healey, who went to Oxford in 1936 and joined the CP in 1937, writes that in his time 'Communists started shaving, tried to avoid being drunk in public, worked for first-class degrees and played down their Marxism-Leninism.'

Had MI5 recognized this shift, and considered its implications, it would have saved itself a great deal of trouble, expense and embarrassment. This new policy was to supply spies right at the heart of the British establishment. Cambridge in the 1930s had several former public schoolboys who were already committed Communists. These included probably the four best known of

Britain's Soviet spies, not unmasked until years after the war: Kim Philby, Guy Burgess, Donald Maclean and Anthony Blunt. There was also James Klugmann.

Klugmann had been at school with Maclean at Gresham's in Norfolk, and took him under his wing when Maclean arrived at Cambridge, carefully nurturing his less intelligent protégé's political opinions. Klugmann came from a prosperous Jewish family in Hampstead. Unlike the others, Klugmann's Communism was never a secret. By 1933, when he took a first-class degree in French and German, he was Cambridge University's best-known Communist and was building the Party carefully under the watchful eye of YCL leader Dave Springhall.

Klugmann willingly sacrificed his excellent chance of a Cambridge fellowship by his uncompromising alliegance. Years later he explained: 'My commitment to the cause was for life, and it was an exhilarating moment to be alive and young. We simply *knew*, all of us, that the revolution was at hand.' He visited a mining village in South Wales and wrote that the Soviet Union would never tolerate 'empty houses furnished with bits of wood and orange boxes, children without shoes, rickets everywhere, small shop-keepers ruined because their customers couldn't afford to buy, tuberculosis and emigration.' An outstanding academic, he both felt and thought his way to Communism. It was – or it seemed to be – a time of simple choices. There was good and there was evil. 'No later generation' writes Healey 'has enjoyed the same political certainty.' Today people tend to focus their idealism on single issues: 'It seems easier to save the whale than to save the world.' Anthony Blunt, after being named as a spy in 1979, said that when he came back after a sabbatical in 1934 to complete his degree, 'all my friends and almost all the intelligent, bright undergraduates had suddenly become Marxists ...'

It was Klugmann who provided the Cambridge link with King Street, and Dave Springhall who guided Klugmann. Springhall visited the University regularly, took the membership lists, and discussed in detail the character and potential of all new recruits. In the late 1930s Klugmann helped organize aid for Spain. Denis Healey remembers a summer holiday in France, when he passed Klugmann a mysterious package on his way through Paris. Thus Springhall and Klugmann helped nurture the spy network which was to cause the British government so much embarrassment years later; but MI5 was looking for subversive activities elsewhere.

Springhall had been dismissed from the navy in 1920 for Communist activities. He was part of the YCL group around Bill Rust which acted as the Comintern's watchdog, stopping the foot-dragging over the introduction of Class Against Class. He joined the CP Central Committee in 1932 and was a political commissar in the Spanish Civil War. He was very particular about ensuring the CP followed Moscow's line correctly. Jack Gaster, when he led his supporters out of the ILP and into the Communist Party in 1935, remembers that Springhall held up their membership. 'I was furious,' says Gaster. 'He was missing the opportunity of signing up 200 new members. He said: "We have to be very careful who we admit."' They were admitted in the end and Gaster met 'a lovely girl called Moira Lynd who had become a Communist at Oxford. Springhall told her to keep an eye on me. But in 1938, when I married Moira and had a party in a Marylebone pub, Springie was there and danced the hornpipe.'

Dave Springhall had the rolling gait of a sailor, and some people thought he looked a little thuggish. He was certainly different from the Cambridge aesthetes around Klugmann: a 'tough hearty', one of them called him. Springhall was arrested in 1943 and sentenced to seven years penal servitude for spying. It was an appalling embarrassment to the CP, which was at that time conducting itself with conspicuous patriotism, and Party leaders expelled him at once. Harry Pollitt was furious with him, and with the Russians. When he was released, a much less bouncy Springhall took his family and went to work in China. He died in Moscow in the 1950s.

Springhall's arrest was not connected with his work with the future Cambridge spies. He was caught obtaining secret information from an Air Ministry employee and an army officer and passing it to the Soviet Union. The information was almost certainly being duplicated by Kim Philby. It was typical of MI5 at the time that they caught Springhall, the working-class lad, at a spot of low-grade spying, but completely missed the Cambridge people; and though they followed Springhall everywhere, they never seem to have asked themselves why Springhall spent so much time in Cambridge. If MI5 looked at Klugmann and his friends at all, all they saw was a few wealthy undergraduates kicking over the traces.

Klugmann had a very different sort of war. While Springhall was in prison, Klugmann joined the army and obtained rapid promotion: captain by June 1943, major by October, lieutenant-colonel by June 1944. He was sent to Yugoslavia to help Tito's partisans. No former International Brigader would have been sent on so delicate a mission. Klugmann might be a Communist, but he was at least a gentleman.

It was in Yugoslavia, some people believe, that Klugmann performed his greatest service for Soviet intelligence. Two competing groups were fighting the Nazis in Yugoslavia. One was the Communist Partisans under Josip Broz, later Marshal Tito, a former International Brigader in Spain. The other was the Cetniks under General Dragoljub Mihailovic. It is alleged that Klugmann played a key part in ensuring that Allied aid went to Tito and not to Mihailovic, thus ensuring that Tito ruled post-war Yugoslavia. Klugmann's defenders point out that he was accurately reflecting reality: Tito's forces, rather than Mihailovic's, were leading the fight against Hitler.

After the war Klugmann became a full-time CP official and wrote the first two volumes of the Party's history. He also wrote a shabby little book called *From Trotsky to Tito* to justify the fact that Stalin had turned against the Yugoslav leader whom Klugmann had once helped and admired.

Years later, after it had missed the Cambridge spies, MI5 briefly became convinced that there must have been an Oxford one too. The unfortunate Bernard Floud, briefly a Communist at Oxford in the 1930s and a friend of Klugmann, was elected. He became a Labour MP and in 1967 Prime Minister Harold Wilson wanted to make him a junior minister, so MI5 interrogated him for weeks on end about his non-existent spying activities. During this period of interrogation, Floud, already depressed about his wife's recent death, went home and gassed himself to death.

It has to be said that Maxwell Knight was beginning to have suspicions of the Cambridge spies by 1940. But he destroyed his credibility by arranging for a man called Ben Greene to be interned for alleged Nazi connections which he did not have. Greene was fingered by one of Knight's less respectable agents, Harald Kurtz, who invented the evidence against him. Greene, who had powerful family connections and was the cousin of the novelist Graham

Greene, was able to prove it, and had to be released. Without this débâcle, Knight's suspicions of the Cambridge spies might have been taken seriously. Instead, MI5 persisted in its futile policy of penetrating the obvious groups – those with unsound political opinions.

Yet the evidence was under their noses. In 1936 the erratic, unstable Guy Burgess, who was indiscreet even on the rare occasions when he was sober, told his friend Goronwy Rees that he and Blunt had been Soviet spies ever since they left Cambridge. Rees seems to have gone round London asking everyone he knew whether Burgess's claim could be true. But no alarm bells rang in MI5, which was busy transcribing Harry Pollitt's telephone calls.

The journalist and future Labour MP Tom Driberg was one of Knight's agents in the CP. In 1940 Anthony Blunt, now working for MI5 and passing information to the Soviet Union, got hold of one of Driberg's reports and worked out who had written it. Blunt's Soviet case officer told King Street and Driberg was promptly thrown out of the Party with no explanation. Driberg went to see Dave Springhall, the most influential Party member he knew, to ask why. Springhall claimed not to know. Blunt was furious with his Soviet case officer and with King Street for using his information so clumsily, and terrified that Knight would find out where the leak had come from. Yet even after this massive blunder, Blunt remained undetected.

Another Knight agent was Bill Allen, an Ulster Unionist MP in the 1929–31 parliament who then attached himself to Oswald Mosley and the British Union of Fascists. He was personally close to Mosley, helped persuade prestigious converts, and even paid the salaries of some of Mosley's staff. But he was also Maxwell Knight's man, reporting to MI5 on Mosley's activities – and Mosley seems to have known this. It is not clear whether Mosley or MI5 got most out of him, but he supplied the evidence on which Mosley was interned.

In 1956, when MI5 was at last closing in on Kim Philby and he had lost his Foreign Office job, his old chum Bill Allen offered him a bolthole. He hired Philby, so they both claimed, to help Allen compile a history of his family's business in Northern Ireland, and Philby stayed with Allen in Ireland for several months until the heat was off.

Whose man was Allen? He probably never knew for certain himself. The business of spying, then as now, was full of men like Bill Allen, Tom Driberg and Harald Kurtz, to whom the game and the power it gives them over peoples' lives are the real reward.

If the security services managed to miss Kim Philby for twenty years, they did not miss his eccentric but relatively harmless father, Harry St John Philby. Philby *père* was a distinguished Arabist and an old associate of T. E. Lawrence. Like many Arabists, he was somewhat anti-semitic and stood in a Parliamentary by-election as an anti-war candidate in 1939. He was locked away for four months while his son continued working inside the secret service and handing information to its Soviet counterpart.

6

Uncle Joe Says Stand on Your Head

O N 23 August 1939 Hitler and Stalin signed a non-aggression pact. The Communist Party had demanded that Britain stand up to Hitler. Now Stalin had made it look and feel both foolish and dishonest. Dutt quickly explained that Stalin had to agree the pact because Britain and France had forced Hitler's attention on to the Soviet Union so that they could watch Germany and the Soviet Union fight it out. This was not hard to believe. The British and French governments had certainly shown no real interest in linking arms with Stalin to contain Hitler.

Hitler invaded Poland on 1 September, and Britain declared war on Germany two days later. The *Daily Worker* declared this 'a war that CAN and MUST be won.' Two weeks later Harry Pollitt's pamphlet *How to Win the War* appeared. The very day it was published, a Moscow press telegram arrived indicating that the war was to be opposed. Pollitt suppressed the telegram for almost two weeks, eventually explaining that he suppressed it because it was contrary to CP policy.

To people who did not know the man, and thought of him as a mere Stalinist functionary, this action was remarkable. He was obstructing the Soviet line. He was being politically unreliable. In Moscow he would have been shot. But for Pollitt it came down, as did most things, to the gut beliefs which motivated his life. Capitalism meant poverty for many so that a few might have great wealth and power. The Soviet Union was the workers' state, run for and by the workers. And Fascism and Nazism were the sworn enemy of the workers, and must be defeated. Moscow was going to demand that the British Communist Party oppose the war. And Harry Pollitt did not see how he was going to be able to do that.

Three days after his pamphlet was published, Russian troops entered Poland. A line in Poland was fixed between the Russian and German armies. Hitler and Stalin had secretly carved up Poland between them – a squalid deal to deprive a small nation of its freedom. Pollitt had fiercely opposed Chamberlain's agreement with Hitler over Czechoslovakia at Munich. The 'appetite of the Fascist beast grows with every fresh kill. Can we be so blind as not to see that our turn will come unless we make a stand now?' Now that the government was at last making a stand, how could he justify trying to stop them? Yet that was exactly what he was expected to do, and without even a pretence of consultation. Pollitt, Dutt, Campbell and Gallacher were on the Comintern executive, but it had not met for four years. Decisions were made in its secretariat, which had no British member.

On 7 September, a week before Pollitt published *How to Win the War*, Stalin told Georgi Dimitrov, general secretary of the Comintern, what he now expected of foreign Communist parties. They should denounce their governments' war plans as imperialistic and reduce anti-Fascist propaganda. Stalin did not want Hitler to be able to accuse the Soviet Union of being anti-Fascist because of the actions of foreign Communists. The Comintern secretariat issued the necessary instructions. It added: 'The Communist Parties, particularly of France, Britain, Belgium and the USA, which have taken up positions at variance with this standpoint, must immediately correct their political line.' The instructions were signed by Georgi Dimitrov, which made Communists everywhere more likely to accept them. Had not Dimitrov, with great courage, denounced the Nazis in a German court in 1933? It was barely believable that the hero of the Reichstag fire trial had gone soft on Fascism.

American Communist leader Earl Browder obeyed at once, turning his Party's policy on its head overnight. French Communists quickly issued a statement declaring to loud Parisian guffaws that the war 'is no longer in reality an anti-Fascist and anti-Hitler war.' In Britain, Harry Pollitt managed to keep the telescope glued to his blind eye until his Central Committee met on Sunday 24 September. Then he explained that the CP's man in Moscow, Dave Springhall, was due to arrive in Britain, probably that evening. Once he arrived, the Party would know what Moscow wanted.

Pollitt cannot have had much doubt what the message was going to be, but a good politician never faces the worst until he has to. He went home depressed, and started to trim the hedge in his front garden in Colindale, North London. Looking over it, he saw Springhall coming up the street. He remembered that moment years later. Springhall must have looked like a figure of doom whom he had hoped, against all reason, might never arrive.

Springhall was one of those Communists who talk like a concrete mixer. His report to the meeting the next day was full of ready-mixed phrases which pass as political analysis. He talked of 'a thesis which will try to concretise the directives for the various countries' and of wanting to 'solidarise' himself with something Dutt had said. Such phrases are often used by those who need to justify the unjustifiable. Stalin said Poland must be jettisoned, so Springhall told his colleagues: 'The situation here is characterised by saying that Poland is a semi-Fascist country ... it would be regarded not as a terrible misfortune if Poland were to disappear from the scene.'

Meaningless slogans such as 'No unity with the Chamberlain socialists' had been concocted by Dimitrov. It is hard to imagine what the British public might have made of this, if it had ever been heard outside the Central Committee. Dimitrov and André Marty had apparently assured Springhall that there was little to choose between Hitler and Chamberlain; that the war was not a just war; that Communists must work 'not only against our own bourgeoisie but for their military defeat'; and Communist MPs like Gallacher must vote against war credits. Dimitrov and Marty understood this was going to cause problems in Britain. You might need to bring 'newer comrades into the leadership of the Party'. The somersault would be made harder by 'the character of Comrade Pollitt's speeches.' This was Comintern-speak for Pollitt Must Go.

If the Comintern wanted to reverse the policy, the rules of democratic centralism meant that the policy had to be reversed. Pollitt could not live with the new line. He handed his responsibilities temporarily to a secretariat – a 'troika' – of Dutt, Rust and Springhall, who accepted the Comintern line. Then he waited until the Central Committee was ready to debate the whole issue at the beginning of October. There, in secret, he would tell his colleagues exactly what he thought, and let them judge. He knew that – for the first and only time in his life – they would have to choose between his position and Stalin's.

But events did not wait for him. On 29 September Britain learned that Stalin and Hitler had agreed a 'Treaty of Friendship and the Delimitation of Borders' which involved carving up Poland between them. They also jointly called on Britain and France to make peace with Germany.

The troika wanted to issue a statement calling for peace, effectively on German terms. The five others in the Politburo, including Pollitt, Gallacher and Campbell, did not. They fudged it, not very successfully. Elements of the old pro-war line were uneasily mixed with elements of the anti-war line which the Comintern was determined the Party should adopt. The working class 'will not allow itself to be led to the slaughter for imperialist aims.' Yet the working class also 'wants the defeat of Nazi aggression.'

The Central Committee met on 2 and 3 October. By this time most of its members had more or less reluctantly convinced themselves that the Comintern, Dimitrov, Stalin and the Soviet Union could not all be wrong, and that their duty was to support the international line. But not everyone. A verbatim note of the meeting was sent as usual to Moscow and only recovered more than half a century later by the CP. Party members knew nothing of what went on, though MI5 quickly acquired a copy. It was a bad-tempered debate, largely because of Dutt's arrogant, hamfisted opening. He demanded 'acceptance of [the new line] by the members of the Central Committee on the basis of conviction. Absolute and complete conviction . . .' This was utterly unrealistic. He proposed a resolution: '. . . In no country can the working class or the Communist Party support the war . . . The international working class can under no conditions support Fascist Poland which has refused the aid of the Soviet Union . . . Operate against the war, unmask its imperialist character . . .'

He rejected the 'foul slander' that the CP was turning just because the Soviet Union was turning. The truth was that Soviet leaders understood quicker than British leaders the need for a new line. 'Nazi Germany has been weakened' by the Hitler-Stalin pact. Only Dutt could have said this with conviction. The Party must 'face frankly and openly that our line was a wrong line.' In a series of highly personal remarks he left no doubt whom he blamed for all this: Pollitt, Campbell and a few others. His call to arms was issued in the usual terms: '. . . merciless ruthless clearing that results in absolute certainty and conviction of every Party member . . . Every responsible position in the Party must be occupied by a determined fighter for the line . . .' The crisis has 'shown dangerous tendencies in our Party' to question the international line.

Bob Stewart mocked 'these sledgehammer demands for whole-hearted convictions and solid and hardened, tempered Bolshevism and all this bloody kind of stuff.' Willie Gallacher was beside himself with fury. Dutt, on behalf of the troika, was violently attacking the Party statement on the partition of Poland – yet all three troika members were on the Politburo which agreed it. 'I have never . . . at this Central Committee listened to a more unscrupulous and opportunist speech than has been made by Comrade Dutt . . . and I have never had in all my experience in the Party such evidence of mean, despicable disloyalty to comrades as has been evidenced by these three. It is impossible to work with them.' Dutt's parroted Comintern phrases 'make him absolutely correct and a devoted servant to the Communist International and surely the Communist International will be very happy to know that.' Everyone knew the verbatim record would be studied closely in Moscow. The CP should not accept mechanically everything that comes from the Comintern. They had mechanically accepted Class Against Class, and look where that got them!

Pollitt, in his more controlled way, was just as furious: 'Please remember, Comrade Dutt, you won't intimidate me by that language. I was in the movement practically before you were born, and will be in the revolutionary movement a long time after some of you are forgotten . . . If you want to have political conviction, Dutt, you must learn to present a case in a different manner to what you did this morning.' The old friendship would never be the same again.

Johnny Campbell, editor of the *Daily Worker*, thought the Comintern was placing the CP in an absurd position. 'We started

94

by saying we had an interest in the defeat of the Nazis, we must now recognise that our prime interest is in the defeat of France and Great Britain ... We have to eat everything we have said ...' If France and Britain were defeated, Europe would become Fascist. The danger was of making the same mistake as the German Communists made in the early 1930s. They refused to ally themselves with social democrats – and the result was Hitler. It might be in Moscow's short-term interest if Hitler defeated Britain and France. But it was not in the interest of British workers.

It did not matter how strong Campbell's arguments were. The Comintern had spoken and that was that. Not for any cynical reasons, but because Communists – intelligent, sincere Communists – believed, as Harry Pollitt had once put it, that the Soviet Union could do no wrong. Maurice Cornforth, one of the few of Klugmann's Cambridge generation to get to the Central Committee and just 30 years old, expressed it most clearly: 'I believe that if one loses anything of that faith in the Soviet Union one is done for as a Communist and Socialist.'

Yet Pollitt, who had taught Cornforth his faith in the Soviet Union, was rebelling: 'I believe in the long run it will do this Party very great harm ... I don't envy the comrades who can so lightly in the space of a week ... go from one political conviction to another.' In this private meeting, for the Central Committee and no one else, he said what was in his heart: 'It is not an easy thing for me not to be sitting at the head of the table ... It would be very easy for me to say I accept ... But I would be dishonest to my convictions.' As for Poland, 'I am ashamed of the lack of feeling, the lack of response that this struggle of the Polish people has aroused in our leadership.' It was 'Polish workers and peasants' who defended Warsaw. The Comintern line was 'a betrayal of the struggle of the labour movement against Fascism.' He told how Georgi Dimitrov once 'explained to Campbell and myself for hours that one of the greatest shortcomings of our Party was that we did not know how to look after the national honour of our country. And I tell you our honour is at stake now.'

Dutt was shaken. The US Party, the Belgian Party, the French Party had done what they were told. The CP's special problem was that 'a group of important leading comrades have taken a position of full opposition to the line decided by the International.' His own opening speech, though aggressive, was, said Dutt, not personal. Pollitt must have recognized the words Dutt used, for they recalled those of Salme Dutt years earlier, in one of the semi-flirtatious letters she was continually writing to Pollitt: 'It is necessary to fight and to make no apologies for it, without kid gloves, without regard to friendship.'

The new line was agreed, only Pollitt, Campbell and Gallacher voting against. Gallacher was still 'seething through and through with disgust.' Dutt, Rust and Springhall had attacked him in an underhand and dishonest way, he said. As the Party's sole MP he needed to be on the Politburo but 'I cannot under any circumstances associate with these three people.' This was awkward. The troika sat immobilized, not knowing what to do, and Pollitt the accomplished politician stepped in and saved the situation. He unostentatiously closed the meeting and told them how to get on with their job quickly and efficiently. Then in a closed session, after Gallacher had left, he tactfully suggested that they record Gallacher as having voted in favour of the new line, so as to keep him on the Politburo. 'All of us know Comrade Gallacher's temperament. No one has had a more difficult job than he has . . . He got rattled because of personal feelings. Actually he is for the thesis . . .'

Pollitt's pamphlet was replaced by Dutt's new pamphlet *Why This War*? Dutt took over from Pollitt, though he was never actually given the title of general secretary. Rust replaced Campbell as editor of the *Daily Worker*, and the paper started to demand that Chamberlain respond to Hitler's peace overtures. A new Politburo was elected from which Pollitt and Campbell were excluded.

Pollitt's mother read in the newspaper that he had been dismissed from his job. She wrote to him at once: don't lose your pride, you can always go back to your trade, I've kept your tools greased. Pollitt used the first weeks of his enforced idleness to write an autobiography, which he dedicated to her. The day he finished it she died. The Dutts wrote characteristic letters of condolence. Dutt wrote: '. . . It is a blow and I am sorry it should happen to you now.' Salme wrote: 'Dear, dear Harry, I feel as if I had lost my own mother . . . My thoughts and feelings are all with her son although he does not care.'

It was not enough for Dutt that Pollitt and Campbell should give up their jobs. They must also be made to recant publicly, like medieval heretics. So the two sat down together and wrote a statement saying that their view 'gave an entirely incorrect estimation of the position and cannot be defended' and declaring support for the new line. It wasn't good enough. Back came a lengthy Duttish letter the next day. A joint statement was no good; they must each sign their own statement. In it they must make 'an examination of the basis of the wrong approach and your persistence in it, and a recognition of the very serious harm done to the Party at a most critical turning point by this opposition and division of the leadership.' Eventually the two men signed individual statements which were sufficiently grovelling to satisfy Dutt. They said they 'played into the hands of the class enemy' by persisting in the 'wrong position.' Years later Campbell told Communist historian Monty Johnstone: 'If you didn't live through that time you can't understand what the pressures were to convince ourselves that the line of the International and the Soviet Union was right, as we had done previously over the Moscow trials.'

In April and May 1940 the Germans swept through Norway, Holland and Belgium. In June France surrendered. In September the Germans started to bomb London. That summer more than 700 Fascists and other right-wing opponents of the war were rounded up and arrested under wartime regulation 18B, which allowed arrest without trial. When Labour joined a coalition government under Churchill, Herbert Morrison, who probably hated Communists more than any other politician of any party and had fought for years to keep them out of the Labour Party, earning himself the title of witch-finder general, became Home Secretary. Morrison itched to imprison Communist leaders, but Churchill restrained him.

French Communists fared worse. The Parti Communiste Français was banned before the fall of France in 1940 and about half of its seventy-two MPs were sentenced to long terms of imprisonment. After France fell the Nazis executed thousands of them.

Morrison suppressed the *Daily Worker* in January 1941. The Party's answer to that was an imaginative one. It set up a news agency called Industrial and General Information (IGI) which sold stories to national newspapers. It got the stories from the *Daily Worker's* extensive network of 'worker correspondents'. IGI also assembled a daily news bulletin which went both to newspapers and to Communist Party offices, thereby keeping Party members in touch. One indiscreet young member working in a Scottish shipyard sent in information which he thought might be useful to the Soviet Union. This was intercepted by MI5 with the result that he finished up in prison.

IGI was run by one of the Party's most trusted underground journalists, Douglas Hyde. Hyde's nose for a story won him friends and customers throughout Fleet Street. He reported to Bill Rust. Hyde was also busy preparing underground presses against the time when all Communist publishing might be banned. If that happened the plan was for Rust to go underground and operate anonymously from the country house of one of the Party's wealthy sympathizers.

On Sunday 22 June 1941 Germany invaded the Soviet Union. That evening the new Prime Minister Winston Churchill said: 'We shall give whatever help we can to Russia.' At once the Communist Party announced full support for the war and brought back Harry Pollitt as general secretary. Secretly many Communists, even those in the leadership, were relieved to be able to abandon a line which they had never in their hearts really believed in. Perhaps it is a measure of the reluctance with which the new line was adopted that no one was ever formally given Pollitt's job while he was out of office, though Dutt performed most of the general secretary's duties. This time there were no agonies of conscience. Those who supported the anti-war stance, like Dutt, did so because they believed in loyal support for the Comintern line, and the Comintern line was now pro-war.

Suddenly the Communist Party was popular and respectable, because Stalin's Russia was popular and respectable, and because at a time of war, Communists were able to wave the Union Jack with the best of them. Party leaders appeared on platforms with the great and the good. Membership soared: from 15,570 in 1938 to a peak of 56,000 in 1942.

Harry Pollitt came back to his post a more accomplished and better connected politician than before. If Dutt had known who Pollitt was seeing while out of office, his dark, jealous suspicions would have given him no rest. Pollitt had been building on the relationships with others on the left which had briefly flowered and then withered during the attempt to agree a popular front. He became a regular and welcome visitor at a flat in Lincoln's Inn owned by Frank Owen, then editor of the *Evening Standard*. There he would talk for hours with Owen and a young left-wing Labour Party journalist who was a friend of the anti-Communists Nye Bevan and Jennie Lee, and even of the hated Fenner Brockway. His name was Michael Foot, and it was here they began a friendship that lasted until Pollitt's death.

Foot and Owen were prominent left-wing supporters of the war and Foot remembers Pollitt as 'a frequent, frustrated drinking companion of those wretched months.' Pollitt confided in them his rejection of the CP's anti-war policy – which, though many must have guessed at it, was not known outside the Party's Central Committee. If there had been a German invasion 'Harry Pollitt would have been fighting it in every possible way, no matter what the Party said', says Foot. 'He had absolutely genuine conviction. Lots of people who were not Communists couldn't help liking him.' Pollitt drew the line at criticizing the Party openly. His frustration only appeared in his private talks with Foot and a few other discreet and like-minded people, and in flashes of irritation in letters to the Central Committee.

Pollitt had gone back to work as a boilermaker, considered essential war work, and when the Party wanted him back, government permission had to be obtained for him to leave it. No one asked how this permission came through at once, but there was certainly swift intervention from people with whom Communists would not normally associate. It was in the interests of the government for the CP to be led by a wholehearted supporter of the war. When Pollitt returned as general secretary there was a period of secret co-operation between Communists and the government which neither side would have cared to admit to at the time. Pollitt had secret meetings with Ernest Bevin and with the minister responsible for aircraft production, Lord Beaverbrook. Pollitt loathed Bevin, but had an instant rapport with Beaverbrook, telling friends years later: 'In the first two minutes we could agree that there was a class war, that he is on one side and I am on the other, and that for the duration of the anti-Fascist struggle there is a truce.'

The Party campaigned for the opening of a second front, so that Britain could help the beleaguered Red Army. Without Pollitt, this would have looked like Communists defending Russia's interests while caring nothing about Britain's interests. 'Because of these meetings we had with Harry Pollitt,' says Foot 'when Churchill took over and Russia came into the war, we had close relations through him with the Communist Party.' Pollitt succeeded in turning the second front campaign into a broad campaign supported by many who had little to do with the CP.

The go-between with Labour's left wing was Wilfred Macartney – the same who had recently emerged from a long stretch in Dartmoor Prison for giving secrets to the Soviet Union. 'He was a remarkable fellow and became my closest friend in the Communist Party', says Foot. 'He used to say that he went to prison for giving information to our allies, he was just a little while ahead of his time.'

There was nothing half-hearted about the change of line. Pollitt told members that the Party was supporting the Churchill government 'wholeheartedly without any reservations.' Communist shop stewards were told to ensure that their members pulled their weight in war production. This made the CP thoroughly welcome in establishment circles. Pollitt shared platforms with local mayors and quelled incipient strikes. Communists and Conservatives joined forces to issue splenetic denunciations of strikers, who were, they agreed, manipulated by Trotskyists.

The Comintern was abolished in 1943, and the same year the CP decided to anglicize those parts of its own structure which sounded foreign and sinister. The Central Committee became the Executive Committee and the names of its members were for the first time since the very early days to be made public. They had been withheld mainly because membership made someone a target for the police. The Politburo became the Political Committee, factory cells became groups and locals became branches.

People admired the sacrifices the Russian people were making to resist Hitler. The BBC, to Communist delight, was under pressure to add the Internationale to the national anthems of Britain's other allies. It resolved the problem in time-honoured BBC style by ceasing to play national anthems altogether, but it did replace the works of Finnish composer Sibelius with those of Russians like Tchaikovsky.

In 1942 CP membership reached its all-time peak of 56,000. It might even have gained affiliation to the Labour Party if Herbert Morrison had not fought hard to prevent this. Morrison was never fastidious about the methods he used to achieve political objectives. As Home Secretary he, like Georgi Dimitrov, saw the report of the October 1939 Central Committee meeting when the CP decided to follow the Comintern line, since the report had fallen into MI5 hands. He had it summarized in a confidential memorandum to the cabinet, which ensured that it became known at senior levels in the Labour Party. His speech to Labour's conference hinted at its contents. This did the trick. The CP's application was thrown out.

Morrison also held out against lifting the ban on the *Daily Worker* long after it was clear to everyone else that there was no security justification for the ban any more. It was eventually lifted in August 1942 after the Labour Party conference had joined many trade unions in putting irresistible political pressure on the Home Secretary.

7

Their Finest Hour

I<small>N</small> 1945 Britain's Communists could feel excited about the future. As in 1918, young men returned from the war determined that things were going to be different. They had not fought and suffered for five years, and seen their friends killed, to come back to the same old unjust society.

Major Denis Healey, former Communist and future anti-Communist, wrote from Italy to a Labour Party selection conference that there were 'millions of soldiers, sailors and airmen who want socialism and who have been fighting magnificently to save a world in which socialism is possible ... If you could see the shattered misery that once was Italy, the bleeding countryside and the wrecked villages, if you could see Cassino, with a bomb-created river washing green slime through a shapeless rubble that a year ago was homes, you would realise more than ever that the defeat of Hitler and Mussolini is not enough by itself to justify the destruction, not just of twenty years of fascism, but too often of twenty centuries of Europe. Only a more glorious future can make up for this annihilation of the past.' The letter persuaded them to give the young Major Healey Labour's nomination in this safe Conservative seat. He told Labour's 1945 conference, which was full of men in uniform: 'The upper classes in every country are selfish, depraved, dissolute and decadent. The struggle for socialism in Europe ... has been hard, cruel, merciless and bloody.'

Wilf Page came out of the RAF after fighting, so he was told, for peace, freedom and justice. He remembered none of these during his childhood in rural Norfolk. His father Billy was a scrap merchant who dreamed of earning enough to get out of the slum his parents lived in. He was conscripted to fight in the First World War, during which time his small savings were spent keeping the family. They were evicted from their cottage and given a tiny, damp one instead.

Wilf watched a local farmworkers' strike in 1923 and asked his Sunday school teacher what it was all about. Wilf writes: 'He got his bible down from the shelf and turned to the book of Deuteronomy and read: "Thou shalt not muzzle the ox that treads the corn"'. The teacher told the boy that the leather muzzle was to prevent the ox eating as much as it wanted. The ox's owner would only allow the animal sufficient food to keep it fit for working again the next day. The farm worker is a human ox, he said, and his muzzle is his wage. He receives only enough to keep him fit to work the next day and to rear children so that when he is too old to thresh the corn the next generation will be there to take over.

A few weeks later Wilf understood. His grandfather turned up at the door, homeless. 'His employer told him that at 62 he was too old and slow to continue humping coal and he would have to get a younger man and give him the sack ... Billy [Wilf's father] said he was finding it difficult to feed the family of six and Grandad would be another mouth to feed. But they could not face him having to finish his life in a workhouse.' So the young Wilf Page shared his bed with his grandfather in a tiny room they shared with Wilf's sister. But a month before his pension was due Grandad died in bed beside Wilf.

'Alice, my mother, had so looked forward to the pension coming in,' writes Wilf. 'Grandad had an insurance for death. It was worth about £25. Billy decided the undertakers were not getting this.' He tied rags round the iron wheels of his cart to deaden the noise and drove his father-in-law to the cemetery under cover of darkness. They waited for the parson, then Billy and Wilf, who was not yet 10, lowered the coffin into the grave using the reins of the pony. Wilf was then lowered into the grave to pull the buckles out. 'Billy worked out that the coffin cost £2 and he had the rest of the insurance money apart from paying the parson and the death certificate.'

These were the sort of experiences that made socialists and trade unionists of men returning from the war. Wilf joined the Communist Party and the farmworkers' union and was a central figure in both for the next four decades.

The Soviet Union was popular in Britain in 1945. The mood of the servicemen was unmistakable, and this time the old men and the old parties were not to be allowed to betray it. The French Communist Party received 26 per cent of the votes in the 1945 election, winning 151 seats, more than the social democrats. It was partly a reward for their heroic part in the resistance, and Harry Pollitt's Party hoped for its reward too. The end of the Second World War was the moment when Britain's Communist Party was to enter into its inheritance.

It did not quite work out like that. Still, two MPs and 100,000 votes was not too bad, especially when some candidates had been withdrawn to give the Labour candidate a clear run in marginal seats. The British electoral system generally stifles small parties to death long before they get that far. But when all the excuses were made, Harry Pollitt's narrow defeat in Rhondda, and Palme Dutt's lost deposit in Birmingham Sparkbrook, were bitter disappointments.

It was some comfort that the Labour Party scored a massive victory and Clement Attlee had the first ever working Labour majority in parliament – despite unremitting hostility from the newspapers and a scaremongering campaign by Winston Churchill. Churchill claimed that no Labour government could survive without a Gestapo. The prospect of socialism brought out all the rotund, terrifying phrases which had served Churchill well throughout his political life and were now part of the national heritage. It was, he chillingly told the electorate, 'abhorrent to British ideas of freedom ... inseparably interwoven with totalitarianism.' But the rhetoric which worked in the 1920s and the 1930s, and would become serviceable again in the 1950s, failed for Churchill in 1945.

There was not only a big Labour majority, but also the most left-wing Parliamentary Labour Party ever. About a dozen of the 393 Labour MPs were either secret CP members or were close to the CP, sharing its beliefs and enjoying the company of its leaders. Just after the election, *Daily Worker* news editor Douglas Hyde writes, 'I answered the phone and the man at the other end announced himself as the new Labour member for his constituency.

He followed it with a loud guffaw and rang off. I had known him as a Communist Party man for years.' By the end of the night 'we knew we had at least eight or nine "cryptos" in the House.'

The size of the Labour majority came as a surprise to everyone. Labour MPs felt they were in at the start of a new era and they were going to shape it. On their first day they and the two Communist MPs broke the rules of Parliament by standing up and singing the Red Flag. 'Tories were horrified,' writes Michael Foot 'and officials of the House went on with the ceremony, much as a polite host continues the conversation after his guest has upset the soup.' Herbert Morrison was annoyed: 'These youngsters will have to absorb the atmosphere of the House.' But to the newcomers it was the 'atmosphere of the House' which had stifled any radical proposals in the first two Labour governments. In 1945 two-thirds of the Parliamentary Labour Party consisted of new MPs, and it was going to be harder to suppress them than it had been before.

Sectarian souls like Dutt could also take comfort in the fact that the Communist Party's old rival, the ILP, was a shadow of its former self. Jimmy Maxton came back to Parliament tired and politically impotent, much loved but no longer a force, together with just one follower, John McGovern. Maxton was ill, and made one speech in the new Parliament before dying the same year. Before the end of that Parliament McGovern had made peace with the Labour Party and was moving rightwards at breakneck speed.

The CP's biggest prize in the general election was the unexpected victory of Phil Piratin, virtually unknown outside the East End of London, in the Mile End division of Stepney. It meant that the regions with the two strongest socialist traditions in Britain had Communist MPs. The East End Jew Piratin joined Willie Gallacher from the Red Clyde, who had represented West Fife since 1935. They made an odd contrast. Gallacher was now 63 years old, a veteran of pre-First World War socialism, the man whom Lenin himself had persuaded to stand for parliament. Phil Piratin, just 38, had come to Communism by a very different route. He was standing outside Oswald Mosley's Fascist meeting at Olympia in June 1934 as mounted police charged the crowd. Someone shouted that the police should stop hecklers from being brutally ejected by Fascist stewards. Piratin heard a senior police officer shout 'Get back to your slums, you Communist bastards', and he went back to the East End and joined the Communist Party that very week.

Many East End Jews like Piratin, whose families had fled the pogroms in Eastern Europe around the turn of the century, saw in the Communist Party a vision of a society where people were not persecuted for their racial origins or their religious beliefs. And when in the 1930s Mosley tried to march his Blackshirts through the East End, and to fight elections there, they saw the persecution they had fled coming to London. They read about Hitler's Germany with horror, and many of them joined the only Party which seemed willing to fight Fascists. It should therefore have surprised no one that the year Hitler was defeated, the East End produced a Jewish Communist MP.

Piratin's career inside and outside politics displays a mixture of fierce courage and conviction and the shrewd cautiousness you might expect from the son of an East End fur trader. He is tall and heavily built, with the unmistakable style of speaking associated with London's Jewish community – the soft voice and flattened consonants, the rotund phrases – 'You want to hear a story? I'll tell you a story.' He followed his father into the trade and became an expert buyer of skins at auctions, married a milliner with her own business, and became a Stepney Communist councillor in 1937. In 1940 he moved into the CP hierarchy as London propaganda secretary. The move was almost accidental, filling a gap in his life: his employer had gone out of business and the fur trade was in a bad way, he had parted from his wife, and he had been turned down for the RAF because of poor eyesight. In 1944 the Party's London secretary Ted Bramley made him London organizer.

He enjoyed the work and, though he was elected to the local council, did not want to be an MP. He tried to persuade Bramley to stand instead. But Bramley might not have won. Like Gallacher's vote in West Fife, Piratin's Stepney vote was at least in part a personal one. Stepney folk were used to going to Piratin for help when they were in trouble. He fought off evictions tirelessly, using legal argument (he was a clever amateur lawyer), political argument as a councillor, and force where necessary in the form of barricades and bags of flour thrown from the top of staircases.

He was especially popular among Jewish East Enders for his part in the battle against Mosley. 'Smashing the fascist bastards' was as far as most Communists had thought it through, but Piratin believed that something more effective than knuckledusters was needed. East Enders joining Mosley must be expressing genuine grievances, he said, and the Party's job was to show that there was a better way of expressing them. It was not an easy message to sell to East End Jews in the 1930s, to whom the sight of Mosley's black-shirted followers brought feelings of almost inexpressible hatred, and Piratin made slow and painful progress with it. But when two families of Mosley supporters were due to be evicted, and some Communists wanted to leave them to their fate, Piratin persuaded his comrades to defend them. They succeeded, and the families tore up their BUF cards and joined the Communist Party. In the 1945 election Piratin's canvassers noted peoples' problems, and he visited constituents' homes in the evenings to try to solve them. It is not the conventional way of running parliamentary elections, but it worked.

Mile End also sent the two first Communists on to the London County Council: Ted Bramley, the CP's London secretary, and Jack Gaster, who in the 1930s had led the Revolutionary Committee of the ILP into the CP. In the borough council elections in 1945 the CP managed to get a creditable 43 candidates elected – 18 of them in London and 14 in Scotland. By the end of 1946 it had increased the number of Communist councillors from 81 to 215. Half a million people were voting Communist. It was far better than anything the CP had ever before achieved. Communists were sure they were on their way.

Once elected, Piratin went to see Harry Pollitt and asked him about the man who was to be his only colleague in Parliament, Willie Gallacher. Privately Gallacher and Pollitt were never close, never quite liked or admired each other, but Pollitt told Piratin: 'You won't learn from him in any organized way, but he's a good man.' The two MPs, different in age, background and temperament, became close friends. 'Gallacher was the straightest man in the world, we were like father and son,' says Piratin.

Gallacher had come out of the war deeply emotionally damaged. Before the war he and his wife Jean had lost their two children in infancy, and they later adopted his brother's two sons after both parents died. The boys were clever, the elder one getting a first-class degree from Glasgow University; both were killed in action.

Afterwards Gallacher and his wife devoted their love and attention to the son of their niece, who was married to the *Daily Worker's* Glasgow correspondent, Phil Stein. Stein's filing cabinet is still full of letters from Gallacher about 'the half pint', most of which contained money to buy something for him together with a demand that no mention should ever be made of the gift.

The Communist Party which emerged from the Second World War was very different from the Party which had been born out of the upheaval of the Great War. In 1920 its leaders were young men who thought the revolution was just round the corner. Gallacher believed Parliament was irredeemably reformist and you could only soil your hands by having anything to do with it. The founding Congress was full of young people. They were proud of being the British section of the Comintern, and saw no shame in putting the views of the International before their own.

In 1945, the leaders were in many cases the same people, but Gallacher was a venerable 63-year-old MP, respected by his parliamentary colleagues. Pollitt was 55 and Dutt almost 50. They were still socialists, but no longer believed Britain was about to have a violent revolution, and they were redefining the whole idea of revolution. It meant a fundamental change in the way society was run – but it no longer necessarily meant violent overthrow of the state. Many of their younger colleagues, like Piratin, had never believed in violent revolution on the 1917 model. Their Party was respectable, thanks to the Soviet Union's battle against Hitler. It was all Herbert Morrison could do to stop the CP from getting affiliation to the Labour Party. The radical-minded 1945 Labour conference only defeated its application by the narrowest possible margin.

Phil Piratin agreed with the Labour government on a great many things – and more often than not co-operated with it. No Communist could have done such a thing in the years after the First World War. The Labour government was the nearest to a reforming socialist government that Britain has ever seen. Aneurin Bevan's National Health Service is its most lasting monument, and the nationalization of major industries at least ensured a more humane management, especially in the mines.

The Party also had great influence in the trade unions. The TUC withdrew the 1934 'Black Circular' designed to prevent Communists from being elected to trade union positions and Arthur Horner became general secretary of the miners' union, the first Communist to lead a major trade union. The TUC's general council had its first ever Communist member, Bert Papworth of the Transport and General Workers Union, and the TGWU itself by 1946 had four Communists on an executive council of thirty-four. The Party practically had full control of the Fire Brigades Union, the Amalgamated Engineering Union, the foundry workers and the Electrical Trades Union.

The Comintern had ceased to exist. The CP was, at least in theory, entirely free to make up its own policy. Freer from Russian tutelage than ever before, it showed a surer touch. Pollitt, Gallacher and Piratin at last had the chance to show that they had a real political feel for the issues that would grab the attention and imagination of the British working class.

After the war the issue was housing, just as it had been in 1918 – though no minister in 1945 was incautious enough to talk about homes fit for heroes, as Lloyd George had done in 1918. Were those to whom the nation owed so much to sleep in the streets with their wives and children? Within four months of the end of the war, Labour's Health and Housing Minister Aneurin Bevan was under siege for failing to get started on housebuilding fast enough.

The problem was massive. Housing for the workers had been ignored between the wars. In the market-driven housebuilding boom of the mid-1930s, houses were built for sale in middle-class areas. Only one new house in fifteen was built to clear slums or ease overcrowding. During the war one in three homes had been damaged, and the rest had gone without repairs for six years, 208,000 houses had been entirely destroyed, 250,000 made uninhabitable, 250,000 seriously damaged. And the post-war baby boom was just starting.

In response, the government built thousands of prefabricated houses – 'prefabs' – on areas of open space throughout the country. These ugly and cramped, but cheap and serviceable caravan-like bungalows were home to many families for years longer than their design life. Bevan then gave priority to repairing damaged homes. He made local authorities the engine of his housing policy, told them to requisition unoccupied premises, and banned the conversion of homes to offices without local authority approval.

But results were slow. Families were still crowded into parents' front rooms and other inadequate accommodation. The CP pointed out that there were perfectly good places to live which, given the will, could be liberated for the homeless. In July 1946 forty-eight families moved unannounced into disused army camps in Scunthorpe. This acted as a signal. Within weeks 45,000 people had occupied vacated army camps. After a moment's hesitation, the government authorized a supply of electricity. Living conditions were primitive, but they were better than these families had known before.

Disused army camps were just a start. Bevan had given local authorities the power to requisition empty premises, but some Conservative authorities in London chose to leave certain blocks of flats empty. So one evening, in September 1946, Ted Bramley called together some fellow Communists and asked them to identify empty dwellings in Tory boroughs. The next day word went out that anyone living in bad conditions should turn up in Kensington High Street two days later carrying some bedding. Hundreds came, not knowing what was planned.

The Communist district committee led them to an empty block of flats called Duchess of Bedford House. Tubby Rosen, a Communist councillor in Stepney and one of Phil Piratin's close friends, slipped in through a back window and opened the tradesman's entrance. As people streamed in, he took their names. One hundred families filled the block and the rest were taken to neighbouring blocks. The next few days saw further occupations.

To Communist leaders, the squatting movement was a welcome sign that the working class was on the move. As squatting snowballed, the CP stayed more or less in control. In some areas, like Birmingham, everyone knew that if you wanted to squat, you should get in touch with the Party. In other areas it threatened occasionally to run out of the Party's control. Noreen Branson remembers leaving her North London house on her way to work at the Labour Research Department when a man appeared from behind some bushes and suggested a block they could squat in. It had been the subject of discussion, she knew, but the committee thought it would be too hard to get into. Nonetheless, she said, she would put it to the committee tomorrow. The man looked at his feet for a moment, then looked up and said one word: 'Crowbars.' Then he vanished as quickly as he had appeared. That night the block was squatted – without sanction from the district committee.

It was all too much for the government. A statement from Downing Street said the government took 'a serious view' of squatting and it was 'instigated and organized by the Communist Party.' Ted Bramley and three other Communist councillors were arrested and charged with 'conspiracy to incite and direct trespass.' Possession orders for the properties were issued. Nye Bevan announced that no action would be taken against squatters who left voluntarily, and they would not lose their places in the housing queue. It was a clear threat against squatters who did not leave voluntarily, and the CP called off the action, knowing that Bevan's carrot and stick approach would leave it with few supporters.

The instruction came in the form of a telegram from the deputy general secretary, Emile Burns, to local organizers: 'No more squatting – explanation follows.' Noreen Branson had it in her hands when, on behalf of the London district committee, she met twenty families who expected to squat in a block of flats near Regents Park. Apprehensively, she passed on her disappointing news. There was stunned silence for a few moments, and Noreen Branson was not sure how her instructions had been taken. Then a soldier in uniform said firmly: 'If you've 'ad orders you've got to obey.' And that was that.

It was a measure of how much the CP had changed from the harsh, sectarian, revolutionary outfit of 1920, when Bevan's statement would have demanded immediate defiance. What had happened to the spirit which created Class Against Class? It still stalked the left. Jettisoned by Communists, it had been eagerly picked up by Trotskyists, and the stage was set for a battle for the soul of the left in Britain which was to last for nearly half a century.

Just as Lenin in 1920 had dismissed the second International as hopeless and created the Third International, or Comintern, so in 1938 the exiled Trotsky dismissed the Third International as a mere instrument of Stalin's foreign policy and created the Fourth International. The FI took on, not just Comintern behaviour, but also its dense and impenetrable language. FI documents are full of theses, and plenums, and all the rest of the jargon. The FI believed that capitalism was about to collapse – just as the Comintern had believed in the early days – and that Stalin would collapse with it. Two years after its creation, Trotsky was murdered in Mexico, on Stalin's orders. But Trotsky the Stalinist martyr was almost as potent as Trotsky the living revolutionary – in fact, in some ways more so, because his followers could attribute their own views to him without fear of authoritative denial.

By 1938 Britain already had three tiny Trotskyist groups, all descended from the Communist Party, mostly consisting of people who had left the CP after one policy change or another, and divided from each other by points of doctrinal disagreement which, to the outsider, seemed so trivial as not to be worth discussing, the equivalent of medieval theologians debating how many angels can sit on a pinhead.

British Trotskyists emerged from the war united in the Revolutionary Communist Party, which was affiliated to the FI. Its 1945 statements could have been Dutt writing in 1920. The RCP thought it was 'on the threshold of the greatest crisis yet witnessed in the history of British capitalism.' The FI seems to have had even less connection with the realities of British political life than the Comintern: it believed that the RCP with less than 500 members was somehow going to lead the working class in revolution. By 1947 it was foreseeing 'a period of economic and political difficulties, convulsions and crises in one country or another' and in Britain this would 'become catastrophic.'

But by then the Revolutionary Communists were well on the way to their first great split – and the issue uncannily recalled the early days of the CP. Like a latter-day Willie Gallacher, RCP leader Jock Haston saw no point in 'entryism'. Entryism meant that, instead of trying to get affiliation, some RCP members joined the Labour Party and kept their real loyalty secret. It was a tactic which the CP had tried briefly in the 1930s, and which was to be made famous in the 1980s by the Militant Tendency. The FI laid down that entryism was the correct line for Britain, and hence, like CP leaders in 1928, Haston found his leadership undermined by the International, which backed his aggressive, forceful 32-year-old rival Gerry Healy.

Healy, who joined the CP in 1928 at the age of 15 and left it eight years later, was short, rotund and pugnacious, with a head too big for his body and a deep scar across his brow. He was given to fits of uncontrollable rage, and had a vast ego and an apparently insatiable appetite for women which persisted into his seventies. As his power within the tiny world of British Trotskyism grew, he took to sending gangs of supporters to beat up members who crossed him.

As a political thinker Healy embodied everything that was worst about Communists, while fiercely condemning them. He was as pedantic, lengthy and tedious as Dutt, and as fiercely unforgiving to anyone who disagreed with him as Stalin. He set the pattern for British Trotskyism firmly in the mould of the CP during the Class Against Class period, with the same determination to begin by destroying potential rivals on the left. The poor old ILP found yet another gun aimed at its head. 'To make a successful revolution in Britain,' Healy wrote 'the working class will require to do it through one party and one programme . . . That is why we are out to destroy all competitive parties such as the ILP.' He was also, of course, out to destroy the Communist Party.

Though Healy's doctrinal intolerance kept the number of his followers to a select few, he does seem to have inspired fanatical loyalty among them. When he died in 1989, Vanessa Redgrave wrote for the *Guardian* the sort of hagiographical obituary which the Comintern used to produce for its leading functionaries: 'Our dear comrade Gerry Healy, central committee member of the Marxist Party . . . studied, taught and fought for materialist dialectics, developing his work continuously on the method and principles of Marx, Engels, Lenin and Trotsky . . .' Her account of his reaction when she telephoned him on the night the Berlin Wall came down bears the hallmarks of a little Comintern-style posthumous tidying up. She claims he said at once: 'No more striking testimony could be imagined to the enormous powers unleashed by the political revolution in the Soviet Union, and no more convincing proof of its entirely progressive character.'

Healy did not bother with the niceties of trying to win his colleagues round to the International pro-entryist line, as Communist Party leaders had done. He simply stated that the line of the majority was wrong. The FI had the same authority for Trotskyists as the Comintern had once had among Communists. The higher body's authority was absolute. Healy hounded Haston out of the Party with furious and incomprehensible denunciations for deviation from the correct line.

In 1951 the FI split. Splitting then became endemic, so that by 1978 there were no less than eight international bodies claiming to be the FI and to carry Trotsky's mantle. Britain saw the same phenomenon. The RCP very quickly split into three sects. Healy led one. There was a group led by Tony Cliff which became the International Socialists and later the Socialist Workers' Party, and started to take the Communists' place in British newspaper demonology in the 1970s. And there was a tiny group which agreed with Healy about entryism – getting members to join the Labour Party and change it from within – but for some obscure reason disagreed with him about the reasons for it. Its leader, Ted Grant, and his followers, joined the Labour Party. In the 1970s this group, by then called the Militant Tendency, started to become very well known indeed, and Grant was eventually expelled from the Labour Party on the insistence of the then Labour leader Neil Kinnock, after – as Grant never tired of telling the national press – more than thirty years' membership.

CP leaders foamed at the mouth about 'Trots' though most other people seemed hardly to notice their existence. It was a hangover from Comintern days when anything that gave Stalin a cold brought the CP down with pneumonia. That spirit seemed in merciful recession in 1945, when the CP had its two best and freest years. But by 1947 the old Stalinist spirit was draping itself around King Street like a pall. The world was freezing rapidly into the Cold War mould in which it was to remain for half a century.

One by one between 1945 and 1948 Eastern European countries fell into pro-Soviet hands: Bulgaria, Hungary, Romania, Poland, Yugoslavia, Albania, and finally Czechoslovakia. The West sent armed forces to crush socialists in Greece. Winston Churchill, now Leader of the Opposition, formally launched the Cold War as early as 1946 with a speech in Fulton, Missouri: 'From Stettin in the Baltic to Trieste in the Adriatic, an iron curtain has fallen across Europe ...'

In Britain, the Cold War smothered the hope and optimism and idealism of 1945 like a frozen shroud. Old anti-Communists like Herbert Morrison started to assert themselves over the idealism of the 1945 intake of MPs. Young anti-Communists like Denis Healey, now the Labour Party's International Secretary, started to remember all that was bad about the Comintern and the old

Stalinist tradition, and forget all the hopes and ideals he shared with the Communists.

Healey had become fiercely anti-Communist as he watched Stalin manoeuvring for control in Eastern Europe. It was Healey who finally scuppered any chance of the CP gaining affiliation to the Labour Party. He suggested an amendment to the constitution ruling out any organization which put up separate candidates at an election, and the amendment was carried in 1946. Ironically, it also achieved an old Communist Party objective: it consigned to oblivion the now tiny and ailing ILP, which lost its last MP before 1950 and eventually turned itself into a publishing house called Independent Labour Publications.

Pollitt meanwhile was engaged in the fight which was to pre-occupy the CP for most of the rest of its life – the fight against Trotskyists and 'ultra-leftists'. At the CP's 1947 Congress he was accused of betraying the revolution by a fiery young Communist from Hertfordshire. 'The perspective of proletarian revolution has been abandoned,' complained Comrade Eric Heffer, later a leading Labour MP. Heffer was not appeased even though the policy to which he most objected – that of helping industry to increase production and discourage strikes in order to aid Britain's recovery – was abandoned the same year.

It was abandoned because new instructions came from Moscow, via a body newly created in September 1947 called the Communist Information Bureau, or Cominform. We now know that Stalin decided to create the Cominform as early as June 1946, when he explained his intentions to two key players in Eastern European Communist politics. One was Georgi Dimitrov, former general secretary of the Comintern, who had somehow survived the purges in Moscow despite knowing perhaps more than almost anyone about them. Dimitrov was now Prime Minister in his native Bulgaria, a post he held until his death in a Moscow sanatorium in 1949. The other was Marshal Tito, former International Brigader, now the ruler of Yugoslavia.

Stalin upset Dimitrov by delivering a torrent of abuse about the uselessness of the Comintern, and explained his plans for a better vehicle. East European Communist Parties were invited to come early to a conference in Belgrade in September 1947 in order to have it explained to them. Then came the second league, the French and

Italians. The British party was not even in the second league, and no one bothered to tell Harry Pollitt what was going on. He received a note of the decisions a few days later, and hastened to welcome the Cominform, and the changes of line which came with it, in a self-abasing way: 'We ... clung to old formulas and agendas,' he told his executive committee apologetically. Communists were forced back to being apologists for Stalin's policies. Harry Pollitt and Michael Foot still drank together and dreamed of a socialist future, but Pollitt no longer talked to friends on the British left about how to achieve it. He went to Moscow and talked to Stalin.

Cominform's real task was to transmit Moscow decisions worldwide. It was a weapon in the Cold War. Its headquarters were to be in Belgrade, probably in the hope that this would ensure the continued adherence of Yugoslavia's ruler, Marshal Tito. Communist Parties were to campaign for their governments to seek peace and friendship with the Soviet Union and the Communist countries of Eastern Europe, and foster hostility to the United States.

In June 1948 the Cominform issued instructions that Tito was to be denounced. The CP obeyed at once. This put James Klugmann in a distinctly awkward position. He knew Tito well and had a high personal regard for him. He had written admiringly of Tito's Yugoslavia. As the British Communist who knew Yugoslavia best, and as a distinguished writer and academic, he was the obvious choice to write the hatchet job which the new circumstances demanded. Being a disciplined Communist, Klugmann wrote *From Trotsky to Tito*. Those of his friends who are still alive testify that he did not enjoy the task, but considered it his duty.

Thus Moscow took control again, stifling the talent of leading British Communists and subordinating their Party to the needs of Soviet foreign policy. The brief honeymoon between the Communist and Labour Parties came to an abrupt end, and Morrison and others could once again vent all their plentiful hatred on the CP. At the same time Britain received a US loan which began to dictate much of its foreign policy.

As if to symbolize the start of the Cold War, and the time when Britain's Communists went into the cold once more, 1947 started with the coldest and harshest winter for fifty years. January and

116

February saw snow and ice blocking the whole country. Many people could not leave their homes, even if they had fuel to run their cars – which they generally didn't, because there was a severe fuel crisis.

When summer came, a nation wearied by five years of war followed by two years of privation and frozen conditions for which no adequate preparations had been made, departed for its joyless summer holiday in damp seaside boarding houses, queuing for tea in dreary cafés and for entrance to cold dance halls and rain-sodden piers. Many of these holidays were in Butlins holiday camps which, as Kenneth Morgan puts it, 'reproduced the crowded, classless solidarity of the Blitz.' British troops were fighting and dying again – in Palestine to stop the Jews gaining control, and in Greece to stop the socialists gaining control.

The cheerful optimism of 1945 was over. People were too tired, busy and cheerless to remember to ask what they had fought the war for, or why the nation had taken its courage in both hands and given Labour a working majority for the first time. The council house building programme was being sharply cut back, the TUC was agreeing a wage freeze to help out the government, troops were quelling a transport strike. The quality of daily life seemed little better than in the hungry thirties. It was at this time, in 1947, when the CP might have made headway, that Stalin once again commandeered it to support his foreign policy, and Harry Pollitt and the rest of its leaders fell back into useless obedience.

The same thing happened to the *Daily Worker*. From 1942 until 1947, free from Comintern tutelage, it enjoyed a renaissance. Editor Bill Rust planned to turn it into a popular mass paper, and started building a new office in Farringdon Road, close to Fleet Street. In 1946 ownership of the paper was formally transferred to a co-operative, the People's Press Printing Society. Forty years later the PPPS, in bitter internecine war, would take the paper away from the Party.

Some famous names in journalism, like Claud Cockburn and Llew Gardner, started their careers on the *Worker*. Allen Hutt, the chief sub-editor and a graduate of Moscow's Lenin School, was the best newspaper designer in the country, but to his disgust every time there was a vacancy for editor or deputy editor the job went to a

King Street official. 'I am only a rude mechanical, dear boy,' he would say bitterly. To Dutt the paper's journalists were suspect: 'The very conditions that have given them their professional training have also given them a technique that is alien to our purposes.' Journalists had a disturbing tendency to condense Dutt's interminable theoretical articles. He fought a bitter and ultimately unsuccessful battle against the introduction of racing tips.

Pollitt urged his colleagues to make the paper more fun, more interesting, and more popular. But Bill Rust made no secret of the fact that on principle he loathed journalists. Once in the *Worker's* newsroom, a colleague gestured round the room and pointed out to Rust that he worked with journalists every day. 'They're not journalists,' said Rust grandly. 'They're Communists.'

Yet it was Rust who planned a popular paper. He was a fine editor: a cynical boss who thumped the table in his furious rages, he nonetheless inspired journalists' best work. A tall and by now heavily built man, Rust was one of the Party's most able people, and one of the least likeable. After a harsh, undernourished London childhood he joined the Young Communist League and quickly became one of its full-time officials. He rose to prominence as one of the strictest defenders of the Moscow line in the 1930s. He grew angry and impatient with Harry Pollitt's occasional questioning of the line and probably believed that Moscow sooner or later would intervene to make Pollitt give way to a younger and more reliable man. He believed that he, not Pollitt, should lead the Party. Ambitious and manipulative, Rust believed as a good Marxist that the Communist Party would win power, and was determined to be at the top of it when it did. Pollitt never entered the *Daily Worker* office while Rust was in charge there. He sent Dutt, now international secretary, to run the weekly briefings for senior *Worker* journalists.

News editor Douglas Hyde remembers those meetings. 'We would sit in a room, just half a dozen of us, and talk about the political issues of the day. When we had all had our say, Dutt would drape his arm over the arm of his chair – he had the longest arms I have ever seen – bang his pipe out on the sole of his shoe, and sum up. Often the summing up was entirely different from the conclusions we were all reaching, but no one ever argued. Did he know things we did not know? We were sure he knew a great deal from Salme

Dutt, but no one I knew ever met Salme.' Hyde once asked Johnny Campbell why everyone obeyed Dutt. 'He's the only man Moscow trusts,' said Campbell.

The post-war *Daily Worker* was Rust's creation, and the ambitious move to the new purpose-built office was his project. They were remarkable achievements, even if they did require hidden Soviet subsidies. These subsidies were not on the scale that the paper's enemies alleged. Half the print-run was bought up by Eastern European countries; a few staff salaries were paid by Soviet front organizations; *Worker* journalists had all expenses paid and preferential treatment when on assignments east of the Iron Curtain. But Rust held together a team of talented journalists and inspired his support staff to ever greater efforts for little reward.

The *Worker*, like the Party, was seriously wounded by the events of 1947. The renewed pressure always to get the line absolutely right, the renewed determination only to cover news which supported the Soviet Union's view of the world, gradually undermined the commitment of the staff and the faith of its readers. The Cold War stifled Bill Rust's dream before the Farringdon Road office was even open.

The next year Douglas Hyde left the Party after several years of growing doubts which he had kept firmly to himself. Two years later he published a book, *I Believed*, which explained his reasons for leaving. Hyde was the last Communist anyone could have believed of apostasy. He was a forceful west countryman who had been one of the Party's most committed workers, often entrusted with difficult, dangerous jobs requiring secrecy and discretion. He was one of the underground members in the 1930s, working inside the Labour Party. He ran IGI, the wartime news agency which substituted for the banned *Daily Worker* in the early years of the war and existed at best on the fringes of legality. When the *Worker* came back, he became its news editor.

Hyde joined the Catholic Church, providing the Catholic community in Britain with a splendid stick with which to beat Communism. He quickly started to write for the *Catholic Herald*. His revelations of Communist machinations in *I Believed* fed Cold War anti-Communism. The book received enormous attention. It was not the ringing denunciation of Communism and all its works

119

which both Communists and their enemies made it out to be, but it was damaging nonetheless. Hyde found, as Jack Murphy had done sixteen years earlier, that the Party was unforgiving to those who left it and unrestrained in its attacks on him. It was twenty years before any old friendships could be re-established. He still tells the story with obvious pleasure of how James Klugmann once again called him 'Douggie' in 1968, at a meeting at the World Council of Churches.

It is worth mentioning, since Hyde was presented by the press as a man who finally saw through the destructive nature of Communism to a purer and saner faith, that when I met him forty-five years later he was alienated from the Catholic faith, had never found there the comradeship and care for the underdog which he had known in the Communist Party, and was much closer to his first faith than to his second.

In 1949, furious at what he saw as the newspapers' constant attacks on the Soviet Union, Bill Rust wrote an editorial headed *Fleet Street Dungheap*. The Central London Branch of the National Union of Journalists was furious and summoned him to a meeting to explain himself. Bill Rust was not the sort of man to crawl along and apologize. He armed himself with the relevant cuttings. On his way to the NUJ meeting, he went to the Party's King Street headquarters, where he had a massive heart attack and died. He was 46. He had just moved into the new office and died thinking the paper had a glorious future. In fact, it had seen the days of its greatest glory. Sales peaked in 1948 at 120,000. By the start of 1956 sales were down to 63,000.

The next editor of the *Daily Worker*, Johnny Campbell, best remembered for the 1925 'Campbell case' which brought down Ramsay MacDonald's first government, and since the 1930s probably Pollitt's closest friend in the Party, never stood a chance. The Cold War, the obsession with getting the line right, slavish subservience to the Soviet Union, and suspicion of the journalistic skills it so desperately needed, spelled the demise of the *Worker*.

As Stalin increasingly used the Party as an instrument of his foreign policy, its popularity and respectability ebbed away. Foreign Secretary Ernest Bevin, busy aligning Britain with the USA in the fast-developing Cold War, had no patience with people he considered little better than Soviet agents, and after 1947 the Labour Party started expelling MPs who were close to the CP and proscribed front organizations like the friendship societies with various East European countries. The TUC started to give serious attention to the matter of trimming Communist influence in the trade unions. Ernest Bevin's successor as general secretary of the Transport and General Workers Union was the strongly anti-Communist Arthur Deakin, who, encouraged by Bevin, pushed through a ban on Communists holding office in his union. Many trade union members thought this both wrong and dangerous, but Deakin was a union leader in the Bevin mould, and did not worry his head with that sort of delicate scruple.

Prime Minister Clement Attlee himself initiated a purge of Communists in the civil service, and civil servants believed to be Communists lost their jobs. This distasteful exercise became acceptable to public opinion when in 1950 the atomic scientist Klaus Fuchs confessed to supplying secrets to the Russians, and in 1951 Guy Burgess and Donald Maclean defected to Russia. None of them were in fact members of Britain's Communist Party – an open Communist was unlikely to be much use as a spy. Burgess and Maclean were members of the Communist Party of the Soviet Union and almost certainly unknown in King Street.

In February 1950 Attlee called an election and scraped home with a wafer-thin majority. Both Communist MPs lost their seats. Peter Fryer, a young *Daily Worker* journalist at the time, remembers being at the count in West Fife and burying his head in his hands as it became clear that Willie Gallacher's fifteen years in Parliament were coming to an end. Suddenly he heard Gallacher's voice behind him, stern and strong: 'Heid up! Heid up! Never let them see you down.'

In the wake of the Party's defeat, any future chance of success required close understanding of the British electorate. But we now know – though it was hidden at the time even from Communists – that the first place Harry Pollitt went to for advice was Moscow. It is a sad reflection on the speed with which the freedom of the immediate post-war years had evaporated. After discussions with Stalin, with whom he now had a real friendship, or what he thought was a real friendship, in June 1950 several drafts were produced, incorporating Stalin's suggestions. In October of the same year

Party members were told that Pollitt had gone for a holiday. In fact he was in Moscow yet again, staying in his own Moscow apartment (he was now too grand to stay in the Hotel Lux with all the other foreign riff-raff). He stayed there for eleven days until Stalin could see him and vet the final draft.

After talking to Stalin, Pollitt wrote to Dutt from Moscow – a long letter on which his then deputy, George Matthews, comments: 'Anyone who knew Harry, or is familiar with his writings, will immediately realise that ... the language of much of this letter is not his. The use of the word 'Labourites' is itself a giveaway, since I doubt if Harry ever used it before.' The stilted, pompous language is the opposite of Pollitt's uncluttered style. It reeks of Comintern bureaucracy.

Pollitt's departure from Moscow has an odd story attached to it. He was driven to the airport by his friend Nikolai Matkovsky, the Soviet liaison for British Communists, who later wrote a hagiographical Russian autobiography of Pollitt. They talked together happily until Matkovsky realized to his horror that he had driven to the normal passenger airport instead of the military airport used by VIPs (even though his Party was not even in the second league of world Communist Parties, the British Communist leader was treated as VIP). So Matkovsky drove at breakneck speed to the airport on the other side of the city. Two members of the Soviet Politburo were waiting to see the great man off, and they pointedly asked the fearful Matkovsky what had kept him. Pollitt jumped in quickly to say that he had been to see Comrade Stalin, and winked and made a gesture of vodka-drinking. The two officials relaxed at once and laughed, and Pollitt said farewell to a relieved Matkovsky and boarded his special military aircraft for London. Pollitt went straight from the airport to his suburban semi in Colindale. He was used to that sort of culture shock. It happened after every one of his sixty or so visits to Moscow.

The British Road to Socialism was published on 1 February 1951 and 150,000 copies were sold in six weeks. It established the principle which Stalin set out five years earlier to a Labour Party delegation: that 'there are two roads to socialism ... the Russian way and the British way' and that 'the Russian way was shorter and more difficult, and had involved bloodshed ... the parliamentary method involved no bloodshed, but was a longer process.' Communists had come a long way since 1920, when they believed that in a matter of months they would be leading the masses in violent revolution on the streets. Slowly, from the time it abandoned Class Against Class and Willie Gallacher stood for Parliament in the mid-1930s, it had turned itself into a party of democratic politicians, placing their policies before the electorate, just like Labour, Conservative and Liberal politicians. Stalin and *The British Road to Socialism* completed the transition.

Eight months after its publication, at the October 1951 general election, the CP fielded just ten candidates. They all lost their deposits, Labour's Communist sympathizers were all turned out as well, and the Conservatives under Churchill were returned with an overall majority of seventeen. The Communist Party never again had a representative at Westminster.

8

1956

IN 1953 Stalin died, and the floodgates of Moscow started to open. There was only a trickle at first, and it was another three years before anything like the full story of the Stalinist terror could be told. We still do not know how many people were murdered, only that the killing went on right up to Stalin's death, that torture was routine, that tens of millions died. Stalin's terror was on such an unimaginable scale that a million or two more or less killed and tortured would barely affect our perception of it. Stalin was defended by sincere Communists for whom the years after 1953 were ones of dawning horror. How they coped, and whether they kept the faith, depended entirely on the individual.

Phil Piratin, out of Parliament and a full-time Party worker, remembers: 'Sometimes at our political committee meetings after Stalin's death, Harry Pollitt would take from his pocket a piece of paper, and say that the Czech ambassador had given him the following names of people who had been . . . what was that word they used? Terrible word! Horrible word! Rehabilitated, that's it.' A terrible word because to be rehabilitated you must already have been condemned and shot, probably after being tortured. 'It used to hurt me. Since then I sometimes try to ascertain how others felt. It's something we all still find hard to talk about.'

At one of these meetings a Czech surname was read out which caused a sudden sick feeling in Piratin's stomach. 'I asked Harry to give us the full name. Harry just looked at me. My wife and

I were friends with this man and his wife, they used to come to our house in Hampstead, we went to their flat in Kensington. Then in 1949, they were due to come over one night, and his wife phoned up and said he'd been called away. A few weeks later my wife phoned the flat. There was a new voice, it said our friends had gone back to Prague. We never heard from them again. Now I knew why. 'I thought: do I tell my wife? I told her in the end. She was very distressed. It was the start of a long period of distress. She felt sick at heart, as I did. Those things live in you, the look in my wife's face when I told her.'

Piratin never left the CP. But his heart had gone out of the work, and he quietly resigned all his Party posts. With a little money of his wife's, they went into business together, and, as he puts it, 'prospered'. But the previous generation of Communist leaders was far closer to it all than Piratin. Harry Pollitt, Johnny Campbell and Bill Rust were all frighteningly close to the terror. Wives, children, lovers – for them the terror laid its cold hand on their lives in the late 1930s and never let go. The leaders of the Comintern generation were now so locked into what happened in Moscow that they must either break with their life's work or rationalize what was happening.

Pollitt's son Brian remembers a happy summer holiday at the home of a Czech friend of his father's, Otto Sling, in 1951. Rather more than a year later Brian, aged 16, read in the newspaper over breakfast that 'Uncle Otto' had been shot as a traitor. He could get nothing out of his father. Some *Daily Worker* journalists who had asked Pollitt to intervene to clear Sling's name got nowhere either, and left thinking Pollitt did not care. They were wrong. Years later it emerged that Pollitt had gone to the Soviet embassy and tried hard to put Sling in the clear. He was ignored.

The year Brian was playing happily in Otto Sling's house, his father's old friend from the early days, Mikhail Borodin, died in a concentration camp. Borodin, alias George Brown, alias Mikhail Grusenberg, an old Jewish socialist, was one of the earliest Comintern representatives in Britain, especially close to Jack Murphy and Bob Stewart. As a young Bolshevik he had survived prisons in Tsarist Russia and Glasgow. He had been in the camp for two years, and the harsh conditions eventually proved too much for a man of 77.

In 1956, now aged 20, Brian joined his father in Moscow. He remembers a meeting with Nikolai Matkovsky. Matkovsky said he was 'glad to report' that a British Communist who had disappeared in the 1930s, and about whom Pollitt was making enquiries, had been 'rehabilitated'.

'Rehabilitated? Is that all I am meant to tell his family?'

'What more can we say? That we are sorry?'

'That might help,' said Pollitt icily. And it is certain that Pollitt conscientiously went to the family and sensitively gave them the news, for he never avoided that sort of duty. But when a Communist journalist fresh from Czechoslovakia went to see Pollitt and told him what he knew about the trials, Pollitt looked out of his office window for a while, then said heavily: 'My advice to you is to forget all about it.'

Bill Rust came closest of all before he died in 1949. In fact, Stalin and all his works can be said to have dominated and shaped Rust's short life. Rust married and had a daughter when he was 22 and a full-time YCL organizer. They named their daughter Rosa after the German Communist Rosa Luxemburg. A few months later Rust was the youngest of the twelve Communists to be sent to prison in 1925, charged with seditious libel and incitement to mutiny, and Rosa took her first faltering steps on a prison table during one of her mother's visits.

Three years later Rust took his family to Moscow, where he worked for the youth section of the Comintern. Rosa grew up speaking Russian and sharing Russian children's experiences. To this day she remembers with horror having her tonsils removed without anaesthetic. In Moscow Rust met and fell in love with Tamara Kravets, and brought her back to London with him. His wife returned later, in 1937, leaving Rosa at a boarding school for foreign Communists and promising to come back for her the following year. But the war prevented her.

In 1941 Rosa, now sixteen, was sent with other young Muscovites to the Volga for safety. But Stalin accused the Volga German Republic of harbouring spies, and decreed that the population be dispersed. Rosa was rounded up with the rest. She spent weeks being herded into primitive boats, trains and cattle trucks. Many of her fellow passengers died before they reached Kazakhstan, hungry, cold and lice-ridden. Some were even driven to throwing dead relatives off the train so that they could go on using the dead person's ration card.

Rosa was strong and a survivor, and helped others who found it harder to stand up to the journey. But at last, sent to work in a copper mine, she became ill from malnutrition and back-breaking work and wrote to Moscow, to a girl she had known at school. Suddenly money arrived, together with travel papers signed personally by Georgi Dimitrov. In the spring of 1943 she started the long journey back to Moscow. There she met Dimitrov and then the *Daily Worker* man there, John Gibbons. 'Bill's been looking for you for years,' Gibbons told her. 'Do you want to stay here or go to England?' 'I want to go home,' said Rosa, though she could neither remember England nor speak English.

A Russian ship took her to Leith and Foreign Office officials smuggled her secretly to London. While the Soviet Union was Britain's ally, they did not want reporters hearing about innocent people being herded round the country in cattle trucks. Neither did the editor of the *Daily Worker*, Rosa's father, whom she met in great secrecy, and who did not recognize her. Rust was now married to Tamara, and Rosa, now very sick, went to live with her mother.

It is one of the few stories to come out of Russia at that time which has a happy ending: Rosa recovered and the remainder of her life has been happy. But Bill Rust never admitted his daughter's existence unless he had to. For that would mean explaining what had happened to her in the Soviet Union – and admitting that she would probably have been left to rot and die if she had not been the daughter of an important foreign Communist. A then *Daily Worker* journalist Alison Macleod said, 'If anyone had described in our office one tenth of what Rosa lived through, Bill Rust would have denounced such anti-Soviet lies and slanders.'

Johnny Campbell, who took over as editor after Rust's death in 1949, was in the great Scottish Communist tradition of worker-intellectuals, a man who could grasp statistical information quickly and accurately and then break off to discuss Robert Browning's use of rhyme; a truly egalitarian editor who would sit in the office canteen and listen to everyone's views. Unlike Rust he was capable of thinking Stalin was wrong – he and Pollitt had resisted the anti-war line in 1939. But his time was past. He was too locked into the thinking of the late 1930s. After Stalin died, you either defended everything, or you rebelled. Campbell had been there too long to rebel. Phil Piratin remembered: 'Johnny Campbell and I were walking somewhere and I said, "All that time when you were in Moscow in the late thirties, what did you sense?"' Campbell muttered something about how he was there to represent the CP and Piratin tried again, then suddenly saw the torment he was causing: 'I realised, Johnny is my friend, let's drop it.'

It was worse for Campbell than Piratin knew. When he worked at the Comintern in the late 1930s, his oldest stepson discovered a talent as a circus clown and song and dance man, and stayed in Moscow when the family came home, eventually performing with the Moscow State Circus as Villi the Clown. Like Rose Cohen before him he made the mistake of becoming a Soviet citizen in 1939, thus throwing away the protection that British citizenship provided. Eventually banned from appearing on stage because of his British origin, he saw his closest friends disappearing into Moscow prisons and daily expected the same fate for himself. He never knew why he escaped. After the war, he got a job with Radio Moscow, and in 1977 he and his Russian wife came to Britain on holiday and never returned.

The atmosphere on the *Worker* was different under Campbell. The staff loved him. Dutt was taken far less seriously than before and stopped going to the office. Used to laying down the line the paper should take, he found Campbell disturbingly immune. One day he telephoned the paper with instructions that an event in China ought to be the splash – the front-page lead story – but Campbell had decided to lead on a speech by Soviet foreign minister Vyshinsky. Allen Hutt, the brusque and often rude chief sub-editor, took the call. 'You want us to splash on China. Well, we're splashing on Vyshinsky,' he shouted, and slammed the phone down. It came as a rude shock to the venerated theoretician.

One of Campbell's first decisions when he became editor of the *Daily Worker* in 1949 had serious long-term consequences, though it seemed routine enough at the time. He sent his best young reporter, 22-year-old Peter Fryer, to Hungary to cover the trial of former Interior Minister Laszlo Rajk. Rajk was accused with seven others of plotting to overthrow the Communist government. Fryer believed they were guilty and sent in the sort of reports the *Daily Worker* wanted. It still haunts Fryer to this day: 'I helped send Rajk to the gallows by my coverage of the trial.'

1. British Communist Party leaders in the early 1920s. *Left–right*: Arthur MacManus, Jack Murphy, Albert Inkpin, Willie Gallacher.

The Allied Philanthropist: 'First, what is your politics?'

2. Cartoon from *The Communist*, 1921.

3. Miners' leader Arthur Cook in 1926

4. Albert Inkpin and his wife emerging from court in 1926. Behind is George Lansbury, later Labour leader.

5. Harry Pollitt leaving King Street after being sacked as general secretary in October 1939.

6. Michael Foot speaking at a Second Front meeting, 1942. *From the left*: Aneurin Bevan, unidentified, Harry Pollitt.

7. Phil Piratin, MP for Mile End, speaks to the Jewish Ex-Servicemen's Association in Stepney soon after the Second World War.

8. *Daily Worker* senior staff meet to plan the next day's paper just after the Second World War. *Left–right*: Allan Hutt, chief sub-editor; journalist Walter Holmes; editor Bill Rust; industrial correspondent Johnny Campbell; news editor Douglas Hyde.

9. Rajani Palme Dutt in the late 1940s, with Johnny Campbell.

10. Arthur Scargill (*second from left*) with other members of Barnsley's Young Communist League. The trophy was for increasing the sales of the YCL newspaper *Challenge*.

11. Bill Rust, editor of the *Daily Worker*, 1940–6

12. The *Daily Worker* building in Farringdon Road, pictured in 1962.

13. In Moscow in the 1960s. *Left–right*: general secretary John Gollan, Soviet president Leonid Brezhnev, Boris Ponomaryev of the Soviet International Department, and *Morning Star* editor George Matthews.

14. James Klugmann, photographed in the late 1960s.

15. Reuben Falber in the early 1970s.

16. Jack Jones, leader of the TGWU, addressing the TUC in the mid-1970s.

17. Tony Chater (1976), editor of the *Morning Star* who refused to print Communist Party statements.

18. Denis Healey (*right*) at the 1981 Labour Party Conference, taking an interest in *Morning Star* support for Tony Benn.

19. Arthur Scargill and Mick McGahey at the 1982 Trades Union Congress.

20. Gordon McLennan launching the Party's campaign in the 1983 general election. On his right is Nina Temple, later general secretary.

DOWN WITH THE COMMUNISTS AND SOCIALISTS!

DOWN WITH THE SOVIET UNION!

DOWN WITH THE PEOPLE'S FRONT AGAINST FASCISM AND WAR!

LONG LIVE THE REVOLUTION!

21. In 1985 British Communists were still denouncing the long-dead Leon Trotsky.

22. Uncomradely comrades: Mick Costello (*left*) and Martin Jacques at the Communist Party Congress in 1987.

23. Ninety-year-old Andrew Rothstein (*left*) accepting membership card number one of the newly formed Communist Party of Britain from its general secretary Mike Hicks in 1988.

24. Soviet leader Mikhail Gorbachev (*second left*) meeting the British general secretary Gordon McLennan (*second right*) in 1989, pictured here with Gerry Pocock, international secretary of the CP (*first left*), and an interpreter.

25. The last general secretary of the British Communist Party: Nina Temple in 1992.

Three years later, in 1952, the Czechoslovak Communist general secretary Rudolf Slansky and fourteen others, including Pollitt's friend Otto Sling, were on trial in Prague. Pollitt had to eat the praise he had heaped on Slansky when holding the Stalin line against Tito: 'Men like ... Slansky, who was tortured at Dachau, are not men who "turn when Joe says turn ..."' Eleven were Jews, and the indictment included a statement that a Jewish charity was an agent of imperialist espionage. Two months later some Russian Jewish doctors were arrested and charged with plotting to assassinate Stalin on instructions from the same Jewish charity. Was Eastern Europe returning to its historic anti-semitism? It was unthinkable to British Communists. Jews had flocked to the CP in the 1930s as a bulwark against anti-semitism. Without Jews from London's East End and Scots from the Red Clyde, the CP would have been a very poor thing indeed.

In the *Daily Worker*'s splendid new office in Farringdon Road there was unease. 'Gosh,' said a young tape boy when he read about the Jewish doctors' 'plot'. 'They never give up, do they?' Journalists shuffled their feet awkwardly. They envied him his faith. They were not sure they could hold onto theirs. The foreign editor, Derek Kartun, left the paper quietly, and Campbell appealed to the staff to rebut any suggestion that it was because he was Jewish, and replaced him with another Jew, Sam Russell. Kartun later told a few colleagues the real extraordinary story. During the Slansky trial *Daily Worker* journalist Claud Cockburn was accused of being a British spy, and Kartun was a particular friend of Cockburn's. Kartun explained all this to Pollitt who told Kartun he must leave the paper.

The doctors were released immediately after Stalin's death. They had been tortured. The *Daily Worker* man in Moscow sent in a story saying that the procedure which allowed the secret police to imprison, deport and shoot people without trial in the Soviet Union had been abolished. He added a message that it ought to be the splash. Foreign editor Sam Russell exploded: 'The bloody fool! We can't even mention it.' The *Worker* had never mentioned that such a procedure existed.

Senator Joe McCarthy's witch-hunt of Communists in the USA was a relief. Here was genuine totalitarian bullying and *Worker* journalists could condemn it to their hearts' content.

By 1955 it was clear that Khrushchev had won the Moscow power struggle. On 25 February 1956 Khrushchev made a four-hour speech to the twentieth Congress of the Communist Party of the Soviet Union, detailing many of the crimes of Stalin. No one in Britain knew about it at the time – not even the British delegation. It was a closed session and foreign delegations were not admitted. Two members of the British delegation were being conducted round a rubber factory. One of them was Harry Pollitt, and months later he deflected criticism in typical style. 'Where was I when Comrade K made that speech? I was being conducted round a French-letter factory. At my age I suppose that was a compliment.' The other was George Matthews, at 39 the youngest of the delegation, and Pollitt's deputy. The third member of the delegation, Palme Dutt, was not at the rubber factory, and no one seems to know where he was. Perhaps he was the only British Communist who knew what Khrushchev said.

But everyone knew that Stalin had been criticized, that crimes had been revealed, that Stalin's 'cult of the personality' had been attacked. Privately, Pollitt and Dutt thought Khrushchev was a little man attacking a great leader now he was safely dead. There were anguished meetings of *Daily Worker* staff, where Campbell struggled to keep his staff loyal, handicapped, some of them believe, by an aching vacuum where his own faith had once been. Peter Fryer remembers him at the end of one meeting: 'This discussion must stop now, we've had it all out and we've got a paper to get out.' And Fryer remembers how Campbell talked about his own doubts: 'I was in Moscow in 1938, I knew a lot was wrong, but the Soviet Union was in danger of attack by Nazi Germany. Was I to break ranks? I was a revolutionary socialist before the Communist Party existed.'

For a month British Communist leaders claimed to know nothing about the secret speech. Campbell's deputy Mick Bennett, desperate to defend Stalin against charges which his colleagues did not know had been made, blurted out more than he was supposed to at a staff meeting: 'In the last three years of Stalin's life he wasn't altogether normal. Beria could do what he liked with him. Hundreds of comrades were shot by Beria. The whole Leningrad leadership was framed and shot . . .'

In March Sam Russell, now the *Worker*'s man in Moscow,

telephoned a six-page summary of the Khrushchev speech. He told the stenographer that it was for Campbell only, but it was soon common gossip in the office. Campbell told Russell to send over another story admitting the speech existed but giving few details, and this story was the splash on 19 March, together with Campbell's editorial: 'Truth and fiction are inextricably linked in the capitalist press accounts of the speech.' Campbell knew that there was very little fiction in them.

On 10 June 1956, nearly four months after Khrushchev delivered it, the *Observer* published the secret speech in full. Stalin was a mass murderer and a torturer, and the Soviet system had allowed him to butcher his people for twenty years. Campbell gathered his staff together. 'A man can be a great historical figure and then a menace,' he told them. Because of the need for unity against Fascism, 'we tolerated the building of Stalin's personal power, which we now ought not to defend.' Now 'the Soviet Union is rid of its suspicious mania. We ought to feel that our burden has rolled away. Why don't we? Because we defended the indefensible.' It was a fine performance and the staff applauded. But Campbell was going far further, far faster than the rest of the leadership. Pollitt could still not bring himself to talk of more than Stalin's 'mistakes'. In the May issue of *Labour Monthly* Dutt mocked the concern people felt: 'That there should be spots on the sun would only startle an inveterate Mithras-worshipper . . . To imagine that a great revolution can develop without a million cross-currents, hardships, injustices and excesses would be a delusion fit only for ivory-tower dwellers in fairyland . . .' Even his own *Labour Monthly* board, composed by this time largely of a tame and ageing fan club which spent its meetings extolling the genius of Dutt's latest Notes of the Month, rebelled. The Party's executive committee, which was less in Dutt's control, sternly told him to withdraw, and reluctantly he did.

Meanwhile Hungarian Prime Minister Rakosi had admitted another 'mistake'. Rajk had been framed. The journalist Peter Fryer now believed that the CP had made him an accomplice to the murder of Rajk. In July Campbell sent Fryer to Hungary to report the rehabilitation of Rajk and 473 other people. Fryer found out how Rajk had been made to confess. Rajk was tortured, then promised that if he confessed he would be looked after in the Soviet

Union for the rest of his life and his child would have a good education. He confessed and they killed him. At Rajk's rehabilitation Fryer saw 300,000 people file past the grave of the tortured Interior Minister and knew that revolt was in the air. He came back and handed in his resignation. Campbell pleaded with him to stay for a year, and Fryer agreed.

The 1956 CP Congress went into secret session to discuss Khrushchev's secret speech. Gallacher thought things had gone wrong in recent years, when he believed Stalin had suffered a stroke. Dutt said comrades had not thought out Stalin's 'positive role'. Campbell thought the injustices done to good comrades should not be minimized: 'If Gallacher had been one of those unjustly condemned, I hope we'd have shed some tears for him.' A few days after the Congress a Jewish newspaper in Poland published an account of Stalin's persecution of the Jews. The CP leadership decided that the account should not appear in the *Daily Worker*: it was only permitted to appear in a Jewish CP publication, the *Jewish Clarion*. Khrushchev abolished the Cominform. The CP withdrew Klugmann's book condemning the now-rehabilitated Yugoslav leader, *From Trotsky to Tito*.

It must have seemed to CP leaders that 1956 would never end. In June riots broke out in the Polish city of Poznan, and martial law was declared. The *Daily Worker* was in complete disarray. On 3 July its first edition carried a headline reading POZNAN RIOTERS HAD BEEN DRILLED IN MURDER. In subsequent editions it read POZNAN WORKERS SPEAK OUT ON GRIEVANCES.

In July Egyptian President Gamal Abdel Nasser nationalized the Suez Canal, because he needed the revenue it could bring in. In October Israel attacked Egypt and occupied Sinai, and the British government under Anthony Eden used this as an excuse to send troops to the canal zone, claiming they were protecting an international waterway in time of crisis. It shows the state the CP had got itself into that few Party members you speak to have any very clear memories of the Suez crisis. The CP position on Suez was clear enough, and today it stands up to scrutiny rather well. The Party thought the Egyptians were entitled to nationalize the canal and British Prime Minister Anthony Eden had no right at all to send in troops. But no one in the CP had the heart for a great campaign about Suez. The Party was too busy feasting on its own flesh.

In October the Poles, defying Soviet leaders, put Gomulka in power, and the *Worker*'s headline was POLAND'S FATEFUL WEEKEND. That, said one journalist, was the equivalent of what schoolboys did when they could not remember whether a French accent sloped forward or back: they put it straight up in the air.

The revolt Fryer predicted came the same month. Russian tanks rolled into Hungary to quell it, and Campbell sent Fryer there. Meanwhile the paper floundered. On 25 October it was calling the demonstration a 'counter-revolution'. By 29 October it discovered that 'the just demands of the people' were also a factor. Phil Bolsover, following Budapest radio, wrote the splash: 'Workers in Budapest factories yesterday formed armed groups to protect the factories and the country against counter-revolutionary formations that had attacked buildings, murdered civilians and tried to start a civil war.' In the privacy of the staff meetings Bolsover later said: 'The Hungarians do not want the Soviet army in the country ... The explanation I wrote was completely wrong.'

George Matthews was sent from Party headquarters to try to calm the situation at the *Worker*, where for the first time the instructions received from King Street were being questioned, though not disobeyed. He said to the paper's staff: 'We have never adopted the attitude that socialist governments must never call in the troops of another country.' The next day, Peter Fryer at last found a phone that worked and filed his story. But the story did not appear. According to Llew Gardner, 'the dispatches became banned reading. Instead of being distributed in the normal way every copy of his story was rushed to the editor's room. Those who had access were forbidden to speak of what Fryer had written.' Instead, the paper reported that Soviet tanks withdrew from Budapest and then 'gangs of reactionaries began beating Communists to death in the streets ... Whole families were dragged from their beds and shot, including children.'

Peter Fryer saw Russian tanks roll into Budapest and overthrow the government. 'I'd never seen a dead body before. I saw a crowd of demonstrators, and the police just mowed them down with machine guns, including women carrying their children.' When Fryer's story appeared, the guts of it had been cut out by George Matthews. Fryer was said to have written 'hysterically', to have threatened to sell his story to another paper, and to have taken refuge in the British Embassy. The first two accusations were false, the third was true and perfectly sensible. All British journalists took refuge in the embassy when the tanks rolled in. Fryer resigned from the staff and wrote his book *A Hungarian Tragedy* in ten days. Nineteen out of thirty-one *Daily Worker* staff signed a petition protesting at the treatment of the news from Hungary.

General manager David Ainley told the staff: 'It was a mistake to send Fryer. He was hysterical on certain questions. A number of our comrades are outraged because a report which he sent is not printed in our paper. But the role of the *Daily Worker* is to express the views of our Party and its leadership.' Mysteriously, rumours started circulating about Fryer: that his wife, who had worked in the *Worker*'s accounts department, had stolen money; that he was seeing a psychiatrist; that he had not done his Hungarian research properly. None of it was true. Fryer joined Gerry Healy's Trotskyists, partly because Healy had a printing machine, and could publish the pamphlets Fryer wanted to write, as well as starting a regular publication edited by Fryer, the *Newsletter*. Fryer was to leave Healy after two years in favour of writing books.

It was hard to see how things at the *Worker* could get worse. But they did. The Hungarian rebels opened the prisons and let out a host of political prisoners who had been left to rot. One, who dragged herself straight to the British Embassy, was a *Daily Worker* journalist, an Englishwoman in her sixties whom no one had heard of for seven years – tortured, half-starved, tormented by arthritis, her guts ravaged by the prison food, ragged and barefoot. She was Hungarian-born British Communist Edith Bone. She had been kept in solitary confinement and, like Rajk, been offered an easy life if she would confess to being a British spy. But she turned it down. What saved her was her difficult, awkward nature, which had irritated her British colleagues.

Communist historians John Saville and E. P. Thompson were now putting out a smudgy duplicated publication called *The Reasoner*. It was open defiance of Party discipline to put out a publication not sanctioned by Party headquarters, but their aim was to teach the leadership the lessons of the events of 1956. It was not going to be an easy message to get across.

Campbell told staff at the *Worker* that 'things went wrong because centralism was stressed, and democracy allowed to become moribund.' The CP's problem, he said, was 'how to avoid the leadership degenerating ... how to enlarge the area of discussion within the Party, without disrupting the Party as a disciplined force ...' He attacked *The Reasoner* because it undermined Party discipline. But the paper's cartoonist Gabriel told him: 'The executive committee is as much to blame for *The Reasoner* as Thompson and Saville.' It had censored so much material that someone had to publish it. 'Stalin got away with it because there was no free press.'

Among those to leave the Party and join the Trotskyists was much of the YCL in Liverpool – which is one of the reasons why, more than two decades later, Liverpool became the heartland of the Militant Tendency. Thompson and Saville did not wait to be expelled; they left. But the leadership viewed more seriously the departure of leading trade unionists including Fire Brigades Union chief John Horner and a future miners' leader, Laurence Daly. Losing intellectuals could be shrugged off, for intellectuals were always a little suspect. Losing workers' leaders was serious.

The *Daily Worker* lost a third of its journalists, including its rising star Llew Gardner, who later became political correspondent for Thames Television. Campbell appealed desperately to the remains of his staff: 'The capitalist press is gloating over every comrade who leaves the paper.' He appealed to anyone thinking of leaving to think it over for twenty-four hours: 'Do not do it in a way which will inflict the maximum injury on our paper ... If a leading member of the staff leaves the paper at this moment it is not an ordinary act but a deadly blow ... This was the best staff we had for a long time. If we hadn't had a high-powered staff of capable people it wouldn't be such a tragedy as it is.'

For those rebels who did not leave the Party, hopes centred on electing a new leadership at the 1957 Congress which would be less slavishly uncritical of Moscow, and would encourage open discussion in the Party. It would not be easy, because the rules of democratic centralism forbade the formation of factions. But it seemed worth a try. The best hope for change rested on the Commission for Inner Party Democracy. This had been set up by the executive committee towards the end of 1956 to counter criticism that the CP's decision-making procedures were undemocratic and likely to produce the dishonesty and confusion that had characterized recent months.

The report was unveiled at the Congress on 19 April 1957. The main report suggested little change, but there were two minor reports. One, from historian Christopher Hill, schoolteacher Peter Cadogan and *Daily Worker* journalist Malcolm MacEwen, attacked the rigid way in which the Leninist doctrine of democratic centralism had been interpreted by the leadership, and it attacked the system of election to the executive committee by the mechanism of the recommended list which delegates had to approve either in full or not at all. It complained that free discussion in the Party was inadequate and asked for the removal of party leaders who could not abandon 'outworn and discredited policies and methods inherited from the past.' The other report came from Kevin Halpin, the one industrial worker on the Commission. Still not yet 30, he was dividing his time between earning a living at Briggs Bodies, a car manufacturing firm in London, leading a fight there for better redundancy payments, and writing his report. He wanted wider policy discussion in the Party, but not the wholesale opening up of policy-making demanded by Hill's group.

Picketing the conference was Gerry Healy, brandishing anti-Communist placards and calling out cheerful abuse of delegates he happened to know like Johnny Campbell. Everyone knew him: for years he was a fixture outside CP meetings. Inside the hall was Peter Fryer, representing the left-wing Labour Party paper *Tribune*. Seeing Fryer, the Executive promptly decided that there would be no room on the press tables for *Tribune*, so Fryer borrowed a press card from the *Observer* reporter, who no longer needed it, and produced a Congress Special each night. Healy duplicated it for handing out to Congress delegates the next morning. Fryer watched his expulsion confirmed by 486 votes to 31.

Meanwhile Dick Clements, later *Tribune* editor and right-hand man to Michael Foot, replaced him as *Tribune*'s reporter, and was allowed in. He remembers Harry Pollitt leaning over the platform and telling him: 'You may think *Tribune* is the voice of Michael Foot and Nye Bevan, but really it's the voice of Gerry Healy and Trotsky.'

Healy's and Fryer's tactics damaged any chance of the reformers carrying anything significant at the Congress. It must have seemed to delegates as though this was just a gang of Trotskyists trying to destabilize their Party. But the leadership did not need Fryer's and

Healy's help to carry the day. They had organized the votes against the reformers just as effectively as Herbert Morrison had organized the votes to prevent Communists getting into the Labour Party. Their methods were little different from manoeuvres routinely carried out at Labour and Conservative conferences.

Kevin Halpin recalls pressure being put on him in the few days before the Congress to withdraw his report and support the majority. King Street refused to type it for him. The leadership also took care to make sure, as far as possible, that reliable people were elected as delegates. Halpin, though a branch secretary, found Party leaders manoeuvring to ensure that he was not elected as the branch's delegate, and he was unable to attend the Congress and argue for his proposals.

Andrew Rothstein attacked 'groups of backboneless and spineless intellectuals who have turned in upon their own emotions and frustrations.' The minority report was heavily defeated. Halpin's report was not put to Congress. Hill, Cadogan and MacEwen left the Party after their defeat, but Halpin remained a member until, thirty years later, he was expelled, ironically for allegedly being a Stalinist irreconcilable.

Pollitt said the Congress had 'cleared the air' and urged delegates to get on with 'mass work.' He and the leaders of his generation knew no other way for a Communist Party to work than the one they had operated for the last thirty-six years. The revolution had stubbornly refused to materialize, but this was no reason for the vanguard Party to relax its guard. Sooner or later the working class was going to need the instrument of steel Pollitt and his comrades had created. They were determined that a line should be drawn under the trauma of 1956, that things should go back to normal.

Of all the old leadership, perhaps only Campbell dimly saw that things had changed for ever, that a new left, unsullied by the crimes of Stalin, was going to emerge whether the CP liked it or not. His colleagues worried about Campbell. He had denounced Soviet anti-semitism and had allowed dissent to surface on the *Worker*. He saw that automatic support for the workers' state could never again make any sort of sense. Democratic centralism, like the rest of the old Party structures, was discredited by Khrushchev's revelations. The Communist Party had worked so hard to be the only real Party on the left. It had stifled the ILP and marginalized the Trotskyists.

In 1957, no longer able to adapt, its leaders consigned to long-term irrelevance the machine they had given their lives to build.

Seven thousand people left the Party, more than a quarter of the membership, because of the events of 1956. Leaving the Party was more than changing politics. It was abandoning one's faith and one's friends – for as Jack Murphy and Douglas Hyde could testify, old friends crossed the street to avoid you. Of course, so many left in 1956 that there was some company. According to Peter Wright in *Spycatcher*, they all remained on MI5's list of Communists, which was compiled from one it had stolen and copied in 1955. CP officials of the time, however, say that MI5 is inventing even this dubious achievement: King Street never had such a list.

John Saville testifies that he and the other historians, E. P. Thompson and Christopher Hill, were deeply reluctant to leave. 'There was tremendous discrimination against Communists. I knew lots of people who did not get jobs because they were in the Communist Party. I was brought up in the thirties so I had no faith in the Labour Party. The Labour Party was tainted nationally and corrupt locally. So we wanted to work inside the CP and reform it from inside.'

Saville, Thompson and Hill, who left the Communist Party, and Eric Hobsbawm, who stayed in it, were historians of a new type – socialists to whom history was not so much the doings of kings, queens and prime ministers, as those of the people. That was what took them into the Communist Party, and those who left were a greater loss to the CP than its leaders could ever bring themselves to admit. In the wake of 1956 a favourite ploy of the leadership was to say, wrongly, that those who left were middle-class intellectuals, while the workers' leaders stayed loyal. One *Daily Worker* journalist who left in 1956 said how nice it was to stop having to feel guilty that she was 'not quite from the bottom drawer.'

1956 also saw the first production of John Osborne's *Look Back in Anger*. Osborne's hero, Jimmy Porter, describes how, as a boy, he watched his father's slow and painful death. He was dying of wounds received while fighting for the British Battalion in the Spanish Civil War, the CP's finest hour. 'There aren't any good brave causes left,' shouts Jimmy Porter. Harry Pollitt would have dismissed that as self-indulgent middle-class angst, with some justification. But he should have listened, all the same. There was idealism in the new generation waiting to be harnessed. The CP should have harnessed it, but instead allowed itself to appear self-deluding, covered in blood.

A 1956 play by Arnold Wesker, *Chicken Soup with Barley*, depicts the faith that British working-class Communists had, the pain of losing it and the pain of clinging to it. It traces an East End Jewish family – like his own – from 1936 up to the eve of the traumatic events of 1956. In 1936 there is the excitement of fighting Fascists on the streets of the East End and in Spain. In the years after the Second World War disillusion grows like a cancer. Sarah Kahn, modelled on Wesker's own mother, listens with horror to her daughter saying: 'How many friends has the Party lost because of lousy, meaningless titles they gave to people. *He* was a bourgeois intellectual, *he* was a Trotskyist, *he* was a reactionary social democrat. Whisht! Gone!'

A young man who has left the Party tells her: 'The whole committee of the Jewish Anti-Fascist League were shot! Shot, Sarah! In our land of socialism. That was *our* land – what a land that was for us. We didn't believe the stories then; it wasn't possible that it could happen in our one sixth of the world.' But for Sarah, the faith is her life: 'All my life I've fought. With your father and the rotten system that couldn't help him. All my life I've worked with a party that meant glory and freedom and brotherhood. You want me to give it up now?

Wesker joined the YCL but, like Sarah Kahn's children, lost his faith in the 1950s. Recently, while researching his autobiography, he found a note from his 1956 diary when he was 24. 'There has been a fantastic spate of letters in the DW [*Daily Worker*] from Party members who are virtually in tears that they had ever been so lacking in courage as to approve...the 'ten doctors', 'Tito' etc. Many are confessing that indeed at the time they felt uneasy and now – now that the new Soviet leadership has given them the lead a great weight seems to lift from their shoulders. Now they can look people in the face. It is as though they had all gone to a mass confessional and with the terrible secrets in their heart now out in the open they feel new people ...

'But Leah, my mother ... does not know what has happened,

what to say or feel or think. She is at once defensive and doubtful. She does not know who is right. To her the people who once criticized the party and were called traitors are still traitors despite that the new attitude suggests this is not the case. And this is Leah. To her there was either black or white, communists or fascists. There were no shades.

'If she admits that the party has been wrong, that Stalin committed grave offences, then she admits that she has been wrong. All the people she so mistrusted and hated she must now have second thoughts about, and this she cannot do ... You can admit the error of an idea but not the conduct of a whole life.'

9

The End of the Old Order

I N the middle of the trauma that was 1956, Harry Pollitt resigned as general secretary of the Communist Party. All the reasons for which Pollitt had joined the Party were still at the top of his mind. He was not the sort of socialist who had forgotten at 66 what brought him into the movement when he was 20. His writing still contained sentences such as 'The Labour movement was built up on the basis of hatred against those who rob the poor,' and 'As long as one man robs another of the full fruits of his labour, there will always be need for struggle against it.' After a visit to India in 1953–4 he wrote of Britons living it up in Calcutta: 'There is only one thing I wish I could do to them. Not murder, not violence. Only just go and make them eat and sleep in the conditions of the working people who live in the other Calcutta.' Nor did he ever lose the optimism of 1920, sustained by what he believed were the achievements of the socialist countries. After a bad by-election performance in 1949 he had a drink with his friend Michael Foot, who still laughs affectionately at the memory of Harry saying: 'We may have lost St Pancras but we've won in China.'

His sense of humour survived an attempt to turn him into a myth on Stalinist lines. His biographer Kevin Morgan provides a splendid description of a celebration for Pollitt's 60th birthday in Lime Grove Baths, Shepherds Bush, at which Pollitt almost disappeared behind a growing heap of presents and panegyrics. 'Leader yes, but also bone of the bone, and flesh of the flesh of the toilers. That

141

is a most important part of his genius.' This nonsense from Pollitt's old friend Peter Kerrigan, former International Brigader, and the Party's industrial organizer, responsible for its work in the trade unions. Morgan finds it sad that they needed to build him up in this pompous Soviet-style way when he had real qualities which they could have applauded: 'Pollitt had by his very humanity earned the deep respect and affection of Communists, whom he in turn regarded almost as an extended family.'

Pollitt's health suffered from overwork as much as from drink and cigarettes. In 1949, with what Morgan rightly calls his 'rather reckless courage', he insisted on fulfilling speaking engagements in Dartmouth and Plymouth just after a British frigate sailing up the Yangtze River had been fired on by the Chinese army. Feelings were running high in the Royal Navy. Both the police and the local Party warned of violence, and they were right. Pollitt was set on by a group of sailors, knocked to the ground and kicked for several minutes, until Peter Kerrigan, who often travelled with him to speaking engagements and acted as unofficial bodyguard, managed to disperse the attackers. Kevin Morgan puts it this way: 'Some brave young sailors decided that what they could not take out on the Chinese People's Army they would take out on this man of sixty instead.' The kicking caused a prolapsed disc in Pollitt's spine; he needed a corset to strengthen his back, and he was never fully to recover from his injuries. By 1956 he was taking strong drugs for high blood pressure, and in April he suffered a haemorrhage behind the eyes which for a few weeks almost blinded him. He decided to retire.

Pollitt was tired, ill and dispirited. Stalin, whom he liked and admired, had given way to Khrushchev, whom he neither liked nor admired, and who had unforgivably attacked the memory of Stalin and, by implication, his own life's work. At 66 he would now be required to denigrate Stalin. He had little time for the agonizing of intellectuals, and there was a lot of it going on in 1956. From the time Khrushchev made his secret speech, according to his son Brian, Pollitt 'grew increasingly unhappy, enjoying most the company of the unreconstructed'. He did not want to face the appalling implications of what had happened.

Harry Pollitt was genuinely angered by injustice and suffering, and devoted his life to putting it right. He was a man of enormous ability who cared for others in both his political and his personal life. But the uncomfortable fact for Communists, and for Harry Pollitt's many admirers, is that there were just two men in Britain who, from about 1937 to 1956, knew a good deal about what was going on in Moscow. They were Harry Pollitt and Johnny Campbell.

They did not know everything. They probably had no idea of the appalling scale of the terror. Perhaps they went to their graves believing that the confessions in the show trials were genuine. Campbell, like Pollitt, a decently motivated and able man, told Monty Johnstone of negotiating with someone who simply disappeared the next day. He was told in a hushed voice: 'He was one of them.' It was harder for Campbell, says Johnstone, because 'he did not have Pollitt's capacity for self-deception.' But they knew that Stalin was butchering old Bolsheviks and foreign Communists who took refuge in Moscow. They knew he killed some of their own friends: Max Petrovsky, Rose Cohen, Mikhail Borodin, Otto Sling and many more. There was hardly a comrade whom they were taught to trust in the 1920s who was still alive in the 1950s. Part of them must even have understood that the preservation of their own lives in Moscow was often little more than diplomatically desirable, though Pollitt did not know that evidence was prepared against him.

If they did not know that Russians could not sleep easy at night for fear that the secret police might turn up at any moment, and that would be the start of weeks, months, years of torture followed by death, it was because they did not wish to know. They knew enough to know that Stalin was a monster, but did not allow themselves to acknowledge it.

Pollitt was used to death. He never once shirked what he saw as his duty, for example to tell an old International Brigader's family how their son had died, or break bad news to the family of one of Stalin's victims. He never tried to pass the duty on to a subordinate, he never missed performing it, and he never took the easy way out and wrote a letter rather than talking to grieving relatives personally. He cared more than anything about people, and that was what made him a socialist. But he never once told what he knew.

There is no need to doubt his motives. Certain that the Soviet

Union was the hope of mankind, Pollitt believed, as did many in the 1930s, that only the Soviet Union stood between the world and universal Fascist dictatorship. On balance, he reckoned Stalin was doing more good than harm; he liked and admired the Soviet leader; and persuaded himself that Stalin's crimes were largely mistakes made by subordinates. Seldom can a man have thrown away his personal integrity for such good motives. But when innocent men and women die miserable, painful deaths because they are thought to hold doubtful political views, then the regime is unquestionably wicked. It was Pollitt and Campbell's self-imposed myopia that they failed to see that. Pollitt's conviction that successful revolutionaries could do 'no wrong against the working class' was self-deception.

Harry Pollitt was a class warrior. Today it is an unfashionable thing to be. We are inclined to pretend that there is no longer any such thing as class, that we live in a classless society. To Harry Pollitt, brought up in a Lancashire textile town sharply divided between the haves and the have-nots, you had to choose your side in the class war. Class was at the root of everything he did. Middle-class intellectuals in the Party needed to be kept strictly in their place, as servants rather than leaders of the Party. When his son Brian won a scholarship to Cambridge, though Pollitt was of course pleased, 'part of him would have preferred me to be a boiler-maker's apprentice and genuinely working class.'

Class dictated his choice of successor as general secretary. Brian Pollitt remembers asking his father whether, since George Matthews was assistant general secretary, Matthews would become general secretary if Pollitt died. 'No, it'll be Johnny Gollan. George isn't working class.' And so it was: the executive committee chose the man Pollitt had been preparing as his successor for years. Pollitt became chairman of the Party. His doctors told him he must not address more than two meetings a month, and while the furious winds of 1956 blew around colleagues' heads, Pollitt quickly regretted his decision to resign. He had a talent for many things, but retirement was not one of them. He sat at home, brooded bitterly, drank far too much, worried about becoming – as his wife once put it – 'useless to the Party, a burden to the family, and financially dependent on the Party.' He travelled as often as his doctors allowed, was fêted in Moscow and Peking as one of world Communism's elder statesmen, but always in the end he had to return to North London, to a suburb of a city where the revolution seemed further away than it had been in 1920.

In 1960 came an invitation from the Australian Communist Party to tour Australia and New Zealand, and he jumped at it. In the departure lounge at Heathrow, in the Gents toilet, he found himself standing next to Douglas Hyde, who had become an untouchable after leaving the Party in 1948 and writing a book attacking it. Hyde, travelling by chance on the same flight, told me he followed Pollitt into the Gents because he knew that his old leader was supposed to cut him dead and a man standing at a urinal cannot easily walk away. On the plane Hyde manoeuvred to get into the seat beside Pollitt, and during an unscheduled overnight stopover in Rome he took him round the Vatican, where Hyde now had an excellent contact. When they parted Hyde asked Pollitt if he could mention their meeting. 'Say what you like after I'm dead but don't mention it while I'm alive,' said Pollitt.

In Australia he was happier than he had been for years, addressing meetings constantly, meeting numerous people, loving their attention and enthusiasm, working far too hard, drinking and smoking far too much, and refusing hospital treatment for his worsening eyesight. But his hosts could see that his health was going downhill and forced him to cut short the tour, booking him on to a boat home in the hope that a long sea voyage would put him right. There is a short piece of silent film of Harry Pollitt boarding the liner for the journey back to England, meeting yet another group, hailing them with the practised yet genuine familiarity of the born politician who also loves people. He looks younger and happier than in pictures taken five years earlier, and there is a spring in his step. The day after the film was taken he had another stroke and died. When his luggage arrived home his family noticed that his packages of medicine – he was supposed to take several pills every day – were unopened.

A month after his death Harry Pollitt made a brief and wholly characteristic final appearance. In his street lived an Irish Catholic family, and he used to go to their house to drink whisky and sing Irish rebel songs. Their daughter was mentally handicapped – in her 20s but with a mental age of about 8. She appeared on the card index which Harry kept of people to whom he regularly sent

145

birthday cards. Before he went abroad, he always went through the names, signing cards for those whose birthdays would occur while he was away and leaving instructions for them to be posted on the appropriate day. So it was that his neighbour received her birthday card a month after Harry died. Her parents told her Harry had sent it from heaven.

John Gollan, the Party's new general secretary, was as different a character from Pollitt as it was possible to imagine. Thin, tense, slightly awkward, chain-smoking, Gollan was a shy and ascetic Scot from Edinburgh. A kind man in private, he lacked the expansive humanity of Harry Pollitt which had bound the Party together. In the King Street office he was as different a boss as it is possible to imagine. Where staff used to take their personal troubles to Pollitt, Gollan pointed out that he was not a marriage guidance counsellor. 'He was very tough and didn't let others interfere with his work,' is the way one colleague puts it. His successor Gordon McLennan sees it differently: 'If you went to him with a problem he would always say, "What would you do?" He would never do your work for you. After all, it's the easiest thing in the world to say, "Right, I'd do this", and send you away without really having done the work.' Another of the Communist Party's Scottish worker-intellectuals in the tradition of Campbell and Murphy, Gollan's speeches and writings showed meticulous research. While Pollitt loved barnstorming from platforms, Gollan had to overcome chronic shyness by sheer willpower. He would shake for half an hour before he had to make a speech, says one close colleague.

When he took over the leadership in 1956, Gollan was 45 and had worked full time for the Party for twenty years. He had a lot in common with the pre-war leadership: he joined the Party at the age of 16 after hearing Willie Gallacher speak, went to prison for six months in his early 20s for distributing a 'subversive' paper to soldiers, and regarded the discipline of democratic centralism as sacred.

George Matthews went to the *Daily Worker* as Campbell's deputy in 1957 and took over the editorship in 1959. Matthews, five years younger than Gollan, was the Party's rising star, and if he had been able to boast a proletarian upbringing would probably have been given Pollitt's job. The son of a farmer, Matthews went to a public school – 'a minor public school' he says today, still a little defensive about it – and Reading University, where he studied agriculture, intending to take over his father's farm. At Reading he took an interest in the hunger marches and the rise of Fascism, and 'the Communists seemed to be the only people who were doing much about it.' He became student union president, a key figure in the National Union of Students, and an underground Communist inside the Labour Party. He was an oddity in the Party: neither Scots, nor Jewish, nor working class, an urbane and amusing speaker. He became assistant general secretary in 1949, a safe pair of hands in those difficult days and the natural choice to talk to *Daily Worker* staff to add political weight and calm jangled nerves.

In 1957 Gollan made what may have been the most important decision any CP leader ever took. He travelled to Moscow and asked for (or at least accepted the offer of) a return to direct subsidies, for the first time since the early 1930s. After 1957 the CP received about £100,000 a year in cash via the Soviet embassy. During the 1970s this sum sharply decreased, and when the subsidy ended in 1979 it was said to be down to about £14,000. Only four people knew about the money: Gollan, Matthews, David Ainley, the chief executive of the *Daily Worker*, and Reuben Falber, soon to become Gollan's deputy, who had the delicate task of meeting regularly and secretly with an embassy official on the streets of London, taking delivery of a huge leather bagful of money, hiding it in his attic, and dispensing it in sums that were not so large as to attract attention.

When this became public knowledge, in 1991, surviving CP leaders explained Gollan's decision by pointing out that the Party had lost a third of its members in 1956. In fact a much more important factor in the financial crisis was the demise of a highly secret section of the Party known as the Commercial Branch, which most ordinary members did not know about. This was a group of about fifty businessmen, mostly Jewish, who joined the Party in the late 1930s and early 1940s. Many of them were important industrialists, and all of them wanted to keep their CP membership secret. Many were in the rag trade, where starvation wages were traditional, and their CP membership did not always persuade them to raise the wages of their employees. One of them is said to have berated his staff for meekly accepting the wages he paid and advised them to join a union until a union organizer begged him to desist, saying: 'They'll never join while you're telling them to.'

The Commercial Branch was set up in the mid-1930s. It met irregularly, and was serviced and held together for most of its life by Reuben Falber. Falber seems from this time to have taken on the role of the shadowy figure behind the Party's finances, and kept this role until the mid-1980s. He is perhaps the only man who ever had a complete picture of its complicated financial affairs, and understood the network of companies and front organizations through which it worked. He was never a public figure, never known at all outside the Party, he never kept written records, and lives now in modest retirement in North London, where his well-organized mind and absolute discretion remain entirely intact.

The branch was the Party's biggest single source of money. Unlike other branches, its members did not pay a fixed subscription. They paid whatever Falber could persuade them to pay. A member might well give enough each year to employ a full-time organizer, and during the war years the Party employed full-time branch secretaries in several London suburbs, collecting subscriptions and organizing Communist activities in the area. Its members were not represented at the Party's Congress or on its executive committee. Like corporate donors to Conservative Party funds, they gave money because they approved of the Party's policies. In 1956 they collectively ceased to approve, mostly because it became unavoidably clear that Stalin had persecuted Jews. The Commercial Branch did not survive 1956. Gollan was forced either to get rid of many of his staff or to take his begging bowl to Moscow.

The crisis was more than financial. Almost all the Party's strategies were in tatters. It had lost both its parliamentary seats in 1950. It did not win any seats at the general elections of 1951 and 1955, at which the Conservatives under Churchill and then Eden were returned with working majorities. 1956 ensured that hopes of electoral success must be indefinitely deferred.

The traditional strategy of destroying all rivals on the left had been broken. The CP had stifled the ILP and the Trotskyists, and turned itself into the natural home for left-wing socialists, but 1956 put an end to that. Now that Britain was testing atom bombs, the Campaign for Nuclear Disarmament had started to provide the cause and the comradeship which former CP members had lost. Leaving the Party lost its sting. So many left after 1956 that they failed to experience the loneliness and 'homelessness' that Douglas Hyde and Jack Murphy remembered so painfully.

It was not easy to find new strategies. Old men whose thinking was shaped by the pre-war years declined to retire gracefully. Gollan did not want to be shackled with an executive committee given to reminiscing about the glorious days of 1920, but it was not until 1965 that the last of the old guard bowed out. Rajani Palme Dutt was with much difficulty persuaded that at 70 he should stand down from the executive committee, though he insisted on carrying on editing *Labour Monthly*. This had in fact lost its influence. A newer theoretical journal, *Marxism Today*, was launched in 1957, edited by James Klugmann. Campbell, who was over 70, left the executive, and industrial organizer Peter Kerrigan handed over to Bert Ramelson. That year, in an even more decisive break with the past, Willie Gallacher died at the age of 84.

The dated mind-set of some Party leaders was painfully clear from the row which erupted over Gallacher's funeral. Peter Kerrigan's suggestion of speakers from the USSR and China had to be sharply vetoed on behalf of Gallacher's family by Phil Stein: 'Experience has taught some of us that lack of awareness of the British situation by both Soviet and Chinese spokesmen could lead to someone putting their great foot in it.' As for Kerrigan's idea that banners be carried, 'we are absolutely astonished that the proposal was ever made.'

The one CP strategy in good shape was the industrial strategy. Throughout its history, whatever troubles the Party brought on itself and had visited upon it, it always had – what many of its rivals on the left lacked – deep roots in the working class, and real influence in the trade unions. In this field the CP's best days were still to come, as it put more and more of its energy into the trade unions. The unions themselves were on the threshold of their best days, and the Party's influence inside them in the 1960s and '70s was stronger than ever.

The Party's new lease of life started badly with the scandalous events inside the Electrical Trades Union. One of the people who left the Party in 1956 was a 35-year-old electrician called Frank Chapple. Chapple maintained that the reason Communists were elected to controlling positions in his union was because they rigged the ballots, and he knew what he was talking about. As a loyal ETU Communist for many years he had helped to rig them, and was elected to the national executive with Communist support. After several preliminary skirmishes, the balloon went up when the Communist general secretary of the Union, Frank Haxell, stood for re-election in 1959 and was challenged by Jock Byrne. Haxell was declared the winner, and Byrne and Chapple went to the High Court to have the election result overturned. Two years later, in July 1961, the High Court ruled that Haxell and his friends had rigged the ballot.

Too many ballot papers had been ordered from the printers, and extra papers, already marked with Haxell votes, were sent to Communist ETU branch secretaries. Envelopes containing ballot papers from unfriendly branches were destroyed, and other substitute envelopes were posted which were then disqualified for arriving too late. Byrne, not Haxell, was the properly elected general secretary. Byrne told the press that this was not the end of Communist control of the union: 'We've only got one less. This struggle could go on for years.' It did. Byrne was the sort of Scottish Catholic to whom Communism was evil because it was godless, and Chapple developed an obsession with Communism that you occasionally find in people who were once particularly dedicated Communists themselves.

Haxell and his friends, used to power in their union, bitterly resented the way in which they were overthrown and were determined to fight every inch of ground. But they were not always wise in their choice of standard bearers. The year after the High Court débâcle they managed to defeat one of Chapple's supporters for a seat on the union's executive council. Their candidate's name was Eric Hammond. He turned out to be one of the few people in Britain who hated Communists more than Chapple did, and eventually became ETU general secretary in 1984.

This was the first example of a peculiar alliance which was to become commonplace. Chapple says today with some pride: 'I told Lou Britz to join the Communist Party while Haxell was general secretary so he could find out what was going on. Britz was really a Trotskyist, and we came together because we were both against Communists.' A standard political joke of the 1960s concerned a Trotskyist who wanted to go to the USA. Communists were banned there, but after an interview at the US embassy he was given a visa, and explained to his friends: 'They asked me what I thought of Communists, and I told them.'

Chapple succeeded Byrne as general secretary, and this tough, thick-set Cockney with black slicked-back hair and a harsh, uncompromising voice and manner became one of Britain's best-known anti-Communists. Communists were banned from holding any ETU office and most of the existing Communist officials left the Party rather than lose their jobs. Fewer posts in the union were filled by election and more by appointment, perhaps on the theory that if there are no ballots no one can do any ballot-rigging. Ten years later it was the Communists who appeared to be the democrats, as they campaigned unsuccessfully for a return to election of union officials and an end to the ban on Communists.

The ballot-rigging case received massive publicity and damaged the CP just as it was starting to recover from 1956. Chapple claimed that King Street knew all about it and it was part of a conspiracy to take over the whole trade union movement. The Party's industrial organizer Peter Kerrigan was behind it all, he said. Chapple now claims that in his Communist Party days he witnessed Kerrigan organize trade union ballot-rigging. Keith McDowall, later public relations officer for the Confederation of British Industry, wrote in the *Daily Mail* that Haxell and his friends were 'puppets who were trained to capture and control the 240,000-strong ETU.' The trainers, apparently, were 'Scots-born Gollan, gaunt, tight-lipped [who] has made several trips [to Moscow] since he took over as Britain's Top Red' and Gollan's 'craggy generalissimo on the industrial front, fellow-Scot Kerrigan.'

But apart from Chapple's testimony, there is no evidence that CP leaders knew what Haxell and his friends were doing. They always insisted they did not, and Haxell was forced to resign from the Party as soon as the High Court gave its judgment. 'We know,' said a CP pamphlet some months later 'that the handling of this election will be presented by reaction as a normal feature of Communist trade union activity. We repudiate this as an absolute lie.'

The balance of probability seems to be that the Party was telling the truth. The ETU's Communist leaders had grown complacent and regarded power in the union as their right, and ETU politics on all sides were particularly vicious. King Street no longer had the power to control its trade union leaders. The days when miners' leader Arthur Horner had been forced to bow to a Comintern directive were long gone. In the 1950s and 1960s King Street was far more likely to take orders from Communist union leaders than to give them. It was not Gollan's style to send out instructions.

Much more his style was the work Bert Ramelson did in Yorkshire before coming to London to be industrial organizer. Ramelson says: 'It was Yorkshire that made the NUM a right-wing reactionary union. To change the NUM leadership you first had to change Yorkshire.' And changing the miners would change all the trade unions, and the Labour Party as well. He succeeded so well that by the time he left Yorkshire to take over from Kerrigan as industrial organizer in 1966, Yorkshire miners were the leading left-wingers in the NUM. Ramelson had nurtured the trade union career of a Young Communist recruit called Arthur Scargill; and he had pioneered the tactic of flying pickets, later made famous by Scargill. Already in 1961 he was being blamed by the press for a strike in the Yorkshire coalfields and attacked by the Labour MP for Barnsley, Roy Mason: 'The miners should be warned that the Communist Party decided a year ago that they must capture the Yorkshire coalfield industrially and politically.'

Ramelson was one of the strangest and most compelling of all those who gave their lives to British Communism. Born Baruch Ramilevich in the Ukraine in 1910, his family emigrated when he was twelve to Alberta, Canada, where he won a scholarship to the University of Edmonton, took a first-class degree in law, read Marx and Palme Dutt, and joined the Canadian Communist Party. His reasons echo those of his future British colleagues: 'I saw unemployment, Fascism, anti-semitism; and the Communist Party were the only people with an explanation for what was happening.' He fought in Spain with the Canadian Brigade and was wounded several times, once nearly fatally. In Canada he had felt intellectually drawn to Communism; in Spain he developed immense pride in his Party, without which Franco would be virtually unopposed.

When the International Brigades were withdrawn the 150 Canadians were quickly taken by train to Liverpool where a Canadian Pacific boat was waiting. Ramelson did not board it; instead he took an instant decision to settle in Britain. During the

Second World War he fought in the British army, was captured at Tobruk, and spent two years in an Italian prison camp where he ran classes in Marxism and from which he eventually escaped.

But he still had the mind-set of a Ukrainian Canadian, used to the harsh world of illegal politics. That was how his faith survived the extraordinary year of 1956. His sister had stayed behind when the family left the Ukraine. In 1945 he sent her a telegram saying he was still alive. He received a telegram back: she was alive too, and would write fully later. But she never wrote. Ramelson went to Moscow on a CP mission in 1956, after Khrushchev's speech, and saw her. She had spent twenty harrowing years in a Soviet labour camp, where her husband died, and she had never seen her brother's telegram, much less answered it. This distressed Ramelson but did not shake his faith, though he was always more critical of the Soviet Union than many of his colleagues. He still believed the Soviet system was fundamentally sound.

A big man with a very wide mouth and an open, honest face, he spoke loudly with an accent which mixed his Canadian and Ukrainian roots. The *Sunday Times* called him 'a charming and erudite man with a keen sense of humanity.' One of his closest friends, trade union leader Ken Gill, says: 'He had the most formidable mind of anyone I know. He was well read but it was all heavy reading, nothing frivolous at all. He was a very powerful and rational speaker and the most confirmed optimist I have ever met.' He, rather than Gollan or Matthews, was to become the face of British Communism in the only place, after 1956, where it really mattered, the trade unions.

Communist progress in the unions seriously alarmed some union leaders. The ETU was the fourth union to ban Communists from holding office. The news that Communists were gaining ground in the National Union of Teachers prompted an American anti-Communist organization, the Twelve Legions of Los Angeles, to issue spine-tingling warnings. 'This bid for power is proof beyond a shadow of doubt that the Communists are planning an all-out assault on the minds of the children of Britain.' Just as the Communist agitator had been the bogeyman of the 1930s, the Communist shop steward became the bogeyman of the 1960s. The Catholic Archbishop of Liverpool, Dr John Heenan, said: 'Wildcat strikes can rarely if ever be justified. You will nearly always find Communists at the back of them.' A Tory MP, Donald Box, called for a ban on a television programme, 'At Home', which, as part of a series visiting celebrities in their homes, featured the Communist leader of the South Wales miners, Will Whitehead.

The most serious attack on Communist influence in trade unions came from the embattled Macmillan government. In 1961 Foreign Office clerk John Vassall was discovered spying for the Russians and George Blake, a lieutenant in the navy, was revealed as a double agent. The government hastened to set up an enquiry under Lord Radcliffe which duly reported that Communist infiltration of civil service trade unions was 'most dangerous to security'. It recommended that any officials of civil service trade unions who were suspected of being Communists should not be permitted to enter civil service departments or negotiate on behalf of civil servants. The Committee said it was 'disturbed at the number of Communists and Communist sympathisers who are holding positions either as permanent full-time paid officials or as unpaid officers or as members of executive committees.' The immediate result was that about half a dozen full-time trade union officials abruptly lost their jobs.

Just as they had done in the 1930s, the security services were staring obsessively in the wrong direction. A decade had passed since the first two Cambridge spies, Guy Burgess and Donald Maclean, defected to the Soviet union. Neither they, nor Vassall, nor Blake had ever tried to negotiate salaries on behalf of civil servants, for it would not have furthered their spying careers in the slightest. As far as espionage was concerned, Communists in civil service trade unions was a red herring.

The Macmillan government had fallen on hard times. Its management of the economy was showing a distinctly uncertain touch, and the Vassall and Blake affairs damaged its reputation further. It was necessary to distance these events from the government. At the same time, ministers were becoming uneasily aware of the growing power of Communists in the unions, and welcomed an excuse to trim this power.

Labour leader Hugh Gaitskell hastened to make it known that he agreed with the Radcliffe proposals. Labour was going through a reassessment after a decade of Conservative government and three election defeats. In 1961 it was trying to jettison left-wing policies and image. It was, according to Gaitskell's close ally, front bencher Douglas Jay, suffering from 'two fatal handicaps – the class image and the myth of nationalization.' Jay thought it should be 'open-minded', by which he meant not wedded to socialism. He even wondered whether the name 'Labour' didn't sound a little old-fashioned and redolent of class warfare. Since Labour was linked in the public mind with the trade unions, Gaitskell wanted the unions to have a moderate image.

Gaitskell did not live to see the rewards of his moderation. He died suddenly in January 1963, and Harold Wilson was elected to succeed him in February. Later that year the Conservatives chose Sir Alec Douglas Home to succeed Macmillan, who had retired on health grounds. The next October Labour ended thirteen years of Conservative rule, scraping home with an overall majority of just four. Wilson's first problem was the economy – and that brought his government into direct conflict with the unions.

The new government inherited a massive and mounting balance of payments deficit. With TUC agreement it set up a National Board for Prices and Incomes, and gave George Brown, who ran the new Department of Economic Affairs, the right to refer any price or wage proposal to it. He could enforce its decisions and delay the implementation of any wage or price settlement while it investigated.

This set the stage for the long-drawn-out struggle over incomes policies which was to last, with occasional respites, until 1979; a struggle which was to give Britain's Communist Party its last and perhaps its proudest battle honours, and was to end in the defeat of both sides and the triumph of Thatcherism.

But that was all in the future. Wilson had solved his immediate problem and was able to call a general election in 1966 with confidence. He came out of it with a very satisfying ninety-six seat majority. Soon after the election came a serious and damaging industrial confrontation. The National Union of Seamen wanted a pay increase larger than the government's approved 3 to $3\frac{1}{2}$ per cent. Wilson, Brown and Chancellor of the Exchequer James Callaghan insisted on fighting the seamen, to the distress of most Labour supporters and some members of the cabinet.

It was a long, damaging strike, and it frayed the Prime Minister's nerves. He declared a state of emergency, and watched as the economy was driven once more into the crisis he had laboured so hard to escape from. As the strike went into its seventh week, he watched his carefully cultivated (and not undeserved) image of economic competence evaporate, and at the end of June he exploded. It was all, he told the House of Commons, a Communist plot.

There was a grim irony to this which no one, least of all Wilson, knew at the time. While Wilson was blaming Communists for destabilizing his government, there was a determined group who really were labouring to destabilize his government – on the entirely false grounds that he himself was a Communist. They worked in the security services.

The strike, said Wilson, was the work of a 'tight-knit group of politically motivated men.' The Communists had at their disposal 'an efficient and disciplined industrial apparatus controlled by headquarters. No major strike occurs anywhere in this country in any sector of industry in which the apparatus does not concern itself ... For some years the Communist Party have had as one of their objectives the building up of a position of strength, not only in the seamen's unions, but in others concerned with docks and transport.' The central figure, claimed the Prime Minister, 'is the Communist Party's industrial organizer, Mr Bert Ramelson.' He went on to name Ramelson's staff, his contacts in the seamen's union, and the address where he met these men. It was a long, detailed statement containing much trivia, and it was too much for the young Labour MP for Liverpool Walton, Eric Heffer, no longer either a Communist or a Trotskyist but in no mood to apologize for his past. He knew all the men the Prime Minister had named, he said. One of them 'is a Communist and a damned good honest working man' and what on earth did it have to do with the House if Bert Ramelson had been seen visiting his flat?

It was the best thing that could have happened to the CP. The message to the seamen was that they owed any advances from the strike to the CP. The advances gained were not that great, but Ramelson's answer to Wilson made the most of them. The concessions were the 'basis for the advance which the seamen, by unity and militancy, can win in the months ahead. The incomes policy, which would have prevented the seamen closing the gap between their conditions and those of other workers, was breached ...

Concessions were made twice after the shipowners had declared that they were prepared to give no more ... By standing up to Wilson, the seamen's executive may deter the Prime Minister from barging into other industrial disputes ... The Communist Party certainly did its utmost among trade unionists and the public generally to win support for the seamen's cause ...'

The same year saw the foundation of the Liaison Committee for the Defence of Trade Unions which owed its birth to the Labour Government's incomes policy. It was a typical piece of Communist Party organization, but rather more successful than most. Its founders and guiding spirits, apart from Kerrigan and Ramelson, were shop-floor Communists like Kevin Halpin of the engineers (who had been the only industrial worker on the 1956 Commission on Inner Party Democracy), dockers' leader Jack Dash and building workers' leader Lou Lewis. It also attracted some important non-Communist trade unionists like print union leader Bill Keys. Dash and Lewis were already well known as strike leaders, and some Communists complained that they did not always follow the Party line in their union work. But Ramelson knew better, and left them alone.

Kevin Halpin was typical of the Party's new industrial militants. His Party activities and his work as a shop steward, in addition to earning a living, took up all his waking moments. If he could have done only one of them, it would have been the union work: 'People used to get two hours' notice that they were out of work, so they could sharpen their tools for the next employer next morning.' When he first joined the Party, Harry Pollitt told him that shop stewards were needed, not full-time trade union officials, so he should stay on the shop floor. That is what he has done ever since. After a 1962 strike at Ford he was fired and spent eighteen months out of work, and several job offers were withdrawn when employers read his Ford record. 'Sometimes the telegram saying the job had gone would be home before I was.' At one motor component factory, 'a chap turned me down for a whole row of jobs I could have done easily, then gave me a cup of tea and said: "You know I can't give you a job – Ford are customers of ours."'

A determined man with a loud voice and a gift for expressing himself clearly and simply, Kevin Halpin explains the success of the Liaison Committee like this: 'We would not discuss anything at all

157

except legislation to stop trade unions from doing one thing or another. Everyone who came to our meetings had to come from an organization and be a delegate. We were against rank-and-fileism. We felt we could win not just grassroots support, but also executives of trade unions if not the TUC itself.

This was a key part of the Ramelson philosophy, and a decisive break with Communist tradition. Pre-war Communists wanted to appeal to the rank and file in the unions over the heads of union leaders. Ramelson left this to the Trotskyists, who embraced it enthusiastically. He pursued precisely the opposite strategy, writing in 1967: 'This was tremendously important for us, the realisation that it's no good having militants at the bottom and not at the top. So there was a move to change who's at the top. For the first time in history there is now a very important minority of left wingers at the TUC.' One of the most important of these was Jack Jones, who became general secretary of the mighty Transport and General Workers Union in 1968 and, though never a Communist himself, ensured that the TGWU ban on Communist officials was lifted.

The Liaison Committee for the Defence of Trade Unions seemed to be the symbol of CP power in the trade unions, and newspapers laboured to make it sound sinister. A *Daily Mail* story in October 1967 began: 'Mr Bill Jones, vice-president of the Transport Workers Union, admitted yesterday that he is chairman of the Liaison Committee for the Defence of Trade Unions.' The investigative techniques required to obtain this 'admission' probably extended no further than asking him. The TGWU's Norman Willis, 'described as publicity officer for the union' (probably because he was publicity officer for the union at the time), declined to comment.

The Prime Minister, the Minister of Labour Ray Gunter, and Engineering Union president Lord Carron also saw the LCDTU as pretty sinister. Lord Carron talked about 'peacetime fifth-column activities.' Gunter said in October 1967 that the Communist Party was trying to create 'a winter of disruption.' If so, it took them another twelve years to achieve it.

10

The New Left

I N the mid-1960s the Young Communist League announced
a meeting to discuss the legalization of drugs. It seemed a
small gesture to the mood of the times, but John Gollan was
outraged and sent for YCL organizer Pete Carter. Carter and a
colleague walked into the general secretary's office and enraged
Gollan and his deputy Bill Alexander by saluting them. Alexander
said that if they held the meeting the YCL would no longer
be welcome in King Street. It sounded as though nothing had
changed since the days of the Comintern. But it had. When Gollan
and Alexander finished, the YCL leaders saluted again, did a sharp
about turn, left the office and held their meeting. And nothing
happened.

Bill Alexander was 50 at the start of the 1960s. In the 1930s he
commanded the British Battalion in Spain. To the new generation
he was an old-fashioned Communist, with all their virtues –
honesty, decency, a rage against injustice and immense courage –
and all their vices – rigidity, ruthlessness, and the ideological
intolerance which Palme Dutt had drilled into the Party. He saw
the Party as a sort of workers' army, and no one knew better than
Alexander the discipline that an army needed.

In Spain during the Civil War, a lesser man might have forgotten
that it was the duty of every Communist to collect money to keep
the *Daily Worker* afloat. But Bill Alexander would choose the
moment when the shelling was at its worst to send a man round

to collect. 'You might not get the *Worker* later on,' he explained. Dead men find it hard to reach for their money.

In 1961 Fidel Castro won power in Cuba and the Soviet Union made Yuri Gagarin the first man in space. John Kennedy became the youngest ever US President at 43 and authorized a disastrous attempt to unseat Castro, the Bay of Pigs invasion. The Berlin Wall went up and the newsreels were full of pictures of East Germans being evicted from their homes to make way for it. 'A last look into the west, then back into the streets of no hope,' reported Pathe News apocalyptically. 'Behind the wall the age of barbarism has returned ... A Soviet type of government, a bullet in the back for anyone who tries to dash for freedom.' Cold War rhetoric, of course, but with enough truth to create a public mood against Communism.

That year the 80-year-old Willie Gallacher sent Phil Stein to East Germany with a letter of introduction that seemed to come from another age: 'Dear Comrade Ulbricht, the bearer of this note is my nephew Phil Stein, the Scottish correspondent of the *Daily Worker*. He is an earnest, energetic fighter for Peace and for a speedy settlement of the "Berlin Question" ... With warmest Comradely Greetings ...' More Cold War rhetoric.

Castro's victory was inspirational for Communists. If socialism could sweep aside a corrupt and brutal American-backed dictatorship in Cuba, what might it not achieve in Britain? Youthful radicalism could be tapped to oppose Ian Smith's Unilateral Declaration of Independence for his white minority government in Rhodesia, or tours of Britain by South Africa's all-white rugby teams. American students on the run for refusing to fight in Vietnam started seeking refuge among British radical students, who often hid them from the authorities and learned from them their unfocused and undogmatic rage. Jimmy Porter's plea in *Look Back in Anger* for good, brave causes had been answered within five years.

But Communist leaders seemed more concerned with Cold War matters: Berlin; and the Soviet success in putting a man in space before the USA. When the two great Communist powers, China and the Soviet Union, fell out, the CP started to tear itself to pieces over the rights and wrongs of the argument. After a little hesitation it reacted as its gut dictated and ranged itself alongside the Soviet

Union. Dozens of people were expelled, dozens more left the Party and regrouped round one of its leading trade unionists, Reg Birch of the Amalgamated Engineering Union. 'Maoist' quickly became as dirty a word as 'Trotskyist'.

The CP seemed to have nothing helpful to say on the matters of personal liberty which concerned the 'sixties generation. Homosexuality and abortion were legalized, censorship was relaxed, Kenneth Tynan placed a few discreetly lit naked bodies on the London stage in *Oh, Calcutta!* and Party chieftains were thought rather to disapprove. A YCL organizer in the early 'sixties was sharply ordered to get his hair cut, which suggests a leadership slightly out of touch.

Meanwhile, the country's political centre of gravity moved sharply to the left. Labour under Harold Wilson took power in 1964 and held it until 1970. It proved too right wing for young radicals of the time, and individual membership of the Labour Party dropped by a quarter of a million. These people would in the past have been natural CP recruits. Now they were more likely to join other left-wing groups or single-issue campaigns, like CND or the growing feminist movement, which the CP hardly seemed to comprehend.

For the first time young people started thinking the Communist Party was quaint, old-fashioned, even a little right wing. To the puzzlement and despair of its friends, the CP hesitated before lending its support to CND, allowing its enemies on the left to claim that it had betrayed the one movement which offered hope for the world. Its instinctive radicalism had deserted it. Its leaders did not seem to understand that 1956 had broken the Party's near monopoly on the left. What they did understand of the new left they often perceived only as a threat.

The CP's natural constituency should have been the young, the impatient, the angry. But increasingly in the 1960s its leaders had little to say to this constituency. In fact it was at this time they launched a determined effort to appear respectable. In the 1966 general election Gollan used his one permitted Party Political Broadcast to present himself to the nation as a sort of trustworthy Scottish family doctor, speaking to the electorate quietly and reasonably in his soft Edinburgh tones. The message was startling in its moderation. Ought we not, he gently asked, to 'nationalize at least some of the key sectors of the economy?' Communists would take Britain 'a step on the road' towards socialism. We could halve the arms bill, but don't think we are not patriotic – think of us as a 'new British peoples' party.' He urged viewers to 'Go one better – vote Communist.' Very few did. Probably very few would have done so whatever Gollan said. But this was not a message to harness the incoherent rage and radicalism which was the mark of the era.

Briefly in the 'sixties, students were radical. Macmillan's Conservative government created a national system of mandatory student maintenance grants in 1962. Before that, student support was the responsibility of local authorities, a few of which were generous while a great many were not. Student grants brought into higher education many young people who would earlier have gone straight into a factory on leaving school. Hence those with the sort of childhood which makes socialists were to be found as much in universities as in factories.

The CP was not used to this. Dutt's student contemporaries helped break the general strike in 1926 by driving buses. In the 'sixties many young people were looking for a vehicle for their instinctive radicalism. The Labour Party had set its face against them, running in the early part of the decade a merciless purge of those who persisted in supporting CND. Many of these became young Communist recruits. As a result the CP grew slowly until 1964, the year Khrushchev was removed by Kremlin conservatives and Labour came to power in Britain after thirteen years of Tory rule. But after 1964 it started slowly and inexorably to shrink again. A large proportion of the new generation of radicals seems to have decided that the CP was not the vehicle they were seeking for revolutionary change.

In the early 1960s a mature student called Mick Costello became president of Manchester University students union, beating the future newscaster Anna Ford to become the first Communist student union president in Britain since the Attlee government. Before he left Manchester Costello was joined there by a very different sort of Communist, a brash, clever, self-assured undergraduate called Martin Jacques. Both confident, fluent and highly educated, they could nonetheless have been born on different planets. Their two cultures were to clash violently for the next twenty-five years, until the battle destroyed the Party which had nurtured them both.

George Matthews explained in 1967 that 'people of the extreme left who use revolutionary phrases are out of touch with reality.' Under his editorship the *Daily Worker* was renamed the *Morning Star*. At its 1967 Congress the CP leadership made sure that 22-year-old Martin Jacques became the youngest member of its executive. 'It was at least a recognition that the youth culture of the sixties could not be ignored, that the YCL was the Party's only success story, and of the importance of the intellectual lobby,' says Jacques. 'There was almost a wall between the generations. People used to talk about the missing generation which left the Party in the 'fifties. There was very little between those of Bill Alexander's generation and those of my generation. It meant that the intellectuals who were dominant had been shaped in the 'thirties, like James Klugmann.'

Bill Alexander made his contribution to giving the Party a more modern image: he resigned. He explains: 'The whole of the political committee were of my sort of age and I am opposed to the old timers hanging on.' But he understood the human problem this represented in a way that aggressive newcomers like Martin Jacques did not: 'I was one of the few who had professional qualifications and could get a job outside the Party.' Alexander had a chemistry degree and had worked before the war as an industrial chemist. At the age of 57 he started a new career as a chemistry teacher in a South London comprehensive, where he worked until he was 72.

In the 1930s it was the YCL under Bill Rust which had forced a more rigid line on the Party. In the 1960s it was the YCL which was to force a more liberal line. The Party of Lenin was not used to having to compete for the loyalty of young radicals. Now there were competing attractions: Trotskyists, Maoists, anarchists, Labour Party left wingers, young Liberals (who managed in the 1960s, such was the libertarian spirit of the times, to look briefly more radical than the Communists).

The year 1968 saw North Vietnam's Tet offensive, the beginning of the end for the USA in Vietnam. It saw President Johnson's announcement that he would not stand for another term as President, a clear victory for the left and for opponents of the

Vietnam War. It saw Enoch Powell being fired from the shadow cabinet for his 'rivers of blood' speech about the alleged dangers of black immigration, showing that even the Conservative Party under its technocratic leader Ted Heath had absorbed something of the spirit of the times. It saw one of Britain's biggest ever demonstrations, against the Vietnam War, ending in a battle between demonstrators and police outside the US embassy in Grosvenor Square.

Unfortunately for the CP, 1968 also saw the Soviet invasion of Czechoslovakia. This put an end to Czech Prime Minister Dubcek's attempt to create a more free and democratic sort of socialist government – 'socialism with a human face'. With shocking suddenness one day in August, tanks from Warsaw Pact countries rolled into Prague. The new regime was crushed and Dubcek arrested. It was a brutal assertion that Soviet bloc countries needed to stay completely in line.

Monty Johnstone, condemned in the higher reaches of the CP ever since 1956 as a revisionist, was staying in Prague at the time of the Soviet invasion. 'I'd gone to spend a holiday to see what was going on – I was attracted by the programme of democratization. On the night of 20 August I was with the director of Czech television, Jiri Pelikan, who was also a member of Parliament's foreign affairs commission. He thought the Soviet Union would invade. I said he was exaggerating – Brezhnev would not be so foolish. As we parted outside the television station at 10 pm he said, "Come and see me again, if I'm still here." I laughed. But he was never to enter that building again.'

At 4.30 am the next morning Johnstone was woken by neighbours saying Russian tanks were outside. A fluent Russian speaker, he joined Czechs asking Russian soldiers to turn their tanks round and go away. 'The soldiers were very embarrassed,' he says. 'People were listening to Czech radio reports on their transistors until the radio station was closed down after a few hours.'

For the CP to support the invasion would have been close to signing its own death warrant. The radicals whom the Party needed were just as disgusted by Russian tanks in Czechoslovakia as by American bombers in Vietnam. Party leaders had been gradually moving away from automatic support for Soviet actions. Even though criticism of the invasion might well cut off the secret Soviet subsidy, the morning the news from Czechoslovakia came through, Reuben Falber, acting general secretary while John Gollan was on holiday, issued a statement calling for the troops to be withdrawn and the Czech government to be left alone to bring in their reforms unimpeded. Falber only criticized what he called the 'intervention' of Warsaw Pact troops. YCL leaders, now determined on a break with the bad old days, called it an 'invasion' and asked Monty Johnstone to draft a pamphlet which they published under the title *Czechoslovakia's Struggle for Socialist Democracy*. Johnstone, shut out of top-level CP affairs for almost a decade for asking awkward questions, was at last respectable again and in demand to address meetings. 'I started to feel it was worthwhile spending all that time in the wilderness,' he says.

Morning Star editor George Matthews sent his foreign editor Sam Russell to Czechoslovakia. Mathews was receiving only stories hostile to the invasion and told Russell to 'give us something of the other side.' But there was not much by way of pro-Soviet stories to be had, and Russell's material could not have fitted the bill, because it was picked up and used by the CIA-backed Radio Free Europe. Moscow was furious. It was keeping the *Morning Star* afloat by buying 12,000 copies a day, paid for a year in advance. When Soviet leaders saw Russell's stories, they cut the order to 9000. 'It was a shot across the bows,' says Russell. 'At receptions people from the Soviet embassy would say: "I hear the circulation has dropped."' The order was restored two years later after some careful fence-building by George Matthews.

Falber insists that the money he was collecting from the Soviet embassy was unaffected. Perhaps it was, but he and Gollan certainly became worried that their dependence on secret Soviet handouts might make it harder to take an independent line. After 1968 the sums collected were progressively decreased, and stopped altogether in 1979. Falber claims that the initiative for reducing and eventually eliminating the subsidies came entirely from London.

The CP's criticism of the Soviet Union brought the 72-year-old Rajani Palme Dutt out of semi-retirement breathing fury. Dutt still edited *Labour Monthly*, and the day before the invasion he left at the printers his Notes of the Month, which poured scorn on speculation that the Warsaw Pact countries might invade Czechoslovakia. On the morning of the invasion he telephoned his managing editor Roger Woddis at the printer and told him to destroy all copies of the article, and never speak of it to anyone.

Labour Monthly by now was looking like something from another age. Its board, mostly men and women in their 60s and 70s, included Dutt's old friends Andrew Rothstein and Robin Page Arnot, both of them as apparently sure the Soviet Union could do no wrong as Dutt himself. They would meet each month in the office of the television technicians' trade union, whose general secretary, Alan Sapper, though never a CP member, was a member of the board and one of those trade union leaders who felt most comfortable, personally and politically, with Communists. After the meeting Sapper would open up his extensive drinks cabinet. They were still warmed by the memory that *Labour Monthly* had been founded on the orders of Lenin himself.

Dutt led a small group of hardliners opposed to the Party line and in support of the Warsaw Pact countries' action. The strongest support came from the Party's Surrey district committee and its full-time official Sid French, who had been unhappy for some time at the growing tendency to distance the Party from Moscow. Czech newspapers and radio stations quoted at length from French's statements, observing that he had taken the trouble to visit the country, unlike some of the British Party's leaders who criticized the invasion. Dutt recalled Lenin's approval of a Latin motto 'salus revolutionis suprema lex' – the revolution's success is the highest law. The row over Czechoslovakia engulfed the CP and virtually took over its 1969 Congress, the first to be called since the post-Hungary Congress in 1957. French told the Congress: 'Today we should be expressing our gratitude to the Warsaw Pact countries and the Soviet Union.' Dutt thought it would be 'a measure of the Party's maturity' if the leadership admitted its mistake. The Dutt-French view was rejected by 295 votes to 118. Official criticism of the invasion kept most members loyal – there was nothing like the 1956 exodus. Nonetheless the invasion made it even harder for the Party to be centre stage in 1960s' radicalism.

In 1968 it looked as though the Trotskyists were more in tune with students than the CP. They, rather than the CP, offered the notion of turning universities into 'red bases'. They launched a Revolutionary Socialist Students' Federation in 1968 demanding 'an end to bourgeois ideology in courses and lectures.' This demand was repeated in sit-ins all over the country. CP leaders could hardly condemn such things, but did not really like students rushing off doing their own thing. Reuben Falber compromised by saying that students should work with RSSF groups where they existed, but should not found any.

Digby Jacks was a student activist in London, joining the CP in 1964. 'In 1968 it became suddenly harder to be a Communist in student politics,' he says. 'I had the feeling that things were passing the Party by.' The CP's straitlaced attitude to drugs did not help at a time when most political and cultural discussions among students took place in smoke-filled rooms where the smoke was of a new and exotic kind. Jim Tait, later the *Morning Star*'s Scotland correspondent, remembers that when a joint was passed to him at a party during the 1970s, he said: 'No thanks, I'm a Communist.' Jacks, with his shoulder-length red hair and long red beard, did not look at all like the traditional Communist, but underneath it he was as precise, disciplined and thoughtful as any Communist intellectual.

Martin Jacques was also finding it hard to be a Communist. Now doing his doctorate at Cambridge University and leading a group of young intellectuals in the CP, his group of Cambridge Communists recruited new members by saying they were nothing like the Party nationally. 'I felt like a Martian on the Communist Party executive. I've got pretty good interpersonal skills but there ... they would turn up in the conservative clothes of the British labour movement. I was dressed in the style of the times, I'd turn up in a sweater. I'd go to the Congress and I'd be the only man in the place not wearing a suit. In those days dress was an important signal.' He was already having ideological doubts, wondering if he should be in the Party at all: 'I was on the executive but mentally up in the air. I had no idea where I'd end up.' He was engaged in a bitter conflict with the student organizer, Fergus Nicholson, a Communist of the old school who, like Harry Pollitt, saw students and intellectuals as having only a supporting role to a working-class leadership. Jacques never saw himself having a supporting role.

A temporarily united left – Communists, Labour Party left wingers, young Liberals, CND supporters, anarchists – harried the leadership of the National Union of Students throughout the decade, finally toppling it in 1969 with the election of Jack Straw to the NUS presidency. Although Straw was not noticeably more left wing than the leadership he replaced, the victory had symbolic importance. Two years later Straw was replaced by Digby Jacks, NUS's first Communist president since 1940.

Student Communists were from then on under siege from Trotskyists, who outflanked them on the left and condemned them for right-wing attitudes. The debate between Communist and Trotskyist students was conducted in esoteric language which recalled Comintern days. To each other they were 'Stalinists' and 'Trots'. They would issue stinging denunciations of each other for having fallen victim to 'an incorrect analysis' and accuse each other of betrayals in immoderate and quaintly dated language. The shadows of Palme Dutt and Gerry Healy lay heavy over student socialists throughout the 1970s.

Increasingly after 1968 Party members identified with one camp or another. Sid French and his supporters were called 'tankies' for their support of the Soviet invasion of Czechoslovakia. In 1971 French was still saying that the Party had not properly understood the titanic achievements of the international Communist movement. He said: 'No country in the world is freer than the Soviet Union'. Dutt thought, as Dutt had always thought, that 'criticism of the world socialist camp ... is alien to our outlook.' George Matthews answered them: 'There have been immense achievements in the Communist world but there have also been mistakes.' That year the tankies suffered another defeat when Fergus Nicholson left and was replaced with an ally of Martin Jacques, Dave Cook.

At the same time there was a mini purge of hardliners in the YCL, and a row about the CP's fraternal delegate at the Czechoslovak Party Congress. Reuben Falber submitted a draft of his fraternal address in advance, and his hosts demanded the removal of the statement that sending troops was a 'grave mistake'. Rather than withdraw it, the CP withdrew its delegate.

The *Morning Star*'s small ads column became a battleground full of coded messages and insults. An old couple in Ipswich had every year placed a black-rimmed advertisement on the anniversary of Stalin's death. In 1977 they added the words 'It suits today the weak and base ...' They knew readers would remember the rest of the verse from the Red Flag:

Whose eyes are fixed on pelf and place
To cringe before the rich man's frown
And haul the sacred emblem down.

The last straw for Sid French and his supporters was the new
version of *The British Road to Socialism*, published in 1978,
drafted by Martin Jacques and the man who was increasingly seen
as the nearest the Party had to a sheet-anchor, George Matthews.
It talked of a 'broad democratic alliance' of the working class and
its allies. These allies included black communities, women's organizations, national movements in Scotland and Wales, and environmental groups. French, a sincere, mild-mannered CP official who
thought Communism had been betrayed, led about 700 supporters
out of the CP to form the New Communist Party. World revolution
had 'obviously taken a bit more time than even Lenin envisaged'
but when the working class, led by a Communist party, came to
power, 'it is ridiculous to pretend that if we were defeated in a free
election we would give power back to the capitalists.'

Dutt had died four years earlier. Would he have gone with
French? Did he ever, for one second, lose the certainty that
Moscow was always right? Did he ever admit to any mistakes? If
he did he never allowed anyone to know. Except once. Stanley
Forman, Communist film maker, made a film about the history of
Labour Monthly, and heard the aged Dutt mutter, before the
cameras were switched on, that the Party had made one fatal
mistake: in the 1920s it thought Germany would lead the way to
world Communist revolution. That was its mistake.

Chris Kaufman, a young graduate from Sussex University,
worked for Dutt on *Labour Monthly* and remembers the great
theoretician in the evening of his life: 'He was very irascible and
in constant pain from his bad back so he always wanted to get
telephone calls over quickly. He was very tall but bent because of
his back.' Kaufman became used to taking down the Notes of
the Month from dictation over the telephone and had his own
shorthand for Dutt's favourite phrases. MWW was 'mad whirligig
of capitalism', UI was 'unparalleled intensity'. As far as he knew
Dutt's attitude to the Soviet Union never changed: 'When Russia
farted Dutt wanted to apologize.'

Yet the Dutt everyone knew was only part of the man. There were

169

several Dutts whom few people believed could have existed. There was the Dutt whom Pollitt and Page Arnot knew in the 1930s, neurotic, jealous, desperate for affection and unable to ask for it. There was the Dutt known to a few close friends and family, humorous and kind. There was the Dutt whom his wife Salme knew and loved, who read poetry to her in bed and could be reduced to tears by the words as he read. History, sadly, will remember only the stiff, monkish, sectarian and ultimately futile Dutt.

Many Communists who were passionately opposed to the new thinking in the Party decided nonetheless to stay rather than go with Sid French. Fergus Nicholson was one of them. In 1977 he led a picket outside an Amnesty International meeting which was discussing Russian political prisoners, holding banners which read 'Amnesty = CIA' and 'Anti-Sovietism is a threat to world peace.' They organized themselves under the title Straight Left. Ranged against them was an increasingly strident Eurocommunist wing led by Martin Jacques. Eurocommunist ideas were heavily influenced by the Italian Communist leader Antonio Gramsci, who was imprisoned by Mussolini and used the years of imprisonment to write his influential *Prison Notebooks*. Labour historian John Foster was one of those Communists who watched the growth of Eurocommunism with dislike and distrust: 'I felt that if you attacked the bases of Marxism the Communist Party would cease to exist as a useful Party – and they were doing that.' The theoretical journal *Marxism Today* started to print more articles by Jacques. When Klugmann died in 1976 Jacques became its editor. Jacques' supporters also ran the Communist University of London each year, using it to press Eurocommunist ideas on the Party's intellectuals.

Jacques was at first appalled by the idea of taking on the job which was to become his springboard in life. He was lecturing in economic history at Bristol University, and if he was going to give up a promising academic career in order to earn less than half as much working for the Party, he wanted a real political job. 'I wasn't a journalist, I had no interest in being a journalist, I thought it was a blind alley.' He insisted, as a condition of taking the job, that he would be on the Party's executive and political committees. 'Klugmann was a behind-the-scenes man, I wasn't.' But in King

Street he found 'a lot of old men brought up in a different world. There was no room for someone like me. They were very complacent. They stuck me on eleven committees and I couldn't do anything. The political committee was every Thursday and there I was back to feeling like a martian.'

Its internal warfare prevented the CP from taking full advantage of the disarray in the Trotskyist camp after 1968. Three warring factions now claimed Trotsky's mantle, none with more than 2000 members. There was the Socialist Labour League run by Gerry Healy, which later became the Workers' Revolutionary Party (WRP); the International Marxist Group; and the International Socialists (IS), later the Socialist Workers' Party (SWP), the biggest and most influential, and the only one to mount a serious challenge to Communists among students.

They were making all the mistakes the CP had made in the early 1930s. Each was making the laughable claim that it was the vanguard party of the working class, and this involved putting huge amounts of energy into attacking each other and the CP, leaving little time for dealing with the small problem of unseating capitalism. Enormous effort and ingenuity went into convincing themselves that their views were more left wing than anyone else's, and other brands would sell you out to capitalism at any moment. Communists, to their fury, found themselves subjected to the sort of abuse which they had applied to rivals on the left such as the ILP in the Class Against Class period. At the game of 'lefter than thou' the Communists had been overtaken.

John Callaghan in *The Far Left in British Politics* lists sixteen activities which a typical member of the International Marxist Group, female and a teacher, would be expected to perform each week, from selling four different publications to her colleagues, attending teachers' fraction meetings, attending branch meetings and 'aggregates', privately studying abstruse journals whose names echoed the ones Palme Dutt once lovingly pored over, and attending the IMG women's caucus. Their very earnestness served to cut them off from the youth they aspired to represent. A young WRP member in the early 1970s became renowned at Communist-dominated NUS conferences for talking in a reedy voice about the need for 'struggle' until one day he approached the microphone and nearly 1000 delegates called out 'struggle' and the huge hall was filled with cruel laughter. Peering uncomprehendingly around him, he yelled through the microphone: 'You don't know what struggle means.' Delegates only laughed more. But he was probably right.

Names like 'fraction' and 'aggregate' served only to distance the Trotskyists further from real life, in just the way that the CP's long-abandoned terminology, such as 'politburo', had once made the Party sound foreign and menacing. And just as the Euro-communists were rejecting the idea that the CP had to be led by people who were recognizably working class, Trotskyists were becoming embarrassed at their student and intellectual following.

The IMG, dissatisfied with its showing among manual workers, removed its best-known figure, Tariq Ali, from the leadership in 1972. It followed this with futile calls for a general strike. The IS was absurdly embarrassed about being able to boast many of the best-known student leaders among its members. In 1969 its leader Tony Cliff ordered his student activists to go and get jobs in factories, just as the CP had done in the early 1930s (and realized its mistake in the mid-thirties). Some of them did so. Others left IS instead.

The student radicals were now at work. Some of them, as a matter of principle, took manual jobs in industry. But the Communists often became trade union officials, for they considered this the highest possible calling. 'It was always the trade union leaders who had the highest status among us when we were students,' says Digby Jacks, who became, and still is, a full-time official for the white-collar trade union ASTMS, now called Manufacturing Science Finance. David Triesman, former LSE activist and a Communist until the 1980s, is the general secretary of the Association of University Teachers.

Others became academics – and in 1977 the Institute for the Study of Conflict, a right-wing think tank, published a report called *The Attack on Higher Education – Marxist and Radical Penetration*, which alleged that these academics were polluting the minds of a new generation of students with left-wing ideas. In the early 1980s some sociology and (improbably) art history courses were reported to undermine western civilization and to be 'Marxist', 'revolutionary' and 'dialectical'. But both right and left were deceived. By that time the advance of Marxism in universities was already in reverse.

John Gollan's health was poor throughout the 'seventies. In 1975 he was told he had lung cancer and did not have long to live, and he retired. The next year, as an ordinary member, he launched a desperate effort to end the warfare inside the Party. He believed that the battle between 'Stalinists' and 'Euros', as the two sides derisively called each other, was likely to become more and more destructive, and could ultimately destroy the Party to which he had given his life and his health. An article in *Marxism Today* to mark the twentieth anniversary of Khrushchev's secret speech was followed by a series of well-attended and noisy meetings for Party members throughout the country.

Gollan died the next year. In Communist circles he is sometimes compared unfavourably with Harry Pollitt. But Pollitt never had to deal with the sort of problems which Gollan faced. The latter took over in 1956 just as the Party was suffering its biggest ever membership haemorrhage. He took on himself the task of asking the Soviet Union for money, and took care that as few of his colleagues as possible knew about it, so that they could always protest ignorance. At the same time he criticized the Soviet Union in a way the CP had never done before.

He was succeeded by another Scot, the national organizer, Gordon McLennan. It did not occur to McLennan in 1975 that by the time he reached retirement, Harry Pollitt's legacy would have broken into several small fragments.

11

Trade Union Power

T HE notion that during the 1970s powerful trade unions pulled the government's strings and the Communist Party's industrial organizer Bert Ramelson pulled the unions' strings is of course a well-travelled myth. But Ramelson himself identified the grain of truth in it when he said the Party had only to 'float an idea early in the year and it will be official Labour Party policy by the Autumn.' He exaggerated, but not much.

The CP had a level of trade union influence that the Trotskyists could not hope for. 'The Trots would just as soon get rid of a union leader as an employer,' says Ramelson. 'They make everyone an enemy, unions as much as or more than capitalists or government.' And the unions still looked on the Labour Party as an errant younger brother. In the early 1970s John Mortimer interviewed Arthur Scargill, then president of the Yorkshire mineworkers. Scargill was quite offended to be asked if he would like to be an MP. 'I was asking King Arthur if he'd care for a post as a corporal. He has been offered four Labour seats, but why should he forsake the reality of union rule for the pallid pretensions of Westminster?'

Labour governments have been known to entice a trade union leader to serve in the cabinet out of a sense of duty, as did TGWU leaders Ernest Bevin from 1940–50, and Frank Cousins in 1964. But union officials prefer their union offices, where they believe the real business of the working class is done. They tend to think of politicians as grubby people who have their occasional uses. They also

174

believe that it is the unions' solid good sense, as well as their money, which has kept the Labour Party on the road for so long. Their block vote in the 1930s and '40s ensured that Labour kept to right-wing policies, and the left railed against the dead hand of the unions in the Party's affairs.

In the 1970s, however, the left found a better tactic than railing against union influence, and that was to work through the unions themselves. Left-wing complaints about the block vote ceased, which bears out Clement Attlee's remark that 'those who make the loudest song about the block vote are significantly silent when it happens to coincide with their own views.' It made sense for Communists to seek influence through the unions. They did it very professionally, and worked hard at it. There was a network of committees – 'advisories' – one in each important union, and Ramelson knew what was going on in all of them. But he did not issue instructions to them. Each committee was assumed to know its own union and to know how far it could be taken. Ramelson knew that Communist union leaders owed their influence to the fact that they put union concerns first. Sometimes the interests of two trade unions conflicted – for example, when they were trying to recruit the same group of members. The Communists always took the side of their own union, even if this meant fighting other Party members. Ramelson was known to try to solve inter-union disputes by acting as honest broker – and such was his reputation in union circles that it sometimes worked.

These committees were about getting people on to union executives and winning policy positions. When any important post in the union fell vacant, the committee would decide on a candidate and work hard to ensure his election. The candidate might be a Communist, or alternatively be someone with whom the Communists felt comfortable. Non-Communist Jack Jones was supported for general secretary by the TGWU Communists, while in the Amalgamated Union of Engineering Workers the Communists rejected a Communist candidate, Reg Birch, in favour of a non-Communist, Hugh Scanlon. Birch later left the CP to lead Britain's Maoists.

These committees caused some tension at King Street because of their independence. Most of their members were not involved in the overall affairs of the Party – their time and energy went into trade union work. A very few – the miners' Mick McGahey, the farmworkers' Wilf Page – were also on the CP executive, but most were not. 'They had more input into the Communist Party than the Party had into them,' says Digby Jacks.

At the end of every year Ramelson would send to each committee a document called *The Needs of the Hour*. This was a list of policies which the Party wanted to see trade unions take up. Over the next ten months he would make sure that the most important of these policies appeared on the agenda of the Trades Union Congress held in September. The weekend before the TUC Ramelson would chair a meeting of all the Communist delegates. It would take the likely course of the Congress apart in fine detail, even down to who should speak on particular motions and what should be said. The objective was to ensure that the maximum gain was made for Communist policies and Communist candidates in elections. Everyone would leave the meeting with the week more or less mapped out – who they should talk to, who they should lobby, what they were expected to achieve. The TUC became a key week in the Communist calendar. Gollan never went to the TUC, but his successor Gordon McLennan never missed it.

Ramelson's key lieutenant was the former Manchester University student politician Mick Costello. The son of a New Zealand diplomat, Costello spent part of his childhood, from 1945 to 1950, in Moscow. He joined the CP as a student, and knew at once that these were the people among whom he wanted to spend his life. 'It had a perspective when no one else had one. I loved the democracy of internal Party life – a trade union baron and an unemployed member were on the same level. And the Party could produce working-class intellectuals as no one else could do. People were taught to respect culture. In a gathering of Communists one can talk on a more intellectual level than among people with much more formal education.'

Tall, thin and dark, Costello was fluent in several languages including Russian and smoked long, thin cigars. So naturally he seemed to many inside and outside the Party to be rather sinister. He cultivated journalists, and his ability to drink whisky all night with them and remain comparatively sober while Fleet Street's best were dropping from their bar stools gave rise to (quite mistaken) rumours that he was a Soviet agent.

These sorts of relationships could turn sour. One of Costello's

journalist contacts, Bruce Kemble, got a job as political correspondent on the *Sun*. Costello says: 'Bruce oversold himself to the *Sun*
and could not produce the stories they wanted. All he had left was
me.' One day the paper ran a full-page article by Kemble headed
THE MOST DANGEROUS MAN IN BRITAIN. It said that Costello 'does not
actually deny being a KGB agent.' It gave Costello's home address,
so that readers could – and did – poke excrement through his letter
box and write obscene letters to his family. 'My lawyer told me it
was no good suing – the paper had only to say I was a Communist
Party official.' The KGB, of course, would have little use for one
of the two or three best-known Communists in Britain. It was
another example of the mentality which followed Harry Pollitt
around and failed to notice Kim Philby.

In 1969 Costello went to the *Morning Star* as industrial correspondent. He had no wish to be a journalist – he wanted to be a
political organizer – but he loyally went where the Party told him
to go. He turned the job into much more than a journalistic one.
Everyone in the trade unions understood that when Costello arrived
at a conference he was not just there to report it. He was an
unattached but crucial part of Ramelson's industrial department.
Not that he ignored his journalistic duties. In fact, he was very good
at them. If you wanted to know what was going on in industrial
relations in those days, you read the *Financial Times* and the
Morning Star each day.

Union members in the 1950s and '60s ceased to be content to
assume that their leaders knew best. Power was inexorably on its
way down through the ranks. One man who saw that very clearly
was Jack Jones, who became general secretary of the TGWU in
1968. Jones not only understood the change, but welcomed it.
His sensitive political instincts as well as his own preferences led
him to place himself at the head of what became known as the
shop stewards' movement. He encouraged, where Bevin and Deakin
would have resisted, a shift of power away from full-time officials
and into the hands of locally elected shop stewards. Labour prime
ministers could butter up the TUC general council, but no union
leader, however eminent, could now deliver unless the shop
stewards said he could. Because he understood and accepted the
growing limitations on the use of his power, Jones became one
of the most powerful people in the land, and, with the exception

of Bevin, the most powerful trade union leader Britain has ever known.

One measure of the change in the unions is that in the mid-sixties Harold Wilson's government had been able to bring in wages policies, in the form of the Prices and Incomes Board. At the end of the decade, the unions destroyed Wilson's and Barbara Castle's proposals, titled *In Place of Strife*, aimed at curbing industrial action by legislation and fixing wages. It was largely a Communist triumph, and Wilson knew it. Ramelson organized the votes on the TUC general council, and the Liaison Committee for the Defence of Trade Unions made sure that the all-powerful shop stewards knew the proposals would be bad for them. Jack Jones was a key figure, ensuring that trade union MPs like James Callaghan saw, as Jones puts it, that 'if they went along with Harold Wilson ... whatever they had in terms of a trade union power base would be lost for ever.' And there was something of the old Union paternalism towards Labour politicians as well. Jack Jones remembers: 'There was a feeling that young Barbara, this upstart of a politician, is interfering in industrial relations – there was some of that, you know.' Wilson was forced to abandon his legislation and settle for a 'solemn and binding' assurance that unions would accept the TUC's guidelines on unofficial strikes. Ever since then, trade union negotiators have invoked 'Solomon Binding' as a name for promises they think will not be kept.

By the time Harold Wilson led Labour into the 1970 election, relations between the unions and the Labour Party were worse than anyone could remember. The Conservatives under Edward Heath won the election and quickly entered into conflict with the unions. Communists were determined that unions would not register under Heath's industrial relations legislation. 'We proved that a law doesn't mean anything if everyone is against it. We got solidarity up and running – if we stick together they can't put us all in gaol,' said Ramelson later. He told *The Times*: 'We've never had a greater influence. Our ideas are getting generally accepted after a shorter and shorter period.' Communists helped in the organization of a dock strike in 1970 and a postal strike in 1971. They were now working together with Labour Party members, but Gollan said: 'We don't want another right-wing Labour government. We are confident that out of [the campaign against Heath's industrial legislation] important leadership changes to the left can be won and a government pledged to a left policy elected.'

The year 1972 saw a breakthrough for the CP. Ramelson helped organize flying pickets during the seven-week miners' strike and helped with organization for strikes of postal workers and dockers; and the TUC lifted a 22-year ban on Communists attending conferences of trades councils. TUC general secretary Vic Feather said the Party was no longer the menace it was said to be in the 1930s and '40s.

That year, too, Communist Jimmy Reid led the famous work-in at Upper Clyde Shipbuilders. Told that the yards must close and that the government would not bail out UCS, the workforce decided to carry on working until their jobs were saved, insisting on no redundancies and no closures. 'The workers of Britain are getting off their knees, getting on their feet and asserting their dignity,' said Reid. 'No one has the right to destroy the aspirations of young men or the security of old men.' After an eight-month work-in the government provided the necessary assistance for UCS to go on working.

After 1972 Communists were an accepted, even a respectable part of the trade union machinery. They extended their influence in the country's two biggest unions, the TGWU and the Amalgamated Engineering Union (AEU) and by 1980 they had their people at the top of several others. Their influence was feared on the right. A rising Conservative politician called Nigel Lawson wrote an article in *The Times* to warn the nation of the growing menace of Communism. He listed dozens of Communist shop stewards and members of union national executives, and their role in events like the UCS work-in, the seamen's strike, and strikes on London Transport. He pleased Communists by saying that Trotskyists 'are insignificant amateurs compared with the highly organized and well-entrenched Moscow-inspired CP.'

Lawson concluded: 'Any government may in time come to wonder whether a system of law which ... lends itself so readily to highly organised Communist exploitation, may not need further amendment.' In fact, by the time the government of which he was a part came to introduce such legislation, the Communist Party was a spent force and the trade union moderates well in control.

A second miners' strike in 1974 led to power cuts and a three-day week. Heath called a snap election in February on the issue 'Who

179

rules Britain?' The right-wing group Aims of Industry took full-page advertisements during the election telling voters that 'the Communists who figured so openly in recent industrial disputes ... want to destroy the system under which we live,' accompanied by a picture of a smiling mask in front of the face of Stalin, though Stalin had been dead for twenty-one years. 'Don't let the extremists wreck our freedom and our economy,' said the advertisement. Aims of Industry even called for a guerrilla campaign against left-wing unions: sit-ins at union headquarters, phone-ins to block their switchboards.

There was a determined attempt to link Labour with Communists, despite Harold Wilson's robust anti-Communism. Sir Richard Powell, director-general of the Institute of Directors, claimed that Britain owed its troubles to Communists, Wilson and women, in that order. Apparently socialists like Wilson encouraged Communists, and women voted socialists into power. The *Daily Telegraph* claimed: 'The Communist Party is leading the extremists in their attempt to penetrate the trade unions, manipulate industrial power and overthrow the democratic system.' Chapman Pincher in the *Daily Express* reported during the election campaign: 'A formidable vigilante group to help protect the nation against a Communist takeover has been quietly organized by former Service chiefs, senior ex-members of the secret service, and MI5 and leading business men.' Cabinet members 'are aware of the group's existence and know the names of some of the leaders.' One of them told Pincher: 'We are not Fascists. We are democratic Britons who put the nation's interests before those of Russia and its political agents.'

Britain's top Catholic, Cardinal Heenan, joined in. 'It is quite clear that some of the miners were determined on disruptive action,' he wrote in a pastoral letter to his diocese. To replace the present social system with Communism would be 'madness'. He begged Catholics to attend all meetings of their unions: 'The militants never miss a meeting.'

The voters decided that whoever did rule Britain, it was not to be Heath. Wilson returned to No. 10 and the new Employment Secretary, Michael Foot, settled with the miners. Foot was a significant choice for the job. As a man from the left of the Labour Party he was not about to forget that the Labour Party and the trade unions were brothers – at any rate as long as the big unions were run by people like his friend Jack Jones. And Harry Pollitt's old drinking companion had no problems about dealing with Communists.

By 1975 trade union leaders were seriously worried that their wage claims posed an inflationary threat to the survival of the Wilson government. Communists campaigned against a pay policy, and Ramelson used all his diplomatic skills to keep the TUC in line. But he ran into direct conflict with Jack Jones, and that was a battle Ramelson could not win. Jones, always in the past a determined opponent of pay policies, recognized, as he put it, that 'something further would have to be done to try to persuade in a voluntary way the trade unions to hold their wage claims within reason, otherwise we were going to have hyper-inflation ... and that was no good to the working people of this country.' He met Ramelson in the hall at that year's Trades Union Congress. 'Keep your fingers out of my union,' he growled. Ramelson, of course, did nothing of the kind – but he was also careful to avoid an irrevocable break with Jones. He knew the realities of power: he was unlikely to have much influence in the unions if he were not on speaking terms with the TGWU leader.

Jack Jones' soft voice and appearance conceal the toughness which saw him through two and a half years fighting in the International Brigade during the Spanish Civil War, and through fourteen years in the harshest and least forgiving job the trade union movement can offer. Only Jones could have delivered a pay policy. By the force of his personality and the transparent certainty of his convictions, Jones could take other unions and union members with him when the take-it-or-leave-it tones of traditional TGWU leaders would have fallen on deaf ears.

His partner in this exercise was the engineers' leader Hugh Scanlon, like Jones a left winger, closer to the CP than Jones, and, like Jones, convinced that inflation was going to do more damage to his members than any pay policy. The Wilson government needed a pay policy. Jones and Scanlon delivered a flat-rate £6 policy, with no increases at all for those earning over £8,500 a year.

When Harold Wilson resigned as Prime Minister in 1976, the Labour Party-TUC relationship continued to flourish. James Callaghan was closer to union leaders than any of his predecessors. He is the only Labour Party leader who was once a trade union official. In 1976 he was the only senior Labour figure who sounded like a trade union official. He was no intellectual, he appeared avuncular to the point of maddening complacency, and behind the scenes he was a fixer and a bit of a bully; to the average trade union official he was almost as good as one of their own.

But the Unions wanted a price for their support. The Alternative Economic Strategy, adopted by the TUC in 1977, was a Communist Party initiative, and was proposed at the TUC by one of Britain's best-known Communist trade unionists, Ken Gill, leader of the draughtsmen's union TASS. From a working-class Wiltshire background, Gill joined the CP in the early 1940s, forming a Communist cell at his grammar school. He has a strong Wiltshire accent, a deep voice and a face rather like an etching. In a profession which is drabber than most – trade union officials typically wear the greyest of crumpled grey suits – Gill's adventurous taste in shirts and ties was very noticeable.

For years Gill was the only Communist on the TUC general council. It was not easy, he says. 'They kept me off the NEDDY six [the TUC's inner cabinet] for years. When they ran out of excuses for this they played the feminist card. They said the NEDDY six could not be all male and put Brenda [Dean, the print union leader] on instead. Very neat. They did at last put me on the international committee as a quid pro quo for letting Frank Chapple on. Jack Jones said to me, we're letting you on because Frank's coming on.'

Briefly he was joined on the general council by other Communists such as Mick McGahey. Communists had never before had that sort of representation at the top of the trade union movement. But they had something they valued much more: a core of union leaders on the general council who, while not Communists, maintained close contact with Ramelson. They were people who felt comfortable with Communists, generally voted with Gill, had a high regard for Ramelson, listened to his advice on policy matters and were happy to be part of a left caucus which he organized. They included the public employees' leader Rodney Bickerstaffe, the seamen's Jim Slater, print union leader Bill Keys, Alan Sapper of the television technicians, Ken Cameron of the Fire Brigades Union and the tobacco workers' Doug Grieve.

The unions held the line on a second, and then a third, period of pay restraint. The government was able to offer some return in the form of legislation to help them defend their members. The first year of Jim Callaghan's premiership saw the lowest number of industrial disputes ever recorded. Inflation fell. Yet it was under Callaghan's leadership that the relationship between the Labour Party and the trade unions came dramatically and disastrously unstuck.

In 1978 the government was in its third year of wage restraint. Trade union general secretaries were making warning noises. Patience, they told Callaghan and his Chancellor of the Exchequer Denis Healey, was wearing thin. Jones and Scanlon, who had held the line for the government, retired that year. No one, except perhaps the government, thought that their successors would have the stature to hold the line. But it turned out to be worse than that. Even Jones could not hold it. At his last TGWU national conference the shop stewards, who owed their power to his leadership, used it to tear him apart. They ignored his prophetic warning that the beneficiaries of their rejection of pay policy would be Margaret Thatcher 'and all the ilk of privilege.'

Bill Keys, then the general secretary of the biggest print union, SOGAT, remembers vividly what he sees as the moment the relationship broke down. It was Autumn 1978, and Keys was in Downing Street with a small group of senior trade unionists to talk about pay policy. 'We were getting 20 per cent pay increases just to stand still. Jim was saying that we must reduce inflation. I said I'd fight for a wages policy, I'd fight for an 8 per cent policy. But Denis Healey said, "No, we've got to have nil inflation." I said: "You must be joking." Later we broke up and had a drink and I said to Albert Booth [who had succeeded Foot as Employment Secretary]: "You've just lost the next general election."'

Ken Gill remembers those meetings, too, though he says he was kept out of the key ones. He once had to telephone his office from 10 Downing Street, and while he was on the phone Denis Healey tapped him on the shoulder. He looked round and the Chancellor of the Exchequer grinned and said: 'Reporting back to King Street, Ken?'

If he had been, the voice at the end of the phone would have been a new one. Bert Ramelson retired in 1978 and Mick Costello took over the job he had always wanted – 'the most exciting job I have ever had,' he says now. He was the perfect man to carry on the Ramelson strategy – he had been a part of it, and talked of Communists influencing the Labour Party by 'participating in the democratic processes of their own unions.'

Gill claims that his opposition to another year of wage restraint brought warnings that he could be responsible for military action to enforce it, but he will not say where the warnings came from. 'They put Jack Jones under a lot of pressure that way and there were suspicious troop movements at Heathrow.'

Callaghan tried to impose a 5 per cent pay rise ceiling without the support of the unions, at which point the relationship between the Labour Party and the trade unions broke down in the most public and spectacular way. The winter of 1978–9 – the 'winter of discontent' – saw bitter strikes aimed directly at the policy of the government.

In 1979 came the débâcle no one wanted: not Jones and Scanlon, not Callaghan, and not Ramelson either. He had not spent a decade and more ensuring that left wingers took crucial decisions in trade unions just so that Margaret Thatcher could dismantle them. Labour's 1979 election defeat by a fundamentalist Conservative government led by Margaret Thatcher – no one yet realized quite how fundamentalist – was the most significant British political watershed since 1945.

After 1979 Labour and the unions changed in ways that Communists neither foresaw nor wanted. Communists were starting to lose control of the trade union left. The Communist Party in trade unions had come to stand for traditional trade union values, and these were not the flavour of the 'eighties, even on the left. There was a price to pay for respectability, and that price was to be outflanked on the left by the traditional enemy, the Trotskyists; by the 'entryists', the Militant Tendency; and by Labour's increasingly sharp-toothed left wing.

The Socialist Workers' Party tactic had been to set up a 'Rank and File organization' within each union. It was a misleading name, for the SWP was not remotely interested in the 'rank and file', only in those few members of it who supported the SWP. The aim was to convince union members that their interests were opposed to those of trade union leaders and officials. The mass of the workers, so the SWP claimed, were straining at the leash to unseat capitalism by industrial action, held back only by their bureaucratic trade union leaders.

To the SWP, Communist trade union officials were the worst of the lot, because they gave the working class the misleading impression that they were left wingers. The spirit of Class Against Class lived on in the SWP. And just as, in the 1930s, Class Against Class succeeded in fatally wounding the ILP but completely failed to build the Communist Party, so in the 1970s the SWP did great damage to Communist influence in the unions but failed to establish its own. The pages of the SWP paper *Socialist Worker* in the late 1970s read like the *Daily Worker* in the early 1930s, packed with indignant abuse for the 'Stalinist bureaucrats' who had betrayed this or that strike, and with hardly a mention of any opponents further to the right.

In each union where it had sufficient influence, the SWP inspired a 'rank and file' newspaper. There were about fifteen of them, mostly in white collar unions: *Hospital Worker*, *Journalists' Charter*, *Rank and File Teacher*. In a civil service union whose official journal was called *Red Tape* there was *Redder Tape*. These made frequent, and generally quite inaccurate, accusations against union leaders – especially Communist leaders – of fiddling expenses, of secret deals which benefited the union official but not his members, of high living at the expense of the members. With similar wild accusations coming both from the left and from right-wing national newspapers, union members could hardly be blamed if they started to think there must be some truth in them.

The SWP had power to damage others on the left, but that was all. By 1982 the number of rank and file newspapers had been reduced to six, and these six had about a third of the circulation they had enjoyed nine years earlier.

If Communists disliked the SWP, they loathed the Militant Tendency, an organization which probably damaged the CP as much as it damaged Labour. Founded in Liverpool in the 1950s by Ted Grant as the Revolutionary Socialist League, it was controlled strictly from the centre. According to its constitution, 'unlike the reformists, centrists and Stalinists, the Marxists decisively reject the theory of the Parliamentary road to socialism . . .'

It adopted the policy of 'entryism' – instructing its members to join the Labour Party and hide the fact that they were members of a conflicting organization. Some of its leading members became Liverpool city councillors in the early 1960s, leading eventually to a Militant-controlled council under Derek Hatton in the 1980s. In 1964 it founded its paper, *Militant*, and began the fiction that it had no members, only salespeople for the paper. By 1970 it controlled the Labour Party Young Socialists. It reserved its fiercest scorn for other Trotskyist sects and the CP – 'the anti-Marxists'. What set Militant apart, it claimed, was 'our understanding of all the myriad factors which determine the attitudes and moods of the workers at each stage.'

Labour's 1979 defeat was Militant's opportunity. Disappointment with the Wilson-Callaghan government made it hard for Labour leaders to hold the line against Militant. In the 1980s Militant was to play a leading part in ensuring the survival of the Conservative government. But it was not the key part. The credit for that went to the bizarre and destructive battle for control of the Labour Party which followed the 1979 defeat, in which neither Communists nor Trotskyists were key players. In fact, they were forced on to the sidelines by the supporters of a former cabinet minister, Tony Benn.

Labour's 1979 conference decided, against the wishes of Jim Callaghan, that the Labour Party leader and deputy leader would no longer be appointed by Labour MPs alone, but by an electoral college consisting of MPs, constituency parties and trade unions. The theory was that this would move the Party to the left. It was a victory for the Bennites, and not something which Communists wanted at all. They could hardly be seen opposing it, but it held all sorts of dangers for them. The CP did not want to be seen to be picking Labour leaders. It preferred to exercise influence without too much publicity. The Bennite system would inevitably attract unwelcome publicity to the way union block votes were cast, the way in which they were influenced by the CP, and the fact that Communist trade union leaders helped take key policy decisions in the Labour Party.

A special conference was arranged to decide the working details of the new system: what proportion of the votes would go to each of the three elements in the electoral college. Callaghan resigned before this conference. The Bennite left was furious. They wanted him to wait, so that the new leader was elected by the new machinery. Callaghan was determined that his successor would be elected by MPs alone, and he wanted Denis Healey to succeed him. But the MPs, already powerfully influenced by the Bennite power in their constituency parties, elected Michael Foot instead.

Foot brought in Jim Mortimer as Labour Party general secretary. Mortimer had as a young man been in the YCL. In the draughtsmen's union, later to become Ken Gill's TASS, where Communists were stronger than in any other union, he had been a trade union official whom they felt comfortable with. He then ran London Transport's industrial relations until Foot, as Employment Secretary, made him the first director of the Advisory Conciliation and Arbitration Service (ACAS), in 1974 – an inspired appointment, for no other candidate could carry the confidence of left-wing union leaders. Two of his closest friends were Bert Ramelson and Ken Gill. Yet such was the topsy-turvy world of Labour Party politics at that time that he found himself fighting a rearguard action on Foot's behalf against Labour's new left, the Bennites, over whom Communists had little influence.

Denis Healey, now deputy leader, was appalled at the appointment. '[Mortimer] had impressed everyone with a reasoned and powerful attack on the Militant Tendency at our Conference,' he wrote later. 'Few in his audience realized that he objected to them primarily because they were neo-Trotskyists, while he represented an older Marxist tradition.' Healey had lost the leadership to Foot largely because he had tried to enforce wage restraint while Chancellor of the Exchequer. 'As student Communists we often debated the question: who would do the dirty work under socialism? Years later I discovered that the answer was: Denis Healey.'

Mortimer, and a lot of Communists in the trade unions, were shocked at the behaviour of the Bennites during the years of the first Thatcher government from 1979 to 1983. Communists had a feel for trade unions. The Bennites seemed to want nothing from them except their block vote at Party conferences, and they were not at all squeamish about how they went about getting it.

At the special conference to decide the new voting system they manoeuvred union leaders into delivering a system in which 40 per cent of the votes for leader and deputy leader of the Labour Party came from the unions. Labour MPs and constituency Labour Parties had 30 per cent each. The Labour left then engaged in an arcane and bad-tempered debate about whether to run a candidate against Denis

Healey for the post of deputy leader of the Labour Party. The post itself had little or no power, but the new machinery needed to be 'tested'. Neil Kinnock thought this was 'a bit like Christmas morning when a kid's given a watch and starts taking it apart to see how it works.' But it was dangerous to argue against an election. Benn's coterie would at once accuse you of being anti-democratic.

For all his talk about democracy coming from the bottom, Benn knew that the people who mattered would be trade union leaders. Not only did they have 40 per cent of the vote; the unions' section of the vote was the only one which could be organized. One constituency Labour Party was hardly worth the effort of visiting for the sake of the tiny proportion of the vote that it could command, but a big trade union was very important indeed. The election, billed as an affirmation of grassroots power, was in fact to be the most public demonstration of the power of the block vote in the whole of the Party's history.

The six-month campaign centred on how the big unions were going to vote. It looked just like what it was: a fight for trade union patronage. Labour's popularity plummeted, and so did trade union membership. The election made the unions look like insolent power-brokers. Union leaders took no significant steps at all to protect their public image, or ensure the loyalty of their members. They seemed not to realize the damage the next few months would do them.

In a House of Commons committee room upwards of twenty unhappy Tribune MPs gathered for a series of anguished meetings about what to do. There was only one way. Another left winger must stand. Then they need not vote for Benn. Even better, they stood a good chance of getting Healey as deputy leader without the odium of having to vote for him. At first Eric Heffer agreed to stand. Now a veteran Labour politician, the former Communist loathed both Benn and his followers. But a weekend in his Liverpool constituency changed Heffer's mind. His constituency party were vehemently opposed to him standing against Benn. He returned to the House of Commons on Monday a changed man – quiet, thoughtful, almost shy, say colleagues who met him that day. Eventually the poison chalice was picked up by John Silkin.

Which voting system unions should use was presented as a matter of high principle. In reality, it was simply a matter of trying to work out which method favoured your own candidate, and then presenting that method as the only truly democratic method. In the white-collar union ASTMS, Clive Jenkins tried to deliver his union's block vote for Denis Healey. He knew that the executive committee could be persuaded to support Healey. So he argued that the executive committee was the only body that was truly representative of the membership. Benn supporters in ASTMS believed that if only they could get the issue to the annual conference, they would win. The conference, they therefore argued, was the only body which was truly representative of the membership. Exactly the reverse argument took place in the TGWU, where the Bennites believed that they had a better chance at the executive than at the conference. And all the CP's nightmares came true when the executive of the building workers' union UCATT took its voting decision. The headline in *The Sunday Times* the next day read HOW THREE TOP COMMUNISTS SWUNG 200,000 VOTES TO BENN.

Healey won narrowly. But it hardly mattered. For the Labour Party, the 1983 election was already as good as lost. Labour entered it exhausted from four years of internal struggle and with no election strategy. Jim Mortimer had to fall back on what he knew, and ran the election as though he were an old-fashioned Communist shop steward. He chaired press conferences from a seat in the middle of the platform, in the plonking style born of a lifetime of trade union meetings. One terrible day, when Foot was under fire, he said: 'At the campaign committee this morning we were all insistent that Michael Foot is the leader of the Labour Party and speaks for the Party and we support the manifesto of the Party.' In a long and distinguished career, Mortimer must have quelled dozens of rebellious meetings like that. 'Brothers and sisters, comrades, committee says Michael's leader and that's all there is to it, so let's not have any more of this argy-bargy.' In a press conference, it enabled unfriendly newspapers to speculate on a non-existent plot to depose the leader.

For the CP, a decade of carefully edging the unions leftwards had been thrown away by people who thought the revolution was going to come if only they could force through a few bureaucratic changes in Labour Party procedure. But by then most Communists were past caring. All their energies were going into their own internal battle, which dominated the 'eighties for them and eventually destroyed their Party.

189

12

The Awful Eighties

JOHN Gollan's successor, Gordon McLennan, was a small, square, dapper man of 50. Precise and methodical, he started by telling the press: 'I don't think my secretaryship will differ at all from Mr Gollan's, in the sense that I will be, along with other members of the executive, carrying out the policies laid down by the national Congress.' So it is easy to see why one young Communist thought him 'vain and pompous.' But it was not really that, more an overwhelming sense of responsibility and perhaps inadequacy at inheriting the mantle of Harry Pollitt – and of John Gollan, whom he calls 'kind, considerate, deep-thinking, a marvellous friend and comrade and adviser.' His successor, Nina Temple says: 'He had a great respect for the job of general secretary. He told me he had been given the Party in trust and had to pass it on in good condition.' Few such modest ambitions have been so crushingly denied.

McLennan grew up in a working-class district of Glasgow and qualified as an engineering draughtsman. He is very much a family man, devoted to his parents, his brothers, his wife and their four children, and an intensely private man. He was appointed partly for his administrative skills. Martin Jacques says: 'Gollan, who was really very arrogant, is thought to have said, "Right, we've got all the political problems sorted out, we just need an organizer to carry it out."' If that is true, it deserves a place among the great misjudgements of history alongside Neville Chamberlain's peace in our time.

As soon as the appointment was made Gollan told McLennan he wanted a private talk. He explained that for almost two decades, in absolute secrecy, the Party had been receiving cash from the Soviet Union, handed over in clandestine meetings between an embassy official and Gollan's deputy Reuben Falber. In recent years the sums had been drastically reduced, and the subsidy was now down from about £100,000 a year in the early 'sixties to about £14,000 a year. McLennan says he told Gollan he wanted it stopped, but it carried on, though McLennan claims he did not know this, for four more years until 1979. The following year the CP sold its biggest asset, its substantial headquarters in King Street, Covent Garden, bought in the 1920s with money donated secretly by Lenin. Lloyds Bank paid more than £1 million for the property and turned it into their Covent Garden branch. The CP moved into more modest premises in nearby St Johns Street.

Gaia Servadio described King Street in the *Evening Standard* shortly before its sale. Gone was the brisk self-confidence of the wartime years and the years of the Attlee government. Inside it was 'shabby and freezing cold, linoleum floors in pieces, typewriters archaic, secretaries few . . .' Spirits rose when a hidden microphone was found embedded in the walls, but MI5 was wasting its time: the CP was not worth bugging any more.

George Matthews, after fourteen years editing the *Morning Star*, was now back at King Street as publicity officer, swapping jobs with Tony Chater. Matthews and Chater were part of an unbroken tradition of appointing politicians rather than journalists to edit the paper. Chater had been a science lecturer in a further education college. He has a quiet, high-pitched voice and a formal manner. But Matthews, like Johnny Campbell and Bill Rust before him, became a journalist with an excellent reputation. Chater's view is that 'editing the paper is primarily a political job.' His appointment caused resentment which served to aggravate the sharpening political battle. In the 1940s and '50s, the chief sub-editor Allen Hutt believed his widely admired professional skill would ensure him the job, but it went instead to non-journalist Johnny Campbell and then George Matthews. In 1974, Sam Russell, who was foreign editor for more than thirty years from 1953 until he retired in 1984 (except for a short period as Moscow correspondent) felt the same, and says: 'People say, old Sam Russell's trouble is, he wanted to be editor. Damn right I did. I knew the trade. Communist Party leaders never completely trusted their own journalists. It was unforgivable. If it was a question of loyalty they couldn't teach me anything about loyalty. The paper looked like just the CP organ. If there was a Central Committee meeting that would be the front page lead story, no matter what else was going on in the world.'

Russell says Chater refused to print his stories from a trip to China in the mid-seventies saying they were anti-Soviet. 'Of course they were anti-Soviet, the Chinese were anti-Soviet,' says Russell. 'He made me interlard it with comments of mine which were pro-Soviet. This was his conception of journalism. But I've no doubt now that one of the motivating forces was large sums of money from Moscow, because Chater was shaking like a dog shitting razor blades, as Allen Hutt used to say.' Chater today does not remember the incident.

By 1980, when it moved offices, the CP had firmly sown the seeds of its own destruction. The Party now consisted of two camps engaged in mortal combat. The two camps were, by and large, the same people as in the days which followed the Soviet invasion of Czechoslovakia in 1968, but the battleground had shifted. The dispute over how you viewed the Soviet Union had been relegated to a supporting role. It had not gone away, of course. The Eurocommunists still found it useful on quiet days to set up shouts of 'tankie' and 'Stalinist' and received equally rich abuse in reply, but the central point at issue now was a seemingly arcane one. The followers of Tony Chater and Mick Costello thought of themselves as class warriors first and foremost, believing that the class struggle was and always should be the centre of the Party's work. The followers of Martin Jacques wanted a 'broad democratic alliance' of the working class, women, gays and ethnic minorities, and were less keen on trade unions. Eurocommunists and class warriors now had their teeth firmly embedded in each others' throats.

No term of abuse was too dreadful, no tactic was unjustifiable, no insult too cruel. Before it was over, old friends would part forever in bitterness, internal ballots would be rigged, comrades would break each others' noses, accusations would be made which libel laws prevent me from repeating. Was this the party Palme Dutt had laboured to create: a party, as he put it during the Second

World War, of '... merciless ruthless clearing that results in absolute certainty and conviction of every Party member ... Every responsible position in the Party must be occupied by a determined fighter for the line ...'

In this sort of battle everyone has to take sides and every issue becomes another battlefield. In 1979 when industrial organizer Mick Costello launched a campaign to win positions of 'trust and understanding' in the trade unions from which it could 'conduct agitation and give leadership', the outsider might think this was part of the CP's day-to-day work, a continuation of the highly successful Ramelson strategy. Insiders knew it was a class warrior strike. Costello's message was that the Party was getting too involved in peripheral campaigns – feminism, anti-racism, the gay movement – and needed to return to its industrial roots.

As Mrs Thatcher stormed to victory in the 1979 election and launched the most radical right-wing programme ever seen in Britain, the battle for the soul of the Labour Party began in earnest. Communists had always wanted to win that battle, but when it came, they were so busy lining up their tanks to fight each other that they were unable to play any effective part. In 1979 Communists were preoccupied with yet another report on Inner Party Democracy, a matter that seemed comparatively trivial outside CP circles.

Yet this, if ever, was the long-awaited crisis of capitalism. Output in manufacturing fell by 14 per cent between 1979 and 1983, masked by large surpluses from North Sea oil and gas. There was urban violence of what Palme Dutt would have called unparalleled intensity in Brixton and Toxteth. As the new government's trade union laws began to bite, there were violent confrontations between police and strikers. Left-wing councils, with policies of which Communists broadly approved, were elected to run London, Liverpool, Manchester and Sheffield. Unemployment rose sharply, easily passing the one million mark which many people had once believed would signal a revolution. The gap between rich and poor widened. And through it all, Thatcherism prospered, Communism declined, and those parts of British society of which Communists approved – the trade unions, the welfare state – were systematically dismantled.

Thatcher succeeded where Heath failed – Bert Ramelson said

just before he died – because 'the Tories learned from their mistakes. Heath's industrial policy had everything in it at one go. So it failed. Since 1979 the Tories have taken it step by step, salami-style, cut a bit here, cut a bit there. It's a good strategy.' Indeed, it is one that Communists pioneered: Rakosi in Hungary in the 1940s called his method of getting power for Communists the 'salami strategy'.

The CP's performance in the 1979 general election was even worse than in 1974. Membership was still falling fast. Class warriors thought the problems were caused by the Eurocommunist policy of pursuing a 'broad democratic alliance' with all progressive groups, of criticizing the Soviet Union, and of not devoting enough priority to the unions. Eurocommunists thought the problems were caused by the old Leninist ways, in particular democratic centralism, and by being too mild in their criticism of the Soviet Union.

What was McLennan to say when the Soviet Union invaded Afghanistan, or a military dictatorship took over the running of Poland? Either defending or condemning was fraught with danger. His statements on both these issues infuriated the class warriors. In Moscow in 1981 in his speech to the Soviet Communist Party Congress he condemned his hosts for trying to dictate policy to Communists abroad. The CP had travelled a long way since Harry Pollitt said the Soviet Union could do no wrong.

Marxism Today became the rallying point for Eurocommunists after Martin Jacques took it over in 1977. It became one of the left's few publishing successes of the 1980s. It adopted a modern design and even started to appear on the shelves of W. H. Smith. Every issue it touched became a battleground between Euro-communists and class warriors. In 1982 it ran an article by a Liverpool University academic, Tony Lane, accusing shop stewards of corruption and of being on a trade union gravy train. They were the 'new working class élite', sitting 'cheek by jowl with managers' and sharing in the 'expense account syndrome'. 'The franchise of perks and fiddles has been widened,' Lane said.

It was to prove the match on the blue touch paper. At 2 pm the day the Lane issue appeared, Mick Costello, from his office a few doors away from Jacques' office, telephoned Tony Chater at the *Morning Star*. They agreed to meet at a nearby Wimpy Bar. This meeting later became mythologized, in the way that Communists since Pollitt and Dutt were alive have mythologized their doings, as the Wimpy Bar Meeting. Over the garish plastic table, the two men took a decision which was to deepen the split in the Party beyond repair. 'Mick thought the article would isolate our comrades in the TUC,' says Chater. 'He wanted to put a statement in the *Star*. Everyone ought to know this was not the view of Communists.' The statement said *Marxism Today* was helping the Tory government to 'undermine the self-confidence of the working class.' Costello and the Communist trade unionists had spent most of their lives defending shop stewards from this sort of accusation when levelled by right-wing newspapers and Trotskyists. Ken Gill says: 'This was the watershed, when the Party fell into the hands of those who had no working-class base.'

Jacques claims that the fuss came as a surprise to him, and that there was a sinister sub-text to it. He had also published an article by Roy Medvedev about lack of democracy in the Soviet Union, and that, he claims, is what really got up Costello's nose. The Soviet Communist Party condemned this article, and he thinks Costello wanted to follow the Soviet line. Jacques calls his old Manchester University chum Costello 'a very hard, bitter Stalinist.' 'They needed to force a breach between *Marxism Today* and the Communist Party. The card they had to play was the anti-intellectual anti-yuppie card.' He told McLennan that if the executive supported Costello he would resign. McLennan found a form of words designed to paper over the cracks, and the executive narrowly agreed it.

Never had the Party's divisions been so open. Pollitt and Dutt would have been scandalized. Here were the Party's two publications in the most public possible confrontation. McLennan was furious with Costello for not consulting him and with Jacques for printing the Lane article with no prior warning. He thought the piece 'very inadequate and poor.' From that moment on the knives were out on both sides for all to see.

A few weeks later Costello came into McLennan's office to hand in his resignation. He explained that following the breakup of his marriage he needed to be more often at home with his children. McLennan said: 'The one thing you mustn't do, Mick, is go back to the *Morning Star*.' He was furious when he heard this was just what Costello did, and thought it was part of a plot.

It was not just the Communist Party which seemed bent on self-destruction. The whole of the British left appeared to be engaged in a hideous battle to strangle itself. Martin Jacques says the CP split 'was the announcement of a split in the rest of the labour movement too.' The Labour Party's ghastly campaign for the deputy leadership was followed by a series of set-piece confrontations between left and right. The New Communist Party, the 1977 pro-Soviet breakaway from the CP, was now regularly purging its tiny membership to maintain ideological purity and surviving on handouts from East European countries dissatisfied with the CP's critical attitude. In 1985 the Workers' Revolutionary Party accused its leader Gerry Healy, now in his seventies, of 'sexual debauchery' – using young female members of his party as sexual playthings – and the Party split in two. The International Marxist Group was split between 'right wingers' who supported Tony Benn and Arthur Scargill, and purists who considered Benn and Scargill too reformist.

It was almost as though Thatcher's 1979 election victory had caused a collective madness throughout the left. There are those who think that the security services, emboldened by the Tory victory, placed *agents provocateurs* in all the left-wing organizations that mattered. Paranoid perhaps, but the security services have a history of keeping tabs on left-wing politicians. Several class warriors think a particular Eurocommunist was an MI5 agent, and several Eurocommunists think it was a particular class warrior, and it is in the nature of spying that they are almost certainly both wrong.

Michael Foot and Gordon McLennan found themselves leading parties which were visibly disintegrating under them. Both were called weak because they could not hold their parties together. But no leader can hold a party together if the members are determined not to allow them to do so.

In the second Conservative election victory in 1983 Communists fared worse than ever. In the world outside the CP Margaret Thatcher seemed unstoppable. In the CP Martin Jacques seemed unstoppable. Each month he printed something to get up the noses of the class warriors. He printed what right-wing people thought of Marxism, such as columnist Peregrine Worsthorne, the director general of the Institute of Directors, and Frank Chapple. He was the subject of admiring profiles in *The Financial Times* and *The Sunday Times*, where he called his critics 'pathetic'. Jacques was now in his mid-30s, balding, slightly built, with a thick moustache and boundless self-confidence. He called himself a 'democratic marxist'. The class warriors believed he ought not to be in the Communist Party at all.

That, secretly, was what Jacques now thought too. After the Tony Lane affair he gave up all hope for the Communist Party, but stayed in it because he needed its subsidy to continue publishing *Marxism Today*. 'I now felt the CP was unreformable. Once the rupture took place the CP had no future. I still collaborated with the people who wanted to change it, but from 1982–83 the organization had had it. It was very small, getting smaller, split down the middle, it had lost its trade union base. You could see it shrinking before your eyes.' No one knew he believed this at the time, and it came as a nasty shock to some of his comrades. Nina Temple, as unhappy as Jacques himself, stayed on only out of loyalty to Jacques. Making *Marxism Today* virtually editorially independent of the Party had needed 'much machiavellian skill' he says, and it is quite believable.

The Eurocommunists rallied round *Marxism Today*, the class warriors rallied round the *Morning Star*, and the two sides started to be identified with the two editors, Jacques and Chater. McLennan tried desperately to reconcile the two sides, but in the end came to the conclusion that if it was to have any future, the Party must move in a Eurocommunist direction – though he never wanted to move as far or as fast as Jacques. Quite why he sided with Jacques when his natural home was probably with the other side we cannot be sure. Partly he thought it was the best way to preserve the Party. But he may have been influenced by personal factors. His son Greg, as an undergraduate at Bristol University, was taught by Jacques. McLennan felt Jacques had given his son both friendship and intellectual stimulus. 'Through Greg he began to find a way of understanding people like me,' says Jacques. McLennan once confessed that without Jacques Greg might have caused his father the ultimate shame, and become a Trotskyist.

But McLennan discovered to his horror that he could not control Chater. The idea, which had seemed so clever in 1946, of distancing the paper from the Party by making it responsible to a front

197

organization, the People's Press Printing Society (PPPS), suddenly exploded in McLennan's face. Legally, if Chater could keep the support of PPPS shareholders, he could do whatever he wanted, whether McLennan liked it or not. Chater announced that he would take orders from the PPPS and not the Party executive.

So in 1984 the battleground shifted to the meetings of the PPPS. The Party demanded Chater's dismissal and the PPPS refused to provide it. Ken Gill puts it this way: 'The *Morning Star* was not the organ of the Communist Party. They behaved as though it was and ordered us to sack the editor. If they had said to Communists on a trade union executive, get rid of your general secretary, that would have been an unwarranted interference in the affairs of the union.' But if he had agreed with the line the Party was taking, Gill would have been the first to insist that the paper reflected it.

McLennan and other CP leaders tried to make sure their supporters were elected to the PPPS management committee. He instructed Party members to vote for them – a binding instruction under the rules of democratic centralism. Circulars poured out of CP headquarters telling members exactly how to use their votes in all conceivable circumstances. They produced a monthly magazine, *Focus*, which devoted most of its pages to furious attacks on the *Morning Star* and instructions on what was necessary to defeat the Chaterite enemy at the PPPS. *Focus* readers wrote angry letters to the *Morning Star*, Tony Chater suppressed them, and *Focus* published them to show that Chater was indulging in censorship. One issue of *Focus* promised on its front cover the tantalising prospect of 'Martin Jacques' full EC report – a *Focus* exclusive!' Apparently the *Morning Star* had distorted Jacques' report. McLennan wrote to the *Morning Star* saying so. His letter was, of course, suppressed, and joined the long list of suppressed letters which appeared only in *Focus*.

It was not, therefore, surprising that hundreds of bad-tempered people, not all of them Communists, turned up for the regional meetings of the PPPS that year. These meetings were crowded, turbulent and sometimes violent. Five hundred people went to the Scottish meeting at Woodside Hall in Glasgow. There were fights, one class warrior was head-butted and had his jaw broken, there was an attempt to rush the platform, and the business was suspended. When the votes were counted the class warriors emerged triumphant with a working majority on the management committee. At the London meeting class warriors recall McLennan running up and down the aisles organizing his votes. But Chris Myant, McLennan's candidate for editor to replace Chater, recalls: 'They were hissing and booing at Gordon, shouting traitor, all sorts of things. It was a generation which came through 1956 and Gordon was part of it and was identified as working class, so they were saying he should be on their side, not siding with those young intellectuals. He was subject to bitter and frightening abuse.' Chater, he says, hated McLennan by now – 'I found it frightening that someone could summon up that much hatred for Gordon.'

As a result, the former *Morning Star* editor George Matthews, now 67 and retired, had to cut down his visits to the opera. Matthews, an opera enthusiast, had taken on the unpaid job of opera critic. You cannot buy many opera seats on a *Morning Star* pension, but the paper's critic got free seats. After speaking against Chater at a PPPS meeting he was fired and told never to enter the building again. Chater said that whenever Matthews wanted to cause trouble in the office he wrote an opera review and brought it round by hand. The same claim was made when firing the 74-year-old science correspondent, the paper's former deputy editor Bill Wainwright. Chater now refused to print the Party's statements. CP headquarters issued a statement headlined MORNING STAR NOT TO CARRY COMMUNIST PARTY STATEMENT which oozed with impotent rage.

The battle for the *Morning Star* became oddly linked with the battle for the left-wing Labour weekly *Tribune*. This started in 1982 when Labour leader Michael Foot recruited the long-standing editor Dick Clements to run his office at Westminster. The paper's staff forced the appointment of one of Benn's advisers, Chris Mullin, in Clements' place. The break from the past twenty years was very sudden. One week the paper broadly supported the Tribune group and Foot's leadership; the next it opposed Foot and campaigned to smash apart the Tribune group, which it said had proved its unfitness to carry the banner of the left by its failure to support Benn, and was full of hopeless reactionaries like Foot.

The sharp-toothed young men round Chris Mullin and Tony Benn reached the bizarre conclusion that the *Morning Star* and *Tribune* battles were linked because they were both about press freedom. So Victor Schonfield of the Campaign for Labour Party Democracy wrote to his members with shares in PPPS asking them to support Chater just as they supported Mullin. In fact, what Chater and Schonfield cared about even more than press freedom was having their respective papers take a line of which they approved. But the Bennite intervention certainly swung crucial votes Chater's way.

It was an odd irony that in its death agony the CP at last realized one of its dreams: to be right at the heart of Labour Party and trade union politics, with Labour politicians and non-Communist trade union leaders becoming deeply involved in its affairs. On the class warrior side there were Tony Benn and his supporters as well as trade union leaders whose views on many issues were close to those of the Communists. These included miners' leader Arthur Scargill; Alan Sapper, leader of the film and television technicians' union; Fire Brigade Union leader Ken Cameron; Barbara Switzer, Ken Gill's deputy and a member of the Labour Party national executive though her views were indistinguishable from Gill's; and the leader of the train drivers' union, Derrick Fullick. There were also the remnants of some of the Trotskyist groups. For the first time ever a Labour politician, Tony Benn, attacked Communists for being too right wing. On the Eurocommunist side there was the Labour Co-ordinating Committee, which was close to Neil Kinnock, who became Labour leader in 1983. Ideas floated in *Marxism Today* helped shape Kinnock's policies in the run-up to the 1987 general election.

The battles for *Tribune* and for the *Morning Star* assumed all the characteristics of holy wars. The two papers constantly carried detailed and bitter invective about the enemy. *Tribune* now read a little like the first few issues of the *Daily Worker* in the early 1930s, in the heart of the Class Against Class period when it could not find space to attack the Conservative Party because it was full of attacks on the ILP.

Chater made a series of trips to Moscow to make sure his guaranteed sales continued. The affairs of Communist parties in English-speaking countries were now watched over by an increasingly troubled English Desk in Moscow, and there Yevgeni Lagutin assured Chater that the lifeline would not be cut off. Moscow would continue to buy 12,000 copies a day, paid for quarterly in advance.

After the PPPS meetings the battleground moved to the London District Congress, controlled by the class warriors under the leadership of a print trade union official, Mike Hicks. It was the Party's biggest district and the votes of the London branches would be crucial when it came to the national Congress. Both sides strained every sinew to win a majority. The class warriors invented members so as to boost the representation of branches controlled by their supporters, and the executive gave instructions that no decisions should be taken. McLennan attended the Congress to ensure that these instructions were obeyed, and sat beside Hicks.

After a long procedural wrangle revolving mostly around the meaning of the term 'next business', McLennan rose from his chair and said: 'All those who support the Communist Party of Great Britain will now leave the hall with me.' He walked out, followed by about half the meeting. The names of those who stayed were noted and many of them were later expelled from the Party. So began the great purges. 'It was the biggest purge, relative to its membership, that any Communist Party anywhere in the world has ever conducted,' says Hicks. 'Whole branches disappeared overnight. Thank heaven they didn't have the power to execute us.'

Hicks was the first to get his letter expelling him from the CP. Over the next year or so expulsions came thick and fast, cutting a great swathe through the top layer of the Party, especially its trade union leaders. Ken Gill, general secretary of the draughtsmen's union TASS and about to become chairman of the TUC, easily the CP's most prestigious and powerful member, was expelled – an extraordinary irony, for Party leaders from Pollitt to Ramelson dreamed of having a TUC president in their ranks, and when for the first time the Party achieved this, it promptly expelled him. He and Chater were expelled for promoting candidates for the PPPS management committee who were not approved by the Party's Executive Committee. Top officials from the engineering, building and tobacco workers' trades unions were expelled. So was the *Morning Star*'s business manager Mary Rosser. The purge did not respect academics: it included John Foster, one of the Party's leading historians. Foster's branch, Govan, was expelled *en masse* for refusing to accept his expulsion. The three full-time London staff were fired from their jobs then expelled from the Party. Twenty-two people were expelled for their part in inventing 'ghost' members before the London District Congress. The *Morning Star* carried bitter attacks on McLennan and Jacques. The Party was slaughtering itself.

Kevin Halpin, one of the Party's key industrial militants, one of those who in 1956 tried to propose a compromise that would minimize the damage to the Party, and who later chaired the Liaison Committee for the Defence of Trade Unions, says: 'We wanted to stay and fight the right-wing opportunist position. We had a good chance of winning the Party. If we had been in a majority we would not have been expelling people.' He managed to hold on until 1988, when he resigned to join Mike Hicks and the *Morning Star* group in forming the Communist Party of Britain.

The CP was now two parties at war with each other. Why not face reality and split? The answer was the one thing no one ever talked about: real estate. The CP might now be living in reduced circumstances, but it was not poor. The Euros were not willing to see the class warriors walk off with the valuable Farringdon Road building which housed the *Morning Star*. The class warriors were even less willing to see the Euros get away with the much more substantial assets owned by the Party itself: offices, businesses set up to facilitate trade with the Soviet Union, a substantial share in Progressive Tours (the specialists in travel to Communist countries). The amounts at stake ran into millions, but no one mentioned the sordid business of money. That was the culture of the Party. Discussion of money and administrative matters was seen as a diversion from issues of politics and ideology.

The Eurocommunists won the battle for the November 1984 Congress and called a special Congress for May 1985 at Hammersmith Town Hall. They won that too, and the expulsions continued. These two Congresses were extraordinary events by anyone's standards. With so many of Chater's allies expelled, the class warriors' banner was carried by the faction called Straight Left, which had so far survived the purges. At the Congress it produced a daily account of proceedings called *Congress Truth*. This was banned, and stewards searched delegates' briefcases to check that they were not carrying copies. One of the Straight Left delegates smuggled *Congress Truth* into the hall in her baby's pram.

The class warriors won the PPPS the following month, even though the Eurocommunists organized coachloads of supporters for the meetings. Thus the Eurocommunists lost their last chance to keep control of the paper which had been the Party's voice for more than fifty years.

Both sides had a brief glimpse of the future as they watched events in the Spanish Communist Party. It split in two, with a pro-Soviet party and a Eurocommunist party, the Eurocommunists then ditching the veteran leader Santiago Carillo. Tony Chater told McLennan from the microphone at the Congress: 'You have gone down on your knees before this minority, Gordon, and it won't be long before they kick you upstairs and treat you like Carillo in Spain.'

'It is like a play in which every single character is miscast,' wrote Martin Linton in the *Guardian*, 'with the Eurocommunists who have long campaigned for more freedom and tolerance crying for the expulsion of sectarians, and the hardliners, for long the advocates of strict discipline and democratic centralism, appealing for justice against the autocratic rule of the executive.' Both sides, of course, were acting in direct opposition to the principles they claimed to stand for. The Eurocommunists used the machinery of democratic centralism, which they opposed, to dislodge the class warriors, and the class warriors, who approved of democratic centralism, used a legal technicality to defy policy decisions taken according to the rules of democratic centralism.

The CP kept its delusions of grandeur to the last. It set up special vetting procedures for membership, saying it feared infiltration. It demanded that members promise allegiance to the Party constitution and to conference decisions. It refused to re-register members at the end of the year if it considered them suspect – a technique previously only used by East European Communist parties to get rid of Eurocommunists. And it made extensive use of the very Stalinist Rule 22, which allowed the executive to dissolve whole branches and make their members re-apply for membership.

All this was going on at the same time as what was arguably the most important industrial dispute of the twentieth century: the miners' strike of 1984–5. It should have been a time when Communists came into their own with a cause round which they could unite, a major event in which the Communist Party could be centre stage, and its view mattered. It turned instead into another stick with which class warriors and Eurocommunists could beat each other.

Everything the Party held dear was at stake in the twelve months of the strike. The National Union of Mineworkers was the union on which the Communists had rested most hope and put in most effort. President Arthur Scargill was a former Communist and was still close to the Party. Vice-president Mick McGahey was probably the most respected Communist in Britain.

Conservative governments had long been wary of the miners. R. A. Butler recalled a telephone call from the then Prime Minister Winston Churchill in the early 1950s. 'He rang me up at 2.30 one morning and said: "I thought you'd like to know we've settled with the miners." "Oh, really, Prime Minister," I said. "On whose terms?" "On theirs, of course," he said. "Dammit, you've got to have electric light."' Butler added: 'If I'd been looking after Ted Heath, I'd never have let him have that confrontation with the miners. Baldwin always said there were two institutions you couldn't possibly fight: the National Union of Mineworkers and the Pope.' But in 1984 the Prime Minister, Margaret Thatcher, saw defeating the miners as an essential step towards curbing over-mighty trade unions.

The impact of the miners' strike on British Communism was enormous. Triggered by the closure of a Yorkshire pit in March 1984, it was over pit closures and redundancies. For the miners, spring was the worst possible time to start a coal strike: they would have to keep it going all the way through the summer before there was any prospect of having an affect on energy supply.

Scargill persuaded the NUM executive that it was not necessary to ballot the miners. McGahey asked the Communist Party to support this decision. Although this was given without a single dissenting voice, it was later to become a point of bitter debate inside the Party. It did the strike great harm. About one in five miners worked throughout, and as Mick McGahey now says, 'other union leaders who wanted to help us had to face the question from their members: why should we sacrifice our jobs when 20 per cent of the miners are producing coal?'

McGahey has a gravelly voice that sounds as though it starts deep in the pit of his stomach and is filtered through thick, dense layers of coal dust and scotch: which it is, for he is most often to be found in front of a half and half – a half of bitter and a large whisky – dispensing trade union wisdom and earthy humour. Today, in his late sixties, he has chronic bronchitis and emphysema, the legacy of a hard youth down the mines and a lifetime of heavy smoking.

He is a sociable, emotional man whose weaknesses are all on display. Tie never quite done up, shave never quite completed satisfactorily, glasses perched at an odd angle to his head, McGahey is nonetheless a shrewd and thoroughly professional negotiator. Born in 1925, his mother was a Catholic and his father a foundation member of the CP who was thrown out of work for his part in the 1926 general strike and had to travel from Scotland to Kent to find a mine which would take him on, returning to Scotland in 1933. McGahey's was a hard and poverty-stricken childhood in an intensely political home.

From the start the strike did not go the NUM's way. Pitched battles between police and miners became the staple diet of television news. Face-saving formulae were to be had but Scargill would have none of them. As early as June the Coal Board's deputy chairman Jim Cowan perceptively observed that 'the Communist Party is ready to settle' but Scargill was not. Cowan started to prepare a peace formula. McGahey knew when a dispute was about to go sour on him, but he would not say so publicly unless he could bring Scargill with him, and Scargill was adamant. Communist leaders were sure the miners' leader was heading for an appalling defeat. There was a fierce private row between Gordon McLennan and Scargill, and the Party leadership in desperation decided to drag Bert Ramelson out of retirement. Ramelson was Scargill's mentor, the man who organized the election machinery which had made him Yorkshire miners' president, who taught him about flying pickets and gave him the springboard to the national presidency. If Scargill would listen to anyone, it was Ramelson. Anyone accusing Ramelson of betrayal would feel pretty foolish. Ramelson wrote a careful appreciation of the situation and took it personally to Scargill. Scargill stopped reading after the first few lines, threw it on the floor and accused Ramelson of betrayal.

Negotiations dragged lazily on through the summer. Scargill told his members: 'The sacrifices and the hardships have forged a unique commitment among our members. They will ensure that the NUM wins this most crucial battle ... Together, we cannot fail.' McGahey knew that they could. Unfortunately for him, the Prime Minister was just as likely as Arthur Scargill to talk in extravagant, confrontationist language. Describing Scargill as 'the enemy within' she boosted his popularity among his members and other trade unionists overnight. Miners rushed to buy T-shirts with THE ENEMY WITHIN proudly emblazoned on the front. How could McGahey move against a leader whom Mrs Thatcher had attacked in those terms? How could a Communist keep his credibility and self-respect if he failed to support such a leader?

The Soviet Union provided money to help the strike and feed the miners, and gave miners' families holidays by the Black Sea, just as it had done in 1926. But as winter began it became plain that the strike was collapsing. In January Bill Keys, the print union leader who had always been close to the CP, opened a private channel with the government through William Whitelaw and went to Edinburgh to see McGahey. They took enormous care that their meeting would not be noticed, either by the press or by McGahey's increasingly paranoid president, and met in a tiny, bare room in Edinburgh's Graphic Club. It was owned by Keys' union and he had given instructions that no one should know they were there. It was unheated and the freezing temperature did nothing to raise their spirits. They both chain smoked and kept their overcoats on.

McGahey was bitterly critical of Scargill. The bones of a deal were discussed. Keys went back to London to see Whitelaw while McGahey talked privately to the NCB's industrial relations director Ned Smith. But the deal leaked and Mrs Thatcher, now scenting total victory, vetoed it. In mid-February Keys witnessed 'an amazing incident between Arthur and Mick. Mick saying that he will chain Arthur's mouth up for three years when this is all over.' It is the only recorded moment when McGahey betrayed what he was feeling. On 1 March 1985, with 95,000 miners back at work, the NUM surrendered.

Ten thousand miners were arrested during the strike. 1000 people were injured and three killed. 100 pits closed, 100,000 jobs were lost, and the NUM was virtually bankrupted and fatally split, with a breakaway union in Nottinghamshire. Scargill told his members: 'The greatest achievement is the struggle itself.' At any other time Communists would have greeted this with contempt as an absurd piece of ultra-leftism. But Scargill was now a totem for the class warriors, and could not be dispensed with.

While the strike was on, Communists kept up a pretence that they were united behind Scargill. The divisions were out in the open within days of the return to work. Quickly Pete Carter, who had replaced Costello as the CP's industrial organizer, produced a document saying that the miners were crushingly defeated, that mass picketing was mistaken, that the NUM should have balloted its members. It was so strongly critical of Scargill that the CP suppressed it, and today McLennan talks as though the divisions never existed. 'After the strike there was a discussion – Mick and I, Arthur and Pete Carter – about how to win unity of the miners in the post-strike situation,' he says blandly. Those four certainly met, but the meeting was much less friendly than McLennan would have us believe.

McGahey even today refuses to endorse Carter's criticisms. But he does not exactly refute them either. He told me: 'When you're in a class battle with the full offensive of the enemy against you and the bullets flying around, it's a luxury to sit back and analyse. I believe, and I accept my responsibility in this, that we underestimated the Conservative government's determination to use the state machine against us. In order to dismember the welfare state they had to break the trade union movement, and they needed to break the miners first.'

Eurocommunists complained that the *Morning Star* gave too much space to Scargill. Class warriors said the Party leadership did not give the miners enough help. And Scargill himself denounced Carter and *Marxism Today* for 'vilifying' the NUM leadership and 'compromising with the class enemy.' He was making sure that loyalty to Scargill would become a firm item in the ideological lexicon of at least one section of the Party.

Scargill was one of many top-rank trade union leaders who had been through the CP and still felt close to it and grateful for the training it had given them. Although no longer a member, he saw himself as a better Communist than many who remained in the Party. In 1956 he supported the Soviet Union over Hungary; he objected when Soviet authorities decided to move Stalin's body out of the famous mausoleum in Red Square where it had lain for decades; he objected when they changed the name of

Stalingrad. He told the *Observer* after the strike that his father was a Communist: 'Not the Eurocommunist variety, not the New Realist variety, but the real Communist who wants to see capitalism torn down and replaced by a system where people own and control the means of production, distribution and exchange ... I'm more passionately in support of that view now than I was then.' He left because he did not like Party discipline. There was a left caucus on the NUM executive, and he made use of it when it supported what he wanted to do and ignored it at other times. Communists did not work that way. They were loyal to collectively taken decisions. Scargill expects loyalty from others; he does not give it.

Scargill, like many union leaders in the 'sixties and 'seventies, needed the CP machine to fight elections for him. His biographer Paul Routledge describes his relationship with the Party as 'a teenage passion that cooled as he grew to manhood and found something more worthy of his ardour: his own destiny as the revolutionary class warrior. But even after the estrangement he would still ask favours of his first love, and she, fool that she was, would oblige in the cause of "left unity".' And she suffered dreadfully for her willingness to oblige. Scargill prepared a battleground over which Eurocommunists and class warriors could beat each other to death.

It was the downside of the Ramelson strategy. In Harry Pollitt's day the CP told Communist union leaders what to do. Ramelson recognized that union leaders knew best what to do in their own unions, and left them alone. Scargill was an extreme example of a union leader using the CP caucus as an election machine without giving anything in return.

Arthur Scargill is an extraordinary man. Ask other union leaders about him, and their eyes go misty and if they trust you they will happily spend the rest of the afternoon telling you their theories about what motivates him and why anyone listens to him. It is something they have thought about a lot. 'You move away from people like Arthur when they start boasting to you in saloon bars,' says John Edmonds, general secretary of one of Britain's biggest unions, the General Municipal and Boilermakers' Trade Union (GMB). 'You know the sort of chap who's always telling you how he put one over the estate agent or his neighbour? A lot of people like that go through life believing their own publicity. Generally

208

they're kept away from any sort of power. When they get power, it's disastrous. After the strike was over, Arthur was telling stories about his victories.

'But, politically, he wasn't a one-off. He represented a serious strand of thinking of part of the trade union movement. That is the strand that says working people will never win anything except by industrial struggle. Even regrouping is dangerous because it weakens the resolve of the working class.'

Bill Keys wrote in his diary the day the miners went back: 'One man and one man alone personified the miners throughout the dispute. It was unquestionably a role he sought and abused ... His rigidity in believing that he and he alone knew what was best set the cornerstone for defeat early on. He attached himself to a belief, and never was he prepared to change his opinion, irrespective that the circumstances that had helped him to form his original views had dramatically altered. Months into the dispute he remained convinced that the coal board were wrong about coal stocks, and that General Winter would come to his rescue ...

'It would be wrong to blame just Scargill, for after all he had a national executive. Here is the greatest dilemma of this whole dispute. Constantly throughout the dispute I would be told by case-hardened officials that they were unhappy at the manner in which the dispute was being carried out. It was not me they should have been telling, it was their executive colleagues ...' The concept of left unity had been hammered into left-wing miners' leaders by the CP. Scargill's achievement was to turn the concept of left unity into an obligation to go along with everything he said.

His defenders come from the CP's class warriors. Ken Gill wrote in the *Guardian*: 'The NUM leaders gave courageous and essentially correct leadership during the strike ... The Labour movement is in a stronger position than at any time since the Falklands war.' Jim Mortimer, now retired and increasingly free with his pro-Communist views, told Paul Routledge: 'Arthur Scargill embodies all the fighting spirit and militancy and solidarity of the mining tradition. His contribution has been a positive one.'

As negotiators themselves, Gill and Mortimer were always careful and professional. You cannot imagine them leading their members to the edge of a steep precipice and then urging them to jump off and be dashed on the unsympathetic rocks below with the rousing battlecry 'One more heave, brothers, victory is round the corner'. It is hard to resist the conclusion that, if Scargill had not become a symbol in the Communist Party's internal power struggle, Ken Gill might have denounced him for ultra-leftism.

The coal board's industrial relations director, Ned Smith, offered Paul Routledge a more down-to-earth view. 'He could put a case across very well indeed. But once his brief was finished, if the answer was no, Arthur was buggered because he wasn't a negotiator. What he said was right and had to be accepted.'

By 1986 the Communist Party was ready to embrace the extraordinary logic of the new position into which the miners' strike had forced its Eurocommunist majority. The Party had said that the biggest and most heroic strike for sixty years was a mistake: called at the wrong time, run with startling tactical incompetence. Yet the miners' strike was, to a considerable extent, the direct result of Communist policies and methods of operation in the unions. So Pete Carter wrote another document attacking the way the CP had gone about creating a trade union left, and condemning the 'hard left'. By this time the term 'hard left' meant Trotskyists, class warriors and most Bennites. As a result of their baleful influence, said Carter, trade unions 'lack . . . any credible, coherent alternative to Thatcherism.' Communist-backed organizations in unions have turned into 'narrow left machines mainly concerned with the election of officers.'

Carter told the *Observer*: 'I can see no future at all for the hard left sectarians. Theirs is a lost cause. We have moved on from the 'sixties and 'seventies.' Mick Costello told the same newspaper: 'The British Party is unique in the world Communist movement. It has lost its newspaper, its industrial power base has virtually disappeared, its youth section does not exist, and it has no close friends left in Third World liberation movements.' The leadership only kept its grip through continual purging of the membership, he said.

That year, during the week of the Trades Union Congress, the CP threw a party to mark Mick McGahey's retirement. It was far and away the best attended event at the Congress, because everyone liked Mick, opponents as well as supporters. The sight of every key trade unionist in the land and every industrial journalist who mattered crammed together, shoulder to shoulder, to pay tribute

to a CP member, ought to have gladdened the heart of Party chieftains, for it had never happened before. Alas, they were celebrating
the retirement of their last representative on the TUC general
council (they had expelled the chairman, Ken Gill) and were never
to have another one.

By now there was a small office in the *Morning Star* building
marked Communist Campaign Group, intended as a base from
which to continue the fight for the CP. By this time, too, *Marxism
Today* had become Britain's leading purveyor of what its enemies
contemptuously called 'designer socialism'. With its consumer
merchandise – leather filofaxes carrying the *Marxism Today* logo,
special-offer futons, Gorbachev T-shirts, and designer boxer shorts
with the word 'proletariat' in Russian; and with its concentration,
not on class, but on feminism and the environment, it seemed to
traditional Communists to embody everything that was loathsome
about the 1980s.

It also embodied the contradiction now at the heart of the CP.
A delegate from Reading, Will Gee, summed it up at the Party's
1987 Congress: 'One time we're told to abide by Party decisions,
the next time we're told that if you're on the editorial board of
Marxism Today or in with their crowd you can write anything
you like.'

13

The King is Dead.

Long Live the Kings

Mоst people think it was the demise of the Soviet Union which killed Britain's CP. Actually, at the end of its life, the Party which had sometimes been slavishly obedient to Moscow was surprisingly little affected by what was going on there. When Mikhail Gorbachev became general secretary of the Communist Party of the Soviet Union in 1985, Gordon McLennan quickly struck up an excellent relationship with him – closer, probably, than the relationship with any Soviet leader since the days of Pollitt and Stalin. McLennan played a key part in persuading Gorbachev to come to Britain and probably helped channel Soviet money into a fund for striking miners in 1984. The night Gorbachev saw Margaret Thatcher he went straight on to a meeting with McLennan, who unburdened himself about his Party's problems. Gorbachev nodded sympathetically and said he understood. 'And of course he understood,' says McLennan. 'He was going through it and he understood more than any previous Soviet leader about the working class.'

The direct Soviet subsidy to the CP may have stopped in 1979, but the disguised subsidy to the *Morning Star*, in the form of guaranteed sales to the Soviet Union, was still coming in. Holidays in the Soviet Union still helped supplement the meagre wages of CP staff. The best Soviet rest homes were still available to key Communists of both factions.

In 1986 Gordon McLennan considered retiring. Press and

212

publicity officer Nina Temple and industrial organizer Pete Carter were in favour of this, but Martin Jacques was not. Nina Temple says: 'Martin argued that it was essential for Gordon to stay, called him the greatest Communist leader in Western Europe.' In reality Jacques considered McLennan a decent enough man of inadequate intellectual quality. He may have considered McLennan's support for *Marxism Today* to be indispensable. Others argued that, with a significant class warrior element left in the Party, McLennan's departure would provoke a fierce and bloody leadership battle. But in 1988 the class warriors finally gave up the struggle for the Party and formed the Communist Party of Britain (CPB) with Mike Hicks as general secretary. The few who had not been expelled from the CP, like Kevin Halpin, left and joined the CPB. So by 1989 it seemed safe to let McLennan retire, exhausted from years of internecine warfare.

The Eurocommunists' victory was complete, and they were able to nominate their own successor. Jacques was discussed, but preferred to carry on editing *Marxism Today*, already secretly sure he was going to leave the Party. Even if he had been a candidate, the job would probably still have gone to Nina Temple, who took over in January 1990 at the age of 33. She insisted on being called the 'secretary' because 'general secretary sounded a bit grandiose for an organization of our size, and a bit Stalinist.' There could hardly be a clearer sign that Temple saw herself, as did her supporters, as a complete break with the past. The CP had spent 70 years talking itself up. For better or worse, it was now going to do the opposite.

Temple was born in 1956 – an ominous year for a future Communist leader to be born. She came from a Communist family (her father Landon Temple still runs Progressive Tours), was brought up on a council estate in North London, and joined the YCL in 1969 when she was 13. She had a classic meritocratic education: Camden School for Girls and a science degree at Imperial College London.

She worked for the YCL until 1982. She was about to leave when the row blew up about Tony Lane's article in *Marxism Today* attacking shop stewards. She felt her friend Martin Jacques, editor of the paper, was under attack. 'So I stayed out of loyalty to

Martin,' she says, now with a tinge of bitterness because she soon
became disillusioned with Jacques, seeing his intellectual acrobatics
and media courting as mere self-indulgence.

In 1982 she took over the CP's press and publicity. She is calm,
understated and engaging, disliking the pomp and ceremony which
distinguished Harry Pollitt's CP. The first thing she got rid of was
the bust of Marx which had adorned the general secretary's office
for more years than anyone could remember. She has mixed feelings about her predecessor. 'Personally he is a very nice man. But
he refused to recognize the problems that were brewing.' As late
as 1979 'he gave me a lecture about how there was no such thing
as Euros and Stalinists, we were all united, all Communists. That
was not my experience.' The showdown when it came was bloodier
than it need have been, she thinks, because McLennan tried to
postpone it, even though 'he was very brave during the crisis with
the *Morning Star* and had to take on people he had been close
friends with.'

The administration she took over was the creation, not of
McLennan, but of Reuben Falber. Falber was born in 1914 and
came from the generation of Jewish Communists who joined in
the 1930s. According to Temple, 'Gordon's attitude always was:
"Reuben's in charge of money, he must be allowed to get on with
it." Gordon would never challenge Reuben about anything. There
was a culture in the Party that it was not political to talk about
money so Reuben had absolute power over millions of pounds. Yet
the Party was always broke. Our wages were ridiculously low.
Working for the Party was an impoverishing experience.'

Part of the reason for this was that the CP maintained its
illusions of grandeur by employing far too many staff – well over
twenty in head office alone and nine in the regions looking after
fewer than 6000 members. The result was what Temple calls, in the
1980s terminology which sent shivers down the spines of all
previous generations of Communists, 'a dependency culture of
members being told what to do by full-time officials.' It had been,
she says, 'a dying movement for decades.' She made a lot of people
redundant and quickly brought the staff down to a total of six. One
of the people who had to go was the all-powerful Falber, now in
his seventies, working part time but still controlling the Party's
money and its companies.

The modest offices to which the CP had moved after it sold King Street were themselves now too expensive and commodious, and it bought a small open-plan office north of Kings Cross Station. The scores of companies, many of them set up in the early years of the Second World War as front organizations in case CP assets were seized, were pared down to six. The Party started to disengage from the big companies which it had owned. Publishers Lawrence and Wishart, book and magazine sellers Central Books, and Progressive Tours all gradually became independent companies.

Temple saw the CP as part of a worldwide revival of a new and freer sort of Communism, combining the social justice which Harry Pollitt dreamed of with the freedom Stalin stifled. But it was not long before the Eurocommunists found their victory turning to ashes in their hands. The rise of Gorbachev and the collapse of old-style Communist regimes in Eastern Europe seemed to herald a glorious future. But quickly this dream started to turn into a nightmare. Eastern Europe seemed to be choosing the crudest sort of capitalism available, and old nationalisms reasserted themselves with ultimately tragic results, such as the brutal war in what used to be Yugoslavia. In Britain the Party seemed irrelevant to the issues of public concern. When in 1990 there was a massive campaign against the poll tax, the sad remnants of Trotskyist groups made the running. The CP no longer had the membership, the people, the organization or the energy. It had exhausted itself in years of civil war. Harry Pollitt must have turned in his grave.

The new dream lacked all the certainty of the old one. The Party was not even certain whether it agreed with the way the poll tax campaigners were carrying on. Illegal activity, so much a part of the lives of early Communists, was dangerous and uncharted territory for Nina Temple and her colleagues. The old Communist Party with all its faults at least had a clear and distinct identity. Members knew what distinguished them from members of all other parties. They knew why, for them at any rate, it had to be the Communist Party or nothing. But the new Communist Party had none of these certainties. Most of its very moderate policies could as easily have been embraced by a member of the Labour Party, or even a Liberal Democrat.

By 1990 they were already thinking about winding the CP up and turning it into a loose network of like-minded people. This was to be the Party's last great internal battle, for the proposal brought out the fighting instinct of the Straight Left group, who shared a great deal with the class warriors but had kept a much lower profile. Temple's job was to try to stop the Party from having one last orgy of faction fighting. She made a brave stab at compromise. The Party, she said, should set up both a political section and a loose network. She called this a 'twin track'. It was, of course, impractical. The Party was not in a state to sustain one organization, let alone two. That did not stop the two factions turning thoroughly nasty on each other, with Straight Left suggesting that their opponents ought in honesty to get out of the Party and leave it to those who still had confidence in it. But they were going through the motions. After the recent strife no one had the energy left for a really good, hard, blood-soaked internal battle. Membership was plummetting: 6000 and falling in 1990. But the Party still had about £4 million, a reasonable nestegg. So both factions thought it worth trying to ensure that the new organisation was run on lines of which they approved.

High noon was set for November 1991, when the executive would recommend the Congress to wind up the CP. But there was one more disaster in store. The new storm blew up in the Party's face just days before the Congress. Reuben Falber heard about it first. Newly retired, he answered the front door of his modest home in Hampstead Garden Suburb late one afternoon and a young man introduced himself as John Davison of *The Sunday Times*. Was it true that Falber had collected substantial sums of money from the Soviet embassy to finance the CP? Nonsense, said Falber, he'd done nothing of the kind, and he'd be grateful if his unexpected visitor would leave straight away as Falber's wife was unwell.

Davison telephoned Nina Temple, who said she was shocked by the allegation and knew nothing about it. When he got back to the office there was a call from Falber. He was sorry he'd been rude, he said. He was sure Davison would understand. The allegations were all nonsense, of course, this sort of story had been around for years. The only time he had been to the Soviet embassy was to protest about human rights. 'He was fast on his feet, the old bugger,' says Davison admiringly.

Davison wrote the story anyway. All he had to go on was a page from a tatty ledger found by the paper's Moscow correspondent which showed two sums of about £15,000 each being paid to a 'Comrade Falber' in 1978. His news editor thought it was too risky, and that week's *Sunday Times* did not carry the story.

What Davison did not know was that after he had talked to Nina Temple, she telephoned Falber and demanded to know the truth. 'There was the longest silence I have ever heard on the telephone. Then he said, no, there was nothing in the story. But it was clear from the way he said it that there was a lot more to know. We decided to investigate.'

But Temple had more urgent things to worry about. There were just a few days to go before she must persuade the CP Congress to wind up the Party. She went to Somerset to work on her conference speech, and was not in the office again until the following Wednesday. 'Without meaning to, I'd left him to sweat. On that Wednesday he phoned up and said he wanted to tell me everything. I went round to his house with two colleagues. He told me the story.' But having told her, Falber insisted the information was to go no further. Temple said it had to be made public at once and drafted an article for *Changes*, the CP's new journal. Falber insisted that no figures should be given. So began a long process of bargaining, with Falber insisting that he had not given certain figures and Temple insisting that he had. They haggled: a few figures were included, a few others left out. Falber said that if the article was to appear, he wanted a personal statement of his own to appear as well. He telephoned Gordon McLennan at home to tell him what he was about to do. McLennan said: 'You know what my position will be, I said to Johnny [Gollan] I wanted it stopped and I thought it had been stopped.' So Falber altered the first draft of his article because it seemed to suggest that McLennan knew about the arrangement. The next day Temple called a press conference and made public the information she had.

Falber's article has been presented as the last word on the matter, coming clean and wrapping up the whole business. In fact it begs as many questions as it answers. Early in 1958, he says, Gollan 'asked me to look after a package containing £14,000.' After that 'I received substantially larger sums annually than those mentioned above, and on several occasions money for Communist parties working in illegal or semi-legal conditions. The latter monies I "laundered" carefully and handed over to representatives of the parties visiting London.' A *Changes* editorial adds a little detail. The payments received throughout the 1960s 'amounted on at least one occasion to £100,000' in one year.

The Soviet Union, he says, offered the money because of the loss of income after the Khrushchev revelations in 1956. It never expected absolute support for Soviet policies in return. Nonetheless, 'after the Czechoslovak events of 1968 John Gollan and I became unhappy about the situation and we began to work out measures to lessen our dependence on help ... and eventually end it ... In the early 1970s we advised the Soviet comrades we wished to make a substantial reduction in the sum paid to us ... I received the last payment in 1979.' The *Changes* editorial adds that some time after 1971 they were reduced to 'between £14,000 and £15,000' a year.

We still do not know how much the CP was getting in the 1960s except that in at least one year it received £100,000. We do not know when the subsidy was reduced except that it happened after 1971, or when it got down to 'between £14,000 and £15,000.' Falber said to me: 'I've said all I know about that. There's no more I can say.' How much did he get? 'I haven't a clue, I never kept a tally. It was cash, it didn't go through a bank account or anything like that.'

We can now add a little more detail. Privately Falber left Temple in little doubt that he was receiving at least £100,000 a year throughout the 1960s. He said that the main flow of money ceased at the start of the '70s and the sums of 'between £14,000 and £15,000' were mainly intended for such matters as looking after British Comintern servants in private nursing homes in their old age.

There are oddities in Falber's account. You can understand the CP taking the risks involved in order to receive six-figure sums, but for much less it was surely hardly worth the risk. And if Gollan and Falber were worried about being beholden to the Soviet Union, why be equally beholden for less money? And did the subsidies really end when Falber says they ended, in 1979? 'We received a large number of legacies in the 80s,' says Nina Temple. 'Now we hardly get any.' It makes her suspicious. When Falber finally retired he continued to administer the CP's pension fund – and this was the fund through which he laundered the money.

In the sixties the *Morning Star* received a Soviet subsidy of £3000 a month. For the rest, Falber did not simply place it in the CP account. The sudden arrival of a large and unexplained sum would have been noticed. Falber is vague. He gave some of it to Party districts, which were often desperately hard up and unable to pay the wages of their full-time officials. But if he did that, he must have been selective about which districts he gave money to. CP district organizers had to raise their own wages, and if they could not do so, they often went without. Many of them were bitterly angry when they heard about the Soviet money, because they felt it should have been used to pay their wages.

Just three people knew, says Falber: himself, John Gollan, and David Ainley, chief executive of the *Morning Star*. In fact, George Matthews also knew. And what about Gordon McLennan? When he was appointed in 1975 Gollan told him about it. McLennan says: 'I said, as far as I'm concerned, I want nothing to do with it. Johnny said, "Good, pleased to hear that."' McLennan claims that he said he wanted it stopped and assumed that it stopped at once. In fact it carried on for another four years. Asked why he never checked, he says: 'I wanted no involvement, all I wanted was it stopped.' There is a sense here that if something is not discussed it does not exist. As Kevin Morgan wrote of Harry Pollitt, you lived in a shadowy world where you knew and you didn't know. Nina Temple says: 'Whenever you needed money Gordon would say, "Go and see Reuben."' When she wanted to dispute one of Falber's decisions McLennan told her: 'If you ever question Reuben you're out. Reuben looks after the money and I trust him totally.' There is one small but perhaps significant discrepancy. McLennan claims he never discussed it with Falber. Falber says there was in fact one discussion.

Why the secrecy? 'Public knowledge that we were receiving financial help from the Soviet Union would have led to a worsening of relations between the British and Soviet governments' and 'might tend to lessen public campaigns to raise money for the Party and our paper.' So why not tell all now? 'People seem to think there's something intriguing about it. These isn't. What we received was peanuts compared with what the Tories have had from their rich friends.'

Soviet funds were not just used for British CP purposes. 'On one occasion we were asked to get a leader of an illegal [Communist] party – threatened with arrest and many years imprisonment – out of his country. We bought a car and a courageous comrade agreed to take the risks involved. On another occasion we were asked to raise money and buy warm clothing for members of a party who were engaged in armed struggle.'

Until the relevant Moscow archive is open the full truth will not be known. It will probably be innocent enough. Reuben Falber, by withholding as much information as he thinks he can withhold, surrounds the whole affair with exactly the aura of intrigue and mystery which he deplores. After fifty-five years in the CP, most of it at the heart of all its most secret affairs, he has the Bolshevik instinct not to give any information that he does not have to give. He does not see that the real problem with the money was not the source, but the secrecy.

Falber ended his *Changes* article: 'I can only say, like that great singer Edith Piaf, "Non, je ne regrette rien."' Martin Jacques' resignation went in the post the day the news came out. Journalist Sarah Benton, who had left the CP a decade earlier, wrote an article in the *Guardian* charged with bitterness: 'The dour men in grey suits who retreated in argument into a clipped assertion of their own authority ... Between the impulse which had brought these leaders into the Communist Party and the execution of their leadership duties lay layers of knowledge about funny money and directions from Moscow ... We raged and laughed at their granite faces, their terrible, deadening language, their suffocation of what was new and lively...' It all seemed rather over the top. But it showed the fatal effect of what Jacques calls 'the missing generation'. The CP had people who were young in the 1930s and 40s, and others who were young in the 1960s and 70s, but very few who were young in the 1950s. Most of them left after 1956, and those who remained – Mick Costello, Tony Chater, Mike Hicks – were in the class warrior camp and out of the CP after 1988. That generation could have provided a buffer between Falber and the younger generation.

The 'Moscow gold' story crystallized the waves of sentiment which were the real divide. To Jacques and Benton, the old men – and, they would have pointed out, they were mostly men – symbolized everything that was wrong about old-fashioned Communist politics:

sullen Bolsheviks in grey suits, class warriors, proud of their contacts with senior trade unionists, for a time more or less a part of the trade union establishment, sombre, secretive, with a certainty that seemed to come from another age. It was typical of them to take secret money from Moscow. To the old men, the sixties generation had annexed their much-loved Party and harnessed it to trendy middle-class issues. They were dilletantes who dismissed class politics; they swam with the tide instead of against it as Communists are supposed to do; they were, in that phrase which carries a world of contempt, radical chic, and it was typical of them to ally with the capitalist press in building Moscow gold into a big issue when no one questioned the Conservative Party's foreign donations. Older Communists talked of having correct politics, while younger Communists were politically correct. The two were a world apart and there was no meeting place.

Shell-shocked, CP members went to their forty-third and last Congress to decide their future, and the Eurocommunists won again. The 1991 Congress closed down the CP after seventy-one years and brought into being the Democratic Left (DL).

The DL has never had more than 1,600 members and is now down to 1,200. Though it calls itself – truthfully, as far as it goes – 'the constitutional successor to the Communist Party of Great Britain', and it has secured the CP's assets, it is in reality only one of several successors.

The CP's assets were wasting. In the nine months before the final Congress it made £100,000 on the money markets and £45,000 from renting out office space, nearly four times as much as it made from membership subscriptions, donations and appeals. It was living off its fat. Worse, at the time of the Congress it cost more to look after each member, supplying regular information and a fortnightly paper, than each member was paying in subscriptions. So if suddenly thousands of people joined, they would bankrupt the organization. Subscriptions rose sharply, from £12 a year to a sliding scale running from £16 to £60.

At the 1992 general election the Democratic Left advised people to vote tactically for whichever candidate was most likely to beat the Tories, whether they were Labour, Liberal Democrat or Scottish National Party. Former Communists were not alone in being horrified. Nina Temple defended the decision in the usual terms of the debate between the DL and the old guard: 'We are trying to create a new culture of politics ... Vanguard revolutionary politics has had its day.' But that was not really what it was about at all. Tactical voting was less part of the DL's Communist past, than part of the left's future. The DL attitude was probably closer to the real feeling of Labour voters, reflecting their reduced ambitions. From demanding Labour governments which would take over the 'commanding heights' of the economy, now most Labour voters felt it would be enough simply to get rid of the Conservatives. No one was demanding that Labour should bring about a social revolution any more – just that it should stop the one that was going on. Yet even that modest ambition was denied. The day after polling day in 1992 the nation woke up to realize that it had, against all its own expectations, given the Conservative government five more years in power.

DL, on the advice of a designer whose father was once Harry Pollitt's chauffeur, now dresses itself in soft blues and mauves, with gentle publicity material designed not to jar the senses. Its soft-focus symbol, three figures holding hands, one green for the environment, one purple for women's rights, one red for socialism, seems a little too deliberately to bring in all the icons of the 'nineties and yet avoid being accused of betraying the icons of the DL's past. In search of its policies, a tasteful blue recruiting leaflet bears the slogan 'caring, sharing, daring' which even by the general standards of political slogans seems to sacrifice meaning to the feelgood factor.

The Democratic Left does not claim to lead. It claims to enable and to empower. It does not aim to be a political party. It is an 'organisation'. One of its leaders, Mike Waite, explains this in its publication *New Times* (the new name for *Changes*): 'Now DL does not seek to be a 'party' alternative to Labour, the Lib Dems, the Scottish Nationalists or anyone else, it can increasingly become a focus for discussions between members of such real political parties about areas of shared concern and interest, which could lead to joint initiatives and campaigns, and to the development of the dialogue and new ideas which political life needs so much.'

It is not an ignoble ambition, though whether, in these harsh times, a 'focus for discussion' is what political life in Britain needs is debatable. Perhaps they mean an anti-Conservative front, a more ambitious and more relevant idea. In any case, with a declining membership, it is a dream, and a dream which Harry Pollitt would not have recognized as having anything at all to do with the Party he led for a quarter of a century.

Harry Pollitt would have recognized Mike Hicks at once. Hicks is the general secretary of the Communist Party of Britain (CPB), formed in 1988 by the defeated class warriors. His father was a docker and a lifelong Communist who once spent six months in Wormwood Scrubs for knocking out Mosley's bodyguard. His mother was a Catholic, so when their son was born in 1937 they compromised between their faiths and called him Michael Joseph Hicks – Michael after St Michael and Joseph after Joseph Stalin. His mother worked as a cleaner at the CP's King Street head-quarters. Hicks remembers sitting on his father's shoulders in Farringdon Street the night they opened the new *Daily Worker* building, and watching as the first copies were thrown out of an upstairs window. He joined the YCL in 1953 when he was sixteen.

He worked as a printer and was active in the print union SOGAT, becoming a member of the CP executive and a full-time union branch secretary. In 1986, when Rupert Murdoch set out to end print union power and moved his papers to the new plant at Wapping, Hicks was arrested during the mass demonstrations outside the plant. During his trial he maintained he was set up by the police, but he spent three months in no less than six prisons – 'they were moving me around because demonstrations kept following me.'

He was expelled from the CP after chairing the London District Congress in 1984 and continuing after Gordon McLennan told him to close it. He is bitter about what happened to the CP. 'They knew we could beat them democratically, so they went for a purge. They used the sort of administrative methods which they con-demned the Soviet Union for using. If they had not we would have won the National Congress and removed McLennan and that lot. Nina Temple and those people made it clear that they were not Marxist-Leninists. But they stayed in the Party and therefore had the benefit of the money, £4 million of it. They were like bees round a honey pot.'

Nina Temple says: 'True, I was not a Marxist-Leninist, but

I believed in *The British Road to Socialism* [the CP policy document rewritten by George Matthews and Martin Jacques]. We were
recruited on that basis and were told that that was what the Party
believed. There were a lot of members like me in the 'seventies who
believed what we were told. Mike Hicks didn't obey his own rules.
He told us: "My loyalty to my class is greater than my loyalty to
the rule book."'

Hicks still works for SOGAT. He is tall and broad, with a soft
voice in private and a loud one for use on demonstrations, and
wears the trade union official's uniform of dark suit and white
shirt, but with a certain style. He is a well-preserved 57 with determination, a forceful personality and absolute certainty. Like Harry
Pollitt his beliefs were formed by a harsh childhood – 'I took a
penny ha'penny tram ride to the West End and saw the difference
between my slum and what they were living in' – and they have
never changed. 'The more I see of trade unions in my job and of
the right wing of the Labour Party, the more I know there has to
be an effective Leninist organization. Capitalism offers no future
for Britain or the world.'

If Harry Pollitt would recognize Mike Hicks as a comrade, he
would also recognize the Party Hicks leads. Just as Bert Ramelson
used to do, its industrial organizer Kevin Halpin publishes *Needs
of the Hour* every year to tell trade union members what policies
they should try to deliver. Halpin, who served on the CP's Commission on Inner Party Democracy in 1956 and was one of the leaders
of the Liaison Committee for the Defence of Trade Unions, is now
retired and putting all his energies into his politics.

The CPB aims to build up its trade union support just as the CP
did in its best days. Of thirty-two people on the CPB executive, nine
are on the executives of their own unions. The Party is strongest
in the rail union RMT. It claims about 1500 members and the only
people with the energy to question this figure are members of the
DL. In the way of small socialist parties the CPB is hardest on those
who are closest: the Straight Left faction, with similar views but
dissimilar tactics, has not been forgiven for walking out of Hicks'
London District Congress in 1984 when ordered to by McLennan.

The CPB was delighted that the CP wrapped itself up and
adopted the name Democratic Left. It would like to call itself the
Communist Party of Great Britain but the DL has legal copyright

on the name. To emphasise continuity with the Party of Harry Pollitt the CPB called its first conference in 1988 the thirty-ninth. And it published a new edition of *The British Road to Socialism*. It published another in 1992 with some amendments 'in the light of the enormous changes which had occurred in the former socialist countries of Eastern Europe.'

At its 1993 Congress there were about one hundred delegates: some very elderly, some quite young, and not many between the two. At the end of the conference Hicks and the chairman, Richard Maybin, a teacher in his fifties, stood side by side, stiffly to attention, arms stretched out in front of them, stiff and dignified, and led the delegates in a complete rendering of the Internationale. Many of them knew all the words. Arthritic arms held up clenched fists and their owners belted out the tune lustily. Hope of a better world was as real for them as it had been when Clement Attlee was Prime Minister and Harry Pollitt produced the first edition of *The British Road to Socialism*.

There is a final horrible, wrenching irony. Mike Hicks and Nina Temple, who can hardly hear each others' names without spitting, are trapped together, side by side, in the murky, glutinous past they share. Much of the CP's money was of secret Soviet origin. Hicks says: 'I didn't know about the Moscow money but it wouldn't have worried me. The ruling class have always done this sort of thing.' Temple, however, thought it corrupt: 'Such substantial secret funds gave vast unaccountable powers to those that held them.' She is nonetheless determined to hang on to every penny and the Democratic Left has strained to ensure that its hold is legally watertight, while Hicks now rails against the moral corruption he claims the money creates.

There was talk of a court case when the DL was founded: the CPB thought it had a case to be seen as the proper descendant of the Communist Party but, says Hicks, 'we decided we would not let a British judge decide the political fate of the Communist Party.' But it looks now as though there will be a case. Just before the 1991 Congress which formed the DL a CP member died, leaving a sum of money in his will to the Communist Party. His executors have interpreted that as meaning the Communist Party of Britain, and the Democratic Left will challenge them in court.

Though the DL has secured most of the assets, the CPB does

have one of the most valuable. The *Morning Star* still insists it is
an independent labour movement newspaper and not owned by any
party, but Tony Chater, who retired as editor in 1995, and most
of the staff are CPB members and the CPB rents office space in
the *Morning Star* building – at a commercial rate, both sides insist.

Until 1991 the *Morning Star* still sold 12,000 copies a day to the
Soviet Union, paid for a year in advance. But in 1988, the year the
CPB was formed, the Soviet Union started paying a year in
arrears – which cut the value of the subsidy enormously. In 1991,
as the Communist Party of the Soviet Union started to lose its
grip, the order went down to 6000. In 1992 Soviet hardliners
mounted a coup against Gorbachev, and its failure strengthened the
hand of the anti-Communists under Boris Yeltsin. In 1992 Moscow
cancelled its *Morning Star* order. Since then the paper has had, for
the first time in its history, to live or die entirely by its own efforts.
Chater and PPPS chief executive Mary Rosser knew harder times
were coming and sold the Farringdon Road building for £2.1
million in 1987. They built a more modest office on the border between Hackney and Islington. New technology enabled them to
reduce the paper's forty journalists to fourteen. After a few shaky
years, they now get paid a tiny salary most months. In these competitive times, with no subsidy and a circulation of 7000, its daily
appearance is little short of a miracle. It now has the reputation
of being a dull, old-fashioned sort of socialist paper but this is
rather unfair. It is actually much brighter, newsier and livelier than
it was in the 1980s, when it could not focus its attention properly
on anything except the dreadfulness of Eurocommunists.

There are other Communist groupings. The Communist Party
of Scotland (CPS) is very like the CPB in approach. It has 360
members, all of whom feel as bitter about the DL as the CPB
people do. Communist Liaison is a loose network of perhaps 150
former Communists, mostly in London, Liverpool and Newcastle
upon Tyne, who did not feel comfortable with either of the main
successor bodies. The Islip Unity Group consists of a few famous
trade union names from the CP's past, most of them now retired,
still meeting to plan how to retrieve something from the wreckage.
Their first meetings were at a member's home in Islip Street in
Kentish Town, hence the name. The select few at the meetings
generally include Ken Gill and Jim Mortimer. Bert Ramelson

attended until he died in April 1994. The New Communist Party, the 1977 Stalinist breakaway, still operates and is thought to have about 200 members. Its weekly newspaper, The *New Worker*, treats China and North Korea in rather the way the *Daily Worker* treated the Soviet Union in its most slavishly uncritical phases. Communists meet under all sorts of other labels: London Communists, Communist Trade Unionists, and others. Straight Left was rehabilitated before the CP dissolved, but rather like a victim of Stalin's purges, it was dead by the time that happened. It is a sad end to an organization that Harry Pollitt saw almost as an extended family. 'One day we'll all get together again,' a *Morning Star* journalist said to me sadly. Then he added: 'Except for those Democratic Left bastards, of course.'

They probably will. At the time of writing it looks as though there will be a grand coming together – just as the various socialist groups came together to found the Communist Party in 1920. This time there will be no Soviet money to help things along. Perhaps that is a good thing.

Gordon McLennan refused to join the Democratic Left. Perhaps he felt betrayed by the people he supported. Certainly Nina Temple and her friends took the Party far further along the path of change than he wanted to go. To McLennan the essence of Euro-communism was independence from Moscow and the ability to criticize the Soviet Union. For Nina Temple and the younger Eurocommunists, and especially for Martin Jacques, it was a great deal more than that – it involved nothing less than the abandonment of Marxism-Leninism. In McLennan's last years as general secretary before his retirement in 1989, it was, says Temple, 'very hard for him to face what was happening. He believes that the problem was that he left.' He offered to continue running the Party on a two-day-a-week basis after she was chosen for the job. She countered with an offer to commission him to write the Party's history. 'Don't insult me,' he told her.

Mick McGahey joined the Democratic Left without any enthusiasm at all. 'I reject Martin Jacques and the intellectuals who don't even know what class struggle is.' He said in January 1994: 'I'm not a member of any Communist Party at the moment, but Mick McGahey is a Communist.' In April, at the Scottish TUC, he joined the Communist Party of Scotland.

Tony Chater and Mick Costello fell out. It was hardly surprising. They were very different people thrown together by circumstances, and the clever, mercurial Costello was bound sooner or later to clash with the careful, autocratic Chater. The last straw was when Chater sent Costello to the Soviet Union to report on changes under perestroika and then refused to publish the results because they were too critical of the pace at which change was proceeding. Chater may have been thinking of his financial deal with Moscow – he had, says Costello, 'few illusions about the Russians.' Costello left the paper and scratched a living in journalism for a while before becoming an adviser on trade with the former Soviet Union, using his fluent Russian, his knowledge of the country and his contacts there on behalf of UK companies. It is not what he wanted to do with his life, any more than journalism was. He wanted to be a Communist political organizer, and was happiest in the few short years when he followed Bert Ramelson as the Party's industrial organizer. He still attracts rumour like a flytrap. In his CP days people used to whisper that he was a KGB agent. Now former comrades whisper that he is a millionaire. He is neither.

Of the founding fathers, only Andrew Rothstein was alive to see the Party wind itself up in 1991. To him joining the Communist Party of Britain in his 90s was as natural as joining the CP when he was 20. He was the only person alive who knew the secrets of the relationship between the CP and the Soviet Union in the 'twenties and 'thirties, and he took them to his grave in September 1994.

George Matthews loyally followed Nina Temple into the Democratic Left, and took over the Communist Party's archive, preparing it for the inspection of historians. Now 77, he says there are 'some things I wish I'd never done and I do regret' and he is 'sorry it had to end as it did.'

Martin Jacques may be the only person in seventy-one years for whom joining the CP turned out to be a smart career move. He never intended to be a journalist, but the success of *Marxism Today* provided him with an instant reputation, and when he wound it up he was immediately in demand as a newspaper columnist. In September 1994 he became deputy editor of the *Independent*.

Postscript

Just before I finished this book, on the morning of 12 May 1994, Labour leader John Smith died suddenly from a heart attack, and many of the fragile hopes of socialists which had survived the 1980s died with him. Smith, though a member of Labour's old right, shared many of the instincts of the people who have mostly populated the pages of this book. His successor, Tony Blair, neither shared them nor even seemed to understand them.

Back in 1992, the Communist Party of Britain (CPB) and the Democratic Left (DL) had both campaigned vigorously and unreservedly for a Labour general election victory. No Labour Party newspaper could have given the Party more unreserved support than the CPB's *Morning Star* and the DL's *New Times*. By the end of 1994 it was clear that Blair intended to change the Labour Party radically. Though they would certainly support Labour again next time, for want of anything better to support, it was going to be hard to do it in the same wholehearted spirit.

This, if ever, was surely the time when the warring remnants of British communism would sink their differences. With socialism increasingly isolated, if there was to be any hope at all, the old disputes would have to be put aside.

There is, however, not the slightest sign that anything of the sort is happening. If anything, they seem to be splitting into ever tinier fragments. The following year, the publication of this book provided a clear demonstration that the trench warfare between the class warriors and the Eurocommunists continued unabated. The *Morning Star* administered a magisterial rebuke to me for not being suffi- ciently uncritical of the class warrior case, while *New Times* published an extended howl of outrage that I should have given any credence to the class warriors at all.

The *Morning Star* at least managed to be dignified. *New Times* was so hyped up and hysterical about the book that it rather took me aback. "One is left wondering whether Beckett cares at all about the truth... We are left with the question of Beckett's motivation. His publishers were evidently motivated by profits... His praise and approval are confined to the wing of the Party most intimately associated with the Soviet Communist Party... The bizarre blend of hagiography and witch-hunting in his prose stems from his determi- nation to exonerate the new CPB..." The bitter, sectarian spirit of Rajani Palme Dutt lives on, though it is strange to find it in the DL, because the DL's main objective is to be as unlike the CP as it can manage. It has decisively rejected the Communist Party, with its solemn, ageing trade unionists, its rigid Party line, its Marxism.

In January 1998 I went to catch up on the DL, and meet once again its intelligent, engaging 41-year-old federal secretary, Nina Temple. She talks constantly about "not doing it the old CP way." The difference in style struck me forcibly as Ms Temple escorted me through the light, airy building to her own small office, with its whitewashed brick walls, its pot plants all along the long window ledge, its computer screen which beeps every hour to remind her to flex her shoulders, and not a picture of a trade union banner or a bust of Karl Marx in sight.

Not only is it not the CP: it insists that it is not a Party at all. It does not stand in elections, and most of its members are in other parties, generally the Labour Party, the Liberal Party, or Plaid Cymru. It is, according to its constitution, "an organisation that seeks to support and initiate coalitions, campaigns and strategic debates." It stands, as one of its leaders, Dave Cook, put it in 1992, at "the point of inter- section between socialist and environmental concerns."

Nina Temple is quite unfazed by the fact that DL is now down to just 960 members. The support it can attract over specific issues, the friends it has, the influence it can exert, the ideas it generates, are far more important, she believes – just as the CP believed in the seventies. She has some stock phrases for its methods. "Ideas grow up and leave home." "We open up spaces that other people find useful." "Because we are so porous, if something good is there it can be contagious." In *New Times* she wrote: "The challenge is to build the flows of communication within and beyond the DL, so that members and friends can get more involved." The DL's slogan is still "Caring, Sharing, Daring." .

They are proudest of their work in the trade unions. "The unions need to reinvent themselves" says Ms Temple. "We don't want to do that by the old CP methods, getting people who had the right line onto key committees." What do they want to do instead? DL set up an association with the trade unions called Unions 21, which, says Ms Temple, helped move the unions away from insisting on a rigid formula for the amount of the minimum wage. This, she believes, has helped keep the minimum wage on Tony Blair's agenda. If Blair had been faced with a demand from the unions for a precise formula, he might have ditched the whole idea, she says. "Unions 21 has helped conversations to happen which might not have happened otherwise."

Like the old CP, DL is very proud of its relationship with senior union leaders, but, again like the old CP, Ms Temple is coy about naming her contacts, except for TUC General Secretary John Monks. Why will she not name names? "It devalues relationships" she said, and old Palme Dutt himself could not have said it with a straighter face.

All old ideas must be ditched, the left must travel ideologically light, vague talk of communicating, the intangible, the touchy-feely – it's all very New Labour, and it is in New Labour circles that DL is probably at its most influential. DL is proud to have provided the first trade union platform from which Tony Blair spoke after his election as Labour leader. The original DL guru, Martin Jacques, welcomed Blair and New Labour enthusiastically in 1994 (though he is much less enthusiastic now). Jacques and his *Marxism Today* writers were influential with the Kinnock circle. Nina Temple is on the editorial board of the influential New Labour journal *Renewal*, which on its October 1995 cover carried a quote from Tony Blair which sounded very like the DL speaking:

"The left I believe is back in business – ready to provide the leadership this country needs. It must now show the confidence and open-mindedness to map out this new course for Britain."

Confidence, open-mindedness, new, caring, sharing, daring,

challenge, communication, spaces. New. Especially new. DL shares with New Labour a liking for the feelgood phrase.

It was at a DL fringe meeting at the Labour conference in October 1997 that Peter Mandelson famously hinted that young people might not benefit as much from the minimum wage as we had assumed. Perhaps the minimum might be lower for them.

Mandelson also told the meeting that New Labour and New Unionism were two sides of the same coin. They are about "building up new membership services and being relevant to individuals at work." The next month one of DL's key figures (and a TUC press officer), Mike Power, asked in *New Times*: "How do the unions become as trusted and respected in New Labour circles as business seems to be?" The answer, Power seems to think, is that the unions should reform themselves so that Blair will find them less unattractive. "Unions are too often seen as unrepresentative of ordinary members. And union services need to be co-ordinated and made relevant to the less secure labour market and new information technologies." Examining this for a precise meaning I found an unrewarding activity, but it crucially contains the word "new".

DL's lack of ideological baggage allows it to do almost anything. This is probably liberating, even if it leaves the outsider feeling a little breathless. "Give this man a seat" trumpeted a *New Times* headline on 18 January 1997, over a long article complaining that 16 months after his defection from the Conservatives to New Labour, former Thatcherite minister Alan Howarth had still not been offered a safe Labour seat for the next election.

It explained what a decent, sincere man Howarth is. It complained that local Labour Parties were reluctant to nominate Howarth, attributing this to "the arrogance of power," and encouraged Blair to impose him on the locals in some safe seat somewhere. "For the constituency that is chosen, and for the nation's poor, Howarth's return to the government benches will probably turn out to be a blessing in disguise." The DL may be able to claim some credit for the fact that Howarth's virtues have not, in the event, been lost to Parliament.

For the foreseeable future, DL will survive because it gained control of the CP's money, £4 million of it. Even now, in 1997 and with only 960 members, DL's finances look quite healthy, although it is still spending a little more than it earns. In 1995 and 1996 it spent

£353,075 and its income was £381,648. But even after the inevitable attrition of the past six years, it is still sitting on money and assets worth more than £2 million.

That makes Mike Hicks, until recently general secretary of the Communist Party of Britain (CPB), angry every time he thinks about it, which is quite often. He believes that the CP was infiltrated by people who did not share its beliefs, and whose motivation was to steal its money. "That money was raised by socialists to fight for socialism. Nina Temple and her crowd haven't any right to it" says Mike Hicks, who still earns his living as an official of a print trade union.

The membership of the CPB has stayed stable at 1200, and it ran three candidates in the 1997 general election, all of whom lost their deposits. In other constituencies they advised their supporters to vote Labour, though Hicks told a press conference that there was barely an inch between Labour and the Tories. So why back Blair, he was asked, and replied quickly: "That inch'll do us." A lifetime in trade union politics leaves you quick on your feet.

Hicks told me in January 1998: "If you believe your position is correct what alternative do you have? Everything goes back to Lenin. Lenin spelled out the logic of what is happening now. Globalisation speeds up the process of imperialism. Now you've got 1.2 billion people in the world unemployed, and 800 million go to bed hungry every night. That's the logical outcome of the accumulation of wealth in the strong imperialist countries."

He did not apologise for the CP's support of the Soviet Union. "What's worse than the Soviet Union? What followed it, that's what" he said. "Look at Uzbekhistan. It's so bankrupt, it had to vote at the UN in favour of the US blockade of Cuba so that the US would bail it out. That blockade only got three votes – the US, Israel and Uzbekhistan."

The deputy leader of the Russian Federation's Communist Party spoke at the last CPB Congress, and Hicks and his colleagues have been guests of the Chinese and Cuban governments. These governments paid their fares, but do not provide any subsidies to the CPB. Broadly, the CPB supports them both. China, says Hicks, has now gone back to Lenin with its new economic policy.

The *Morning Star* has a circulation of 7,000 and is proud of the well known non-Communists who write for it: Tony Benn, Ken

Livingstone and a handful of other Labour MPs, as well as TUC general secretary John Monks. It is the only daily communist paper in the English language, now that the US *Peoples Daily World* has been reduced to a weekly. All its 13 journalists, including the editor, and all its support staff, receive the same wage, which in 1998 is £10,500 a year.

Its appearance is a minor daily miracle, because it now has nothing to live on except the cover price and the fighting fund. Its main problem is the distribution system in Britain, which is increasingly geared to the needs of the big distributors. But that is not what, in 1998, looks capable of killing it. In 1995 the CPB stormed into a good old-fashioned internal power-struggle which, at the time of writing, threatens to destroy both the Party and the *Morning Star*.

The troubles seem to have begun with the arrival of a new faction from the old CP. The CPB and the Straight Left faction had been divided by the long-dead tactical issue of the best way to fight the Eurocommunists inside the CP. They agreed about everything else. Straight Left had kept aloof from the CPB when it was founded. But by 1995, to most people on both sides, the dispute was more or less forgotten, and many former Straight Left luminaries were inside the CPB.

But not everyone wanted to bury the hatchet. The diehards in the CPB, led by Hicks, his wife the *Morning Star* chief executive Mary Rosser, and the paper's editor Tony Chater, had neither forgotten nor forgiven Straight Left's ideological turpitude. "Straight Left was neither straight nor left" Mike Hicks told me. "We opened our doors to people who had venomously attacked us in the past. They have now said they accept the programme and rules of our party and we trust this turns out to be true." His voice made it clear he did not believe for a moment that it was true. He has not forgotten old grievances. "They ended up selling *Marxism Today* instead of the *Morning Star* and justified it because the executive told them to" he says with contempt.

At the 1995 CPB Congress Straight Left did remarkably well in elections to the executive, and Mary Rosser, Tony Chater and some of their hardline supporters were voted off it. Straight Left people were accused of running slates, or factionalism as it was called, contrary to the Bolshevik rules by which communists since Lenin are supposed to operate.

A commission of enquiry was set up to examine the charge, and its report makes depressing reading. The Party's most distinguished trade union leader, and its most experienced and formidable tactician, Ken Gill, will no doubt be careful whom he allows to use his spare bedroom in future, because the commission reported: "A comrade, staying at Ken Gill's house, alleged that he had seen a list in the house. Comrade Gill was interviewed and said that the list was of comrades on the outgoing EC, any marks made beside names were entirely his own. He denied being given a list by anyone ..."

In the same year, Tony Chater retired as editor of the *Morning Star*. Hicks, Rosser and Chater were determined that news editor Paul Corry, Mary Rosser's son in law, should succeed him as editor. Corry was defeated by an alliance led by Ken Gill, then the chairman of the Peoples Press Printing Society. Gill, it is said, called a snap vote while a couple of crucial opponents were out of the room, and deputy editor John Haylett got the job.

Just as in the days of the CP, the *Morning Star*, though an avowedly CPB paper, is owned by the shareholders of the Peoples Press Printing Society (PPPS), not by the CPB. And just as in the last days of the CP, the shareholders, not all of them CPB members, all had pretty strong views, one way or another.

The commission of enquiry looked at this contest too, and examined some more depressingly trivial accusations. "Stan Dalby of the North West District was accused of circulating an alternative list to that of the party's at the Manchester AGM... Comrade Dalby admitted advising two party members on how to vote..."

According to the commission of enquiry, the old guard – Hicks, Rosser, Corry and their friends – think the problems are caused by "the existence of a left-sectarian current which seeks to narrow down the party's political positions. In some cases, it was alleged that this was the direct result of the infiltration into the party of straight left/communist liaison members." The commission thought that, if there was a danger of sectarianism, it could as easily come from Hicks and Rosser as from their enemies.

On 11 January 1998, the CPB removed 60-year-old Mike Hicks as general secretary and put in his place a man who, if the word had not already been claimed by another political party, might have been called a moderniser. 45-year-old Rob Griffiths is a senior lecturer in labour history and trade union studies at the University of Wales

College, Newport. He is a Welsh speaker, has campaigned for devolution and leasehold reform, and has written books and television scripts on working class history in both English and Welsh.

The problem, said Griffiths, was that Hicks's "style of work had become divisive and highly personalised, discrediting individuals and undermining collective leadership." He had "allowed and even encouraged a dangerous polarisation to take place, based on the misrepresentation of comrades' views – and in particular on the notion that an anti-British Road to Socialism faction was at work (and had taken over the EC) alongside a Straight Left faction."

Just one week later, the Hicks faction took its revenge, persuading the PPPS to fire John Haylett. The journalists went on strike, with the support of the CPB, and the paper was off the streets.

During the five week strike, the journalists were supported by the CPB as well as by the National Union of Journalists (NUJ). The battle was fought with a bitterness which recalled the early eighties, when socialist often did not speak unto socialist except in a threatening growl. The editor of the NUJ journal *The Journalist*, Tim Gopsill, himself a veteran of many left wing battles in the old days, wrote about "megalomaniac dyed-blonde *Morning Star* chief executive Mary Rosser" while the family relationship of Hicks, Rosser and Corry prompted one national newspaper to speculate that Socialism in One Country had been replaced by Socialism in One Family.

It was Gopsill who drew attention to the oddest feature of the affair. Rosser and Hicks, on behalf of the CPB, had formed an informal alliance with a group called Socialist Action, which is what remains of one of the mushrooming trotskyist groups of the seventies, Tariq Ali's International Marxist Group. Socialist Action now enjoys the patronage of left wing MP Ken Livingstone, and in recent months Livingstone had been a frequent contributor to the Morning Star. Livingstone, amazingly for a man who still nurtures hopes of being London's mayor, actually tabled a parliamentary motion accusing Haylett of anti-Semitism for supporting an event at which American black nationalist Louis Farakhan was to speak. Unsurprisingly, no other MP backed the motion.

Back in the real world, Rosser agreed to a new appeal before an independent panel, which on April 1 threw out the rather trivial charges she had levelled against Haylett. It was the end of the road.

The *Morning Star* is back on the streets, with Haylett in the editor's chair.

That's now quite the end of the affair. Rob Griffiths and his allies are now determined to break the grip of the Hicks-Rosser group on the *Morning Star*'s management committee, and as I write, both sides are busy organising for the elections to be held in June. Perhaps Hicks and Rosser hope to repeat the triumph of more than a decade ago, when they and Tony Chater held the paper against the Party. But this time the odds are stacked against them.

After that, Griffiths hopes to see an end to all that, and a return to the main business of the day, which is a campaign to save the welfare state from the depredations of the Blair government. Who knows, he might just get it.

The CPB does not represent all the Communists who rejected the DL route and stayed true to Marxism. There is still a separate Communist Party of Scotland, and several other communists thought the formation of the CPB was a mistake.

Bert Ramelson tried hard to persuade the CPB people not to go ahead. Ramelson was one of the founders of the Islip Unity Group, with Ken Gill and Jim Mortimer. Some of these, including Ken Gill, decided after some hesitation to join the CPB. Others stayed out. George Anthony, a retired trade union official who sends out the Islip group's regular newsletter, speaks for them:

"I'm still a Communist but I'm not in any political party. If there's going to be change in Britain it must be through the Labour Party – there's no alternative at the moment, if there ever will be. So we give New Labour critical support. Mo Mowlem is doing a good job, at any rate, but the attack on lone parents was a monstrous error. The big Labour vote at the 1997 election was an anti-Tory vote, and people are not going to waste their vote on small parties until there is a dramatic change in the political situation – a major strike, for example."

Some of the 300 or so people who receive Anthony's newsletter have joined the CPB after some hesitation, but Anthony and Mick Costello stay out. "The CPB behaves like a sect" says Anthony. Costello says: "The absence of a powerful CP is bemoaned across the labour movement spectrum except for the extreme right of Tony Blair. The trade union right wing is disoriented. People who hated the USSR are now bemoaning its absence; they don't like the USA having a free hand. Eastern Europe produces the biggest Communist votes in the world – and these are the people who have allegedly suffered under communism."

They are sure that eventually a real socialist left will emerge. Costello says: "The absence of an ideological powerhouse has to be resolved, and will be resolved by the coming into being of a broad left organisation." But Anthony cautions: "A Communist Party has to grow organically out of the struggles of the working class, otherwise it's just an appendage."

When Arthur Scargill left the Labour Party he could have gone to the CPB. Instead, he chose to start yet another tiny political party. In theory, the division between Scargill's party and the CPB is that Scargill believes there is no hope of change within the Labour Party, while the CPB does not go quite that far. The real reason may be, as George Anthony speculates, that "in the CPB, Arthur felt he wouldn't be the governor."

Anthony and his friends, as well as the CPB, are furious with Scargill. They still hope that those on the left of the Labour Party will eventually break away and form a party to the left of Blair's New Labour. Scargill, he thinks, has made this harder, because he has already done it and failed. I do not know how Scargill would answer his critics. He is one of only two people who refused to talk to me for this book (the other was Andrew Rothstein).

The CP had of course already been deserted, many years before the nemesis of the 1980s, by people who thought it had already diluted the true faith. Back in the late 1970s, Sid French, believing that the CP had betrayed communism and the Soviet Union, led about 700 supporters out of the CP to form the New Communist Party.

The NCP, inevitably, split quickly. The older communists, Soviet Union loyalists who were tired of trench warfare against the eurocommunist advance, fell out with the younger ones, who cared little about the Soviet Union and more about the revolution. After a brief faction fight, many of the younger members were expelled, and in 1981 four of them published a theoretical journal called *The Leninist*. The first issue had a plain, rather striking blood red cover with a small black picture of Lenin, and underneath the title the words "Communist Theoretical Journal – Without revolutionary theory there can be no revolutionary movement."

It was one of those dense, unreadable publications that tiny socialist sects often produce. There were nine pages of a founding statement explaining why the NCP was no longer at the revolutionary vanguard: "...The NCP... sprung into existence ready-formed, like Athena from the head of Zeus, but instead of being fully armed and ready for war, the NCP was nothing but an epigone, quickly degenerating into a small 'pro-Soviet' sect..." The next 17 pages were taken up with the authors' denunciation of views recently put forward by a Communist economist called Sam Aaronovitch. "...The task of Communists, comrade Aaronovitch, is not with you, but against you. Your road to reformism and opportunism is not the Communist road to revolution..."

The founders of the *Leninist* decided to call their Party by exactly the same name as the CP – The Communist Party of Great Britain – which is why, today, it is the only organisation in the country which has the same name as Harry Pollitt's party gave itself in 1920 and abandoned in 1992.

It was they who picketed the last Congress of what was now Nina Temple's CP, with their angry, mocking chant "No matter how you change your name, You still play the bosses' game." It was they who announced to the press that the baton so recklessly dropped by Nina Temple and her friends was, after all, in safe hands. The next year they briefly relaunched the *Daily Worker*, a name not used since George Matthews renamed it the *Morning Star* in 1967. Believing that communism had been betrayed by Mikhail Gorbachev, they ran four candidates in the 1992 general election, "with one aim – to smash capitalism."

Today they claim no more than 500 members, but point out that you are either an active member, or you are not a member at all. These 500 raise enough money for their leader to work full time and still keep a wife and young child.

He is from a working class South Wales Communist family. His earliest memories are of CP meetings in Swansea, and how cold and uncomfortable and tedious they were for a child. He joined the CP's Young Communist League at 13, rising to become part of the YCL leadership. He could not find work in Swansea, and made his way to London, where he went to college and studied politics and government. He fell in love with London's left wing bookshops – "it was like letting a child loose in a sweetshop."

I do not know his name. In 1998, still only 36, he introduces himself as Mark Fischer. But he told me that all members of his party use "cadre names" as "a security measure against fascists and the old CP bureaucracy."

From all this you might suppose that Mark Fischer was a humourless man lacking in a humanity and a sense of proportion. You would be quite wrong. He is witty, intelligent, and transparently sincere. He believes that one day, he and his friends will make their contribution to a better world, in a revolution that happens, at least in part, on the streets and violently.

"The world is an awful place and it could be changed" he says. "Relationships are all wrong – men and women, adults and children. But there is love trying to break through. There are great human beings shining through the eyes of most people you meet, but they live in a world which is ugly and warped." But scientific Marxism? "We got rid of smallpox by scientific precision. It's the same with politics. There's a scientific basis to Marxism just as there's a scientific basis to Beethoven."

His Party has now entered into a bitter battle with Arthur Scargill's Socialist Labour Party. The whole of the December 1997 issue of the CPGB publication *Weekly Worker* is devoted to an attack on Scargill's party. The SLP, says the CPGB, is simply Scargill's personal fiefdom, controlled by Scargill through the NUM's block vote, in which ordinary members have no say.

When you publish a book, your errors are kindly and discreetly pointed out by your friends, or inflated and magnified by your enemies.

I was pleased that the mistakes were kept firmly within bounds. The worst, I think, came to my notice by way of a private and kind letter from Miss S.J. Saklatvala, now the only survivor of Shapurji Saklatvala's five children. She recorded the book for the RNIB. My description of her father is inaccurate, she says: "He was neither aristocratic nor wealthy. His uncle and cousins were very successful founders of the firm of Tatas in India. My father worked for the firm as a clerk until 1925 when he resigned from the family firm because they objected to his political views.

"In fact he and my mother brought us up in meagre circumstances and both of them made great sacrifices to enable us five children to have a good education."

Her letter led me to look at my references to Saklatvala, and they do not reflect adequately his importance in the history of British communism. This is partly because – as Eric Hobsbawm pointed out in a generally very kind review – the history of the Party's attitude towards India is not told here. But, India apart, Saklatvala was a key figure in the migration of many ILP figures towards communism in the 1920s; a key socialist organiser in south London; an effective MP and, until Willie Gallacher was elected MP for West Fife in the 1930s, communism's only significant parliamentarian. He was also a remarkable and interesting man, and the book should have reflected that.

There are some small factual errors which are worth putting right. I wrote Lionel Blair as one of a list of people associated with the Unity Theatre: I meant, of course, Lionel Bart. I am grateful to Avril Fox, who worked there, for pointing out that Cominform headquarters was in Bucharest, not Belgrade. J.T. Murphy is listed in one passage as one of the Scots in the movement, but he came from the north of England (as noted elsewhere in the book.) Bill Rust didn't die of a heart attack, but a stroke, and Phil Piratin wasn't tall, but short.

The Marx Memorial Library's bulletin was inexplicably furious that I called Palme Dutt's book *World Politics* 1918–1935 when it was really *World Politics* 1918–1936, and that I have it as the Left Book Club's first publication when another publication came out three months earlier. This bulletin was also furious about my use of slang words – "Lousy, on the hoof, cash stacked, ready wrapped, riff raff are not the appropriate language to be used" – and incandescent about the title – "the final infamy." It is a shame when communists insist on playing up to their popular, but usually mistaken, image of being pompous and humourless.

People emerge whom you would love to have talked to, and new information surfaces about your characters. I told the story of Rosa Rust in chapter eight: how she was taken to Moscow at the age of three when her father, Bill Rust, was given a Comintern job; how she was left at school in Moscow during the war and mistakenly sent to one of Stalin's labour camps where she almost died; how she made her own way across Russia to Moscow and was secretly sent back to

Britain; and how the Communists and the government collaborated to keep her story out of the newspapers, because they were both denying that Stalin had any labour camps.

I told the story entirely on the basis of Alison Macleod's information, and only afterwards had the great pleasure of meeting Rosa. This would have been a better book if I had met her before. She married George Thornton in 1949, soon after Bill Rust's death, and they live in Redcar, on the north east coast, where for 20 years they were the mainstays of a local drama group.

Today, in their early seventies, they still talk with excitement and passion about the productions they took to the Edinburgh Festival: their *Antigone* which had the drama critic of the Scotsman in tears, their *Shweik,* their *Midsummer Night's Dream,* which was packed out every night and in which they played Oberon and Titania. "'So is mine eye enthralled to thy shape, And thy fair virtue's force perforce doth move me' – that's very hard for a foreigner to say, you know" says Rosa, whose accent still sounds Russian.

George is a retired civil servant with a neat moustache discreetly covering the nakedness of his upper lip. When not reciting poetry, they play music, and walk by the sea, and talk of cricket and of their four grown up children and four grandchildren: George in his light, dry, quietly humorous voice, Rosa with great, gay Russian-sounding gusts of poetry and laughter. The grandchildren call Rosa Babu for Babushka, the Russian for grandmother. In the summer they generally take a package holiday to Bulgaria, where Rosa can use her Russian. She would love to show George St Petersburg, but their pensions don't stretch to it.

I spent a happy afternoon with them, drinking wine and laughing and talking, and listening to Rosa talk about her extraordinary life. Here is one brief vignette out of many: 16-year-old Rosa on the train, with thousands of Volga Germans, crammed in like cattle, being forced to travel thousands of miles across the vast country, making friends with a young German woman who was nursing her four month old baby girl.

Each time the train stopped, the woman rushed to search for hot water for the baby's feed. One terrible day the train started without her, and Rosa was left holding the baby. "I was 16 and the baby was screaming. We gave her some milk with cold water, she didn't like it very much, and someone had a water melon, and I remember cutting

242

a bit of water melon and her sucking it.

"I remember once washing her in the lake. It was so cold! There were no disposable nappies or anything like that, just some rags, but my friends went to the driver and said, try to stop the train where there is a lake or a bit of water, we've got to wash nappies." She laughed happily as she remembered. "The driver did that because he liked us, because we were cheerful. The conditions were so grim and depressing, to be young and alive was something important. The baby was all right, she didn't even get diarrhoea. I was very pleased with myself."

The mother was frantically hopping from train to train trying to catch up with the refugee train. After a week she made it. "She looked about 90 years old, she said" – Rosa comically mimicked the mother holding the baby and weeping – "Oh Rosa, oh my little one. I said, I'm afraid she's a bit stinky. She said Oh-oh-oh she's alive."

Bibliography

This is not a comprehensive list of every book about British communism. Rather, it is a list of books I have found useful. It includes key textbooks like Noreen Branson's excellent two volumes of Party history and Kevin Morgan's biography of Harry Pollitt; books giving the texture and feel of communism, like Alison MacLeod's study of 1956 or Arnold Wesker's famous trilogy; and key primary sources, such as autobiographies by the likes of Pollitt, Bob Stewart and J.T. Murphy.

For those coming fairly new to the subject, the best books to start with (in my very subjective opinion) are marked *.

* Bill Alexander, *British Volunteers for Liberty (Spain, 1936–9)*, Lawrence and Wishart, 1982.
Tom Bell, *The British Communist Party*, Lawrence and Wishart, 1937
* Noreen Branson, *History of the Communist Party, Vol 3 (1927–1941) and 4 (1941–51)*, Lawrence and Wishart, 1985 and 1997.
Fenner Brockway, *Inside the Left*, Allen and Unwin, 1938
Fenner Brockway, *Towards Tomorrow*, Hart-Davis MacGibbon, 1977
Gordon Brown, *Maxton*, Mainstream, 1986
John Callaghan, *Rajani Palme Dutt*, Lawrence and Wishart, 1993.
* John Callaghan, *The Far Left in British Politics*, Blackwell, 1987.

Bibliography

John Carswell, *The Exile: A Life of Ivy Litvinov,* Faber, 1983.

Frank Chapple, *Sparks Fly!*, Michael Joseph, 1984.

Phil Cohen (Ed), *Children of the Revolution,* Lawrence and Wishart, 1997.

Judith Cook, *Apprentices of Freedom,* Quartet, 1979

Andy Croft, *Red Letter Days*, Lawrence and Wishart, 1990.

Paul Davies, *A.J. Cook,* Manchester University Press, 1987.

Bernard Donoughue and G.W. Jones, *Herbert Morrison,* Weidenfeld and Nicholson, 1973.

Michael Foot, *Aneurin Bevan,* McGibbon and Kee, 1962

* Geoffrey Goodman, *Strike!*, Pluto, 1986.

Dennis Healey, *The Time of My Life,* Michael Joseph, 1989

Eric Hobsbawm, *Age of Extremes – The Short Twentieth Century*, Michael Joseph, 1994.

Patricia Hollis, *Jennie Lee,* OUP, 1997.

* Jack Jones, *Union Man,* Collins, 1986.

Walter Kendall, *The Revolutionary Movement in Britain 1900–21*, Weidenfeld and Nicholson, 1969.

James Klugmann, *History of the Communist Party Vol 1 (1919–1924) and 2 (1925–1926)*, Lawrence and Wishart, 1969.

Branko Lazitch and Milorad Drachkovitch, *The Comintern: Historical Highlights,* Frederick Praeger (NY), 1966.

Branko Lazitch, *Biographical Dictionary of the Comintern,* Hoover Institution Press, 1986.

* Alison Macleod, *The Death of Uncle Joe,* Merlin, 1997.

Anthony Masters, *The Man Who Was M,* Blackwell, 1984.

* George Matthews and Francis King, *About Turn*, Lawrence and Wishart, 1990.

Seamus Milne, *The Enemy Within,* Verso, 1995.

Kenneth Morgan, *The Peoples' Peace – British History 1945–89*, OUP, 1990.

Kevin Morgan, *Against Fascism and War*, Manchester University Press, 1989

* Kevin Morgan, *Harry Pollitt,* Manchester University Press, 1993.

J.T. Murphy, *New Horizons,* The Bodley Head, 1931.

J.T. Murphy, *Preparing for Power,* Lawrence and Wishart, 1934.

Henry Pelling, *The British Communist Party*, A&C Black, 1958.

Barry Penrose and Simon Freeman, *Conspiracy of Silence*, Grafton, 1986.

Kim Philby, *My Silent War*, McGibbon and Kee, 1968.

Ben Pimlott, *Hugh Dalton,* Cape, 1985.

Phil Piratin, *Our Flag Stays Red*, Lawrence and Wishart, 1978.

* Harry Pollitt, *Serving My Time*, Lawrence and Wishart, 1940.

Paul Routledge, *Scargill,* Harper Collins, 1992.

Bill Rust, *Britons in Spain*, Lawrence and Wishart, 1939.

John Scanlon, *Decline and Fall of the Labour Party*, Peter Davies, 1932.

L.C.B. Seaman, *Life in Britain Between the Wars,* B.T. Batsford, 1970.

* Mike Squires, *Shapurji Saklatvala,* Lawrence and Wishart, 1967.

H.F. Srebrnik, *London Jews and British Communism*, Vallentine Mitchell, 1995.

Bob Stewart, *Breaking the Fetters,* Lawrence and Wishart, 1967.

Paul Thompson, *The Edwardians,* Weidenfeld and Nicholson, 1975.

Willie Thompson, *The Good Old Cause*, Pluto, 1992.

Hilary Wainwright, *Arguments for a New Left,* Blackwell, 1994.

* Arnold Wesker, *The Wesker Trilogy,* Cape, 1960.

Francis Wheen, *Tom Driberg*, Chatto and Windus, 1990.

Index

247

Index

Index

Index

252

Index